# TWENTY-FIVE YEARS ON THE ND&C

# TWENTY-FIVE YEARS ON THE ND&C

## A History of the Newburgh, Dutchess & Connecticut Railroad

Bernard L. Rudberg

PURPLE MOUNTAIN PRESS
Fleischmanns, New York

*Twenty-five Years on the ND&C:*
*A History of the Newburgh, Dutchess & Connecticut Railroad*
First Edition 2002

This book is fondly dedicated to the memory of the people who created and ran the railroads. Among them were my great grandfather, Carl Johan Carlsson, who, in 1894, was stationmaster in a small town called Polcirkeln, where the tracks cross the Arctic Circle in northern Sweden and my grandfather, Carl Ferdinand Ahlstrom, who was station foreman at the strategic railroad-junction town of Boden a few miles south of the Arctic Circle. Railroads opened up communications between formerly isolated places. Railroads carried rural products to cities, but they also brought city culture and life to the farms, even beyond the Arctic Circle. Railroads influenced daily life in countless subtle ways. For many of us, commuting to work became a way of life made possible by railroads. Our modern life-style owes much to men like my ancestors and the men in this book, George Brown, Charles Kimball, G. Hunter Brown, and William Underhill. They probably did not realize it in their own time, but they changed the world simply by doing what they did best: running a railroad.

Bernie Rudberg

Published by
Purple Mountain Press, Ltd.
1060 Main Street, P.O. Box 309, Fleischmanns, New York 12430-0309
845-254-4062, 845-254-4476 (fax), purple@catskill.net
http://www.catskill.net/purple

Copyright 2002 © by Bernard L. Rudberg
All rights reserved under International and Pan-American Copyright Conventions. No part of this publication may be reproduced or transmitted without consent in writing from the publisher.

Library of Congress Control Number:   2002113065

ISBN 1-930098-37-5 (limited-edition hardcover); 1-930098-38-3 (paperback)

Manufactured in the United States of America on acid-free paper

5 4 3 2 1

Half-title page and frontispiece:
Details of drawings by Victor Westman from the collection of Robert B. Adams presently in the collection of Heyward Cohen of Amenia, New York.  See Appendix D.

Cover print by Peter Tassone.

# Contents

Preface  7

Introduction  9

Before There Was an ND&C  10

East-West Rails in Dutchess County  11

ND&C Letterbooks  23

The ND&C Gets Started  25

Dutchess Junction  35

The Clove Branch Railroad  49

Buying and Selling Equipment  60

The BH&E Returns as the NY&NE  71

Bridges of the ND&C  85

More Rails Into Hopewell Junction  94

Meanwhile, Back at the East End  110

The Milk Business  119

The Coal Business  130

Coping With Weather  136

The Lighter Side of Railroading  142

After The ND&C RR  153

Appendices  158

Appendix A: Locomotive Rosters  159

Appendix B: N&C RR Maps  171

Appendix C: Adams Photographs  182

Appendix D: Adams-Westman Drawings  189

Sources  197

Index  199

# Preface

THERE have been many books and magazine articles describing the railroads of Dutchess County, New York. This volume will not attempt to trace over that same path except as background to the Newburgh, Dutchess & Connecticut Railroad story.

Recently, the old headquarters building of the ND&C Railroad in Matteawan (now part of Beacon, New York) was renovated, and the workers found the railroad record books. There are forty-eight volumes with seven hundred pages in each for a total of over thirty-three thousand pages of office correspondence. Some of the volumes are missing, and the earliest book is dated 1879; the latest is 1904.

Larry Way, a member of the Beacon Historical Society, donated the books to the organization. The books are now available to anybody who has the interest and the time to read them. Many of the pages are handwritten script, so a bit of the personality comes through. You can read this book to get a taste of what the ND&C volumes contain. For a real trip into 1800s railroading, you are welcome to go to Beacon and absorb all thirty-three thousand pages with your own eyes.

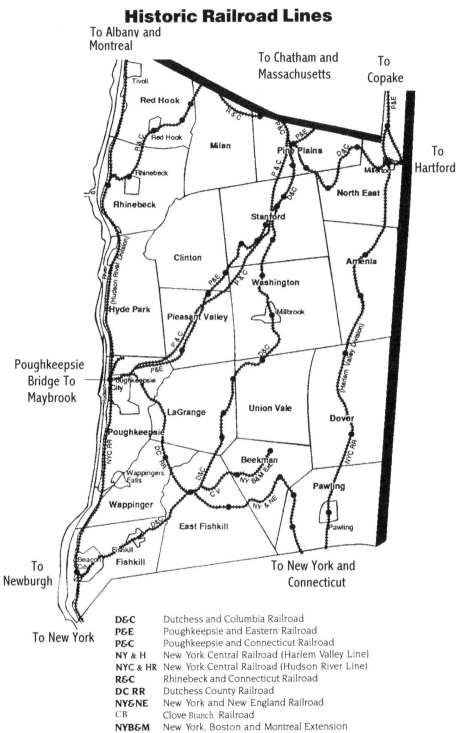

**Historic railroad lines of Dutchess County, N.Y.**
Map from the Poughkeepsie Dutchess Transportation Council.

# Introduction

IN THE EARLY YEARS OF RAILROADING, grand schemes and dreams sprang up in almost every county and town. Dutchess County, New York was no exception. This was particularly true in Dutchess County because of the geographic location. North to south, Dutchess is between New York City and the state capitol of Albany. East to west, Dutchess is the gateway between southern New England and the coal fields of Pennsylvania or the western states. Dutchess also is bordered on the west by the Hudson River, which provided water access but at the same time was a barrier to east-west rail travel. When the idea of taking advantage of this economic potential took hold, there were plenty of people with high hopes ready to join in and get rich. As in any new undertaking, there were lessons to be learned and often, people had to cope with a dose of reality. Some actually did get rich, but for most the lessons were unfortunate.

The earliest railroads in Dutchess County were the north-south routes that served New York City, Albany, and Montreal. These routes were relatively stable and successful. With that success as added incentive, an east-west railroad was chartered and built. The first nine years of east-west railroad operations in Dutchess County saw turmoil, conflict, and multiple financial failures. The railroad tracks that ran from Dutchess Junction and Matteawan (Beacon, New York) through Hopewell and Millbrook to Millerton and to Connecticut at State Line had several different names in their first few years of existence. Out of that chaos grew the Newburgh, Dutchess & Connecticut Railroad (ND&C). The leadership of the ND&C Railroad, John Schultze and Charles Kimball, established an operation that survived through good times and bad for over twenty-five years until it was absorbed into the Central New England Railway (CNE) and eventually became part of the New Haven Railroad (NH). Later, eleven miles of the old ND&C line became part of the ill-fated Penn Central, next Conrail, then the Housatonic Railroad, and currently, Metro North.

Early sections of this book set the stage for the entrance of the ND&C Railroad. The heart of this book is the twenty-five years of ND&C operation from 1879 to 1904. The ND&C record books are a window into the everyday events and problems of running a railroad in the late 1800s. The books contain everything from compensating farmers for cattle that were run over by trains to dealing with the great blizzard of March 1888, as well as ordering locomotive repair parts or reporting that the office washroom drain was clogged again. After spending over a year of my spare time reading the books, I felt as though Schultze and Kimball were old friends, even though both have been gone for over one hundred years.

I have tried to convey some of the human side of the struggle to build a successful business. Along with that I also have tried to preserve a bit of the contribution that Schultze, Kimball, and the railroads made to the world we live in today. How much different would the world be if railroads had never been invented?

# Before There Was an ND&C

DISCUSSIONS AND PROPOSALS for railroads in Dutchess County date back to 1826 or earlier. The first north-south rails came in 1848, but the first east-west rails were not laid until 1868, over forty years after the first rumblings.

The Dutchess County Railroad Company obtained a charter in 1832 to build a railroad from Poughkeepsie to Connecticut. It was never built.

In anticipation of railroads not yet built, and profit to be made, a Poughkeepsie Locomotive Engine Company was organized. Plans for the company included a large building and the construction of seventy-five locomotives per year. The company managed to build one locomotive before they went broke in the financial panic of 1837, before any tracks were built in Dutchess County.

One of the factors that slowed the progress of railroads was the success of the Erie Canal, which opened in 1825. Investors saw a proven profitmaker in the canals as more attractive than the unproven and often failure-prone railroads. At one point, there was a proposal to build a canal from Sharon, Connecticut, through Dutchess and Putnam Counties to the Hudson River. It was never built. Some Poughkeepsie people pushed for a canal through Pine Plains to Massachusetts. It was never built.

The idea of an east-west railroad through Dutchess County did not always come from within. In 1847, the Hartford, Providence & Fishkill Railroad was chartered. Their plan was to build rails from Connecticut across Dutchess to Fishkill Landing, which is now part of Beacon, New York. At that point, they would establish a ferry service to transfer train cars across the Hudson River and connect with the Erie Railroad in Newburgh, New York. This would connect industrial New England with the coal fields of Pennsylvania and the wide open market of the western states. For a variety of reasons this connection did not materialize until the 1880s. When this connection finally was built, it became quite a problem for the ND&C Railroad, as we will see later.

The first rails actually laid down in Dutchess County were for the New York & Harlem line (NY&H). The Harlem Railroad had started out as a horse-drawn line from Greenwich Village to Harlem in Manhattan in 1831. By December 1848, the Harlem had extended as far as Dover Plains in Dutchess County. The line continued north and reached Amenia and Millerton in 1851. They continued building to Chatham in Columbia County and connected to the Albany, & West Stockbridge Railroad to reach Albany in 1852. At Albany, the line connected with the Erie Canal, which opened up trade to the West.

In December 1849, about a year after the Harlem line came to Dutchess, the Hudson River line reached Poughkeepsie. This had been a difficult line to build because of drilling and blasting through solid rock at Breakneck Ridge and having to add fill and build bridges over the marshy spots along the river. On this new line the travel time from Poughkeepsie to New York City was cut to two and a half hours, which was about half the time of the same trip on a steamboat.

# East-West Rails in Dutchess County

## Dutchess and Columbia

FROM THE EARLIEST east-west railroad proposals in Dutchess County there was disagreement over exactly where the tracks and terminals should be. As early as 1831, there were factions advocating locations along the Hudson River such as Poughkeepsie, Fishkill Landing, and Rhinebeck. Even after the Harlem and Hudson lines were built, the squabbling continued. The success of the two north-south lines in the 1850s held out a greater incentive for building east-west lines, but there was still disagreement. As it turned out, there were lines constructed to all three locations along the river by 1872, but the first east-west rails actually laid down were on the southernmost line, in 1868, near what is now the city of Beacon.

The new railroad was called the Dutchess & Columbia (D&C). After organizational meetings in Verbank and Millbrook, the line filed articles of association in Albany on 4 September 1866. A Millbrook resident named George H. Brown was elected president. With five hundred thousand dollars of financial backing, Brown enlisted the help of Oliver Weldon Barnes to design the new line. Barnes was perhaps the best known and most successful civil engineer and railroad designer of his day. By 1867, the line had been surveyed and preliminary contracts arranged.

A much older survey had used a surveyor's plummet (actually a pointed weight on a string) to place a "Plumb Point" marker along the banks of the Hudson River south of Fishkill Landing. For whatever reason, the letter "b" was lost from the old map, and it became Plum Point. There was no point and not a plum tree anywhere nearby. This Plum Point became the starting location of the new rail line and later was named Dutchess Junction.

Grading began in 1868, and teams of horses pulled wagon loads of rails to be distributed along the right of way through Matteawan, Glenham, Fishkill, and Brinckerhoff to nearby Hopewell. Bridges were built over Fishkill Creek and Sprout Creek. After this section was in place, more rails would be hauled by trains to complete the line. Construction reached Millerton in the northeast corner of the county in November 1871.

## Clove Branch Railroad

A short four-mile connecting railroad called the Clove Branch (CB) was chartered in 1868 and opened in 1869. The CB connected with the D&C near Old Hopewell, and its main purpose was to haul iron ore out of the mine at Sylvan Lake. Later, the CB was extended another four miles and ran passenger and freight service to a few customers and an iron furnace in Clove Valley. The president was the same George H. Brown who was president of the D&C Railroad.

## Boston Hartford and Erie Railroad

The first name change for the new D&C Railroad came before the first revenue run. The Boston, Hartford & Erie Railroad (BH&E) had

**Building the railroad, 1868.**
Collection of P. McLachlan. Courtesy of J. W. Swanberg.

purchased property at Dennings Point a mile north of the Dutchess Junction starting point of the D&C Railroad. The BH&E also bought one half of the right of way of the D&C from Hopewell to Wicopee. In a surprise move, with about eleven miles of D&C track built, George H. Brown leased the entire operation of the D&C to the BH&E in November 1868. Part of the agreement stipulated that the D&C had to finish the construction of the line in ten-mile increments for a compensation of two hundred thousand per year. Railroad historians are still speculating about the reasons behind this sudden change of plans.

The D&C Railroad continued building the line and bought a used locomotive from a railroad in Pennsylvania, naming it Tioronda. It was a 4-4-0 wood burner that had been built in 1856. It arrived at Dutchess Junction on 8 February 1869. A week later, on February 15, two more used wood burners arrived from New Haven. These were named Washington and Pine Plains for the towns that the D&C and BH&E ran through.

The station at Plum Point/Dutchess Junction was not yet completed. On Monday, 21 June 1869, the first trip on the line left Fishkill Landing. The chocolate brown coaches were lettered BH&E Railroad. They ran south along the Hudson River line to Plum Point/Dutchess Junction and then ran east on the new rail line. Trains used this route for a short time in 1869 until the station was finished at Dutchess Junction. By the winter of 1869-70 the rails had reached Bangall.

**Dutchess & Columbia RR locomotive Washington at Bangall Mills, 1870. Built in 1857, purchased used in 1869, wrecked in 1883, and sold in 1884.** Collection J. W. Swanberg.

**Winchell Mountain cut was filled with snow and ice every winter. This rock cut was dug mostly with hard labor for the D&C RR.** Collection of the Beacon Historical Society.

The grand plan of the BH&E was to connect New England cities with a shipping terminal on the Hudson River. They owned Dennings Point and set in place a curve of pilings from the east bank of the river across a small bay to Dennings Point with the intention of laying track. As late as 1957, these pilings were still shown on a US Government Geological Survey map. The right of way from Hopewell to Waterbury Connecticut was partly graded, but not yet completed. The BH&E had started to lay track eastward from the D&C main at Hopewell toward Connecticut. This was not to be. In March 1870, the BH&E failed.

**Above: Boston, Hartford & Erie RR special train, September 1869.** Collection of the Beacon Historical Society.

**Right: Boston, Hartford & Erie RR timetable #3, October 1869.** Collection of the Beacon Historical Society.

**Below: Postcard view of Bangall RR station.** Collection of Heyward Cohen.

## The D&C Returns

George H. Brown did not hesitate when word came about the BH&E failure. About midnight on 22 March 1870, he roused up locomotive fireman Roswell S. Judson and the two of them got steam up in the engine Washington. At 2:00 AM they started for Hopewell. At Hopewell they captured the BH&E rolling stock and locomotives by removing the connecting rails to the construction site just east of Hopewell. With the BH&E immobilized, they proceeded to occupy the stations along the line and placed guards. Within a few days, the D&C was again in operation with borrowed coaches. Three BH&E locomotives trapped at Hopewell were later returned to the BH&E. Of course the BH&E attempted to reclaim the line through the courts, but withdrew after several months of wrangling. The line was once again the Dutchess & Columbia Railroad with George H. Brown as the boss.

To tap the Pennsylvania coal traffic, the D&C built a ferry terminal at Dutchess Junction. Railroad cars were transferred across the Hudson River on car floats to connect with the Erie Railroad in Newburgh. There was also passenger and general freight service using Hudson River steamboats and barges. A steamboat called *Fannie Garner* shuttled freight and passengers back and forth across the river to and from Newburgh. Loads of coal from the Delaware and Hudson Canal came down the river from Rondout Landing near Kingston, New York, and were transferred from barges to train cars at the long dock. Dutchess Junction became a busy place with all that activity plus connections with the Hudson River Railroad, which included a pedestrian bridge over the main line.

Construction of the D&C Railroad continued at the northeast end of the line. In November 1871, the tracks reached Millerton. In the original plans, the D&C was supposed to go north to Hillsdale in Columbia County. Instead of building to Hillsdale, the D&C turned east just north of Pine Plains to Millerton. They built a one-mile connector from Millerton to the Connecticut border at State Line, where the rails joined the Connecticut Western Railroad (CW). In hindsight, this move would prove to be unprofitable for the D&C because the CW Railroad made agreements with the Rhinebeck & Connecticut Railroad (R&C) after 1875,

**Postcard view of Bangall, NY.**
Collection of Heyward Cohen, Amenia, NY.

when the R&C Railroad made direct connections at State Line. Then much of the coal business went through Rhinebeck instead of Dutchess Junction.

But we are getting ahead of our story. Let's get back to the D&C. Ironically, by 1871, the tracks of the Dutchess & Columbia Railroad ran fifty-eight miles diagonally across Dutchess County from corner to corner and ran less than one mile from the northern line, but never actually reached Columbia County.

### The New York, Boston & Northern Era

George H. Brown had grander dreams. In December 1872, he became president of the New York, Boston & Northern Railroad (NYB&N) with the intentions of connecting several smaller railroads together to run trains from New York City to Northern New York State. It lasted only about a month into January 1873 when he extended the scope of this new venture to include Montreal in Canada.

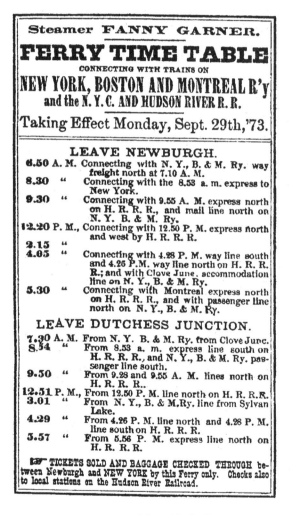
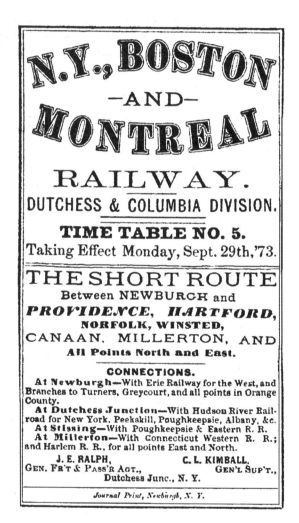

New York, Boston & Montreal timetable, September 1873.
Collection of the Beacon Historical Society.

### The New York, Boston & Montreal Era

In January 1873, George H. Brown became the president of the New York, Boston & Montreal Railway (NYB&M). The plan was to build a few short link railroads to connect existing lines into a complete route from New York City to Montreal via Rutland, Vermont. The D&C and the CB were to be segments of this route. New links were to be built from Brewster, New York, to the CB near Hopewell and also from Pine Plains to Chatham, New York. These links were never built. The financial panic of 1873 ended George H. Brown's dreams of a Canadian American railroad empire. The NYB&M failed, and the linked railroads reverted back to independent lines. One of the NYB&M segments became the four-mile-long extension of the CB out to Clove Valley. The CB did not actually own the extension. They leased the line from the NYB&M court trustees. NYB&M equipment was divided up

**New York, Boston & Montreal timetable, September 1873.**
Collection of the Beacon Historical Society, Beacon, NY.

between the smaller lines or simply sold to the highest bidder. In 1874, there were twelve brand new NYB&M Railroad locomotives stored at Dutchess Junction awaiting their fate. Three of them eventually went to work on the D&C and ND&C.

## The Aftermath of the NYB&M Failure

Some years later, in 1885, the ND&C letterbooks contain a sort of hindsight view of events following the failure of the NYB&M. Superintendent Kimball wrote two long letters to President Schultze detailing the disposition of NYB&M property. The actual records were destroyed in a fire at Dutchess Junction in 1876, so a good bit of the description is from Kimball's memory.

### Volume 21, Pages 241-243, 1 December 1885
*Very long (three full pages) letter to Schultze:*

In regard to the history and final disposition of the rails, fish plates, bolts and track spikes sent here by the NY&BM Ry. in 1873. I submit the following.

Our records having been destroyed by fire in April 1876, I am unable to say, positively, just how much of this material was sent to Dutchess Junction in 1873. But in a copy of a report to you dated 5 Feb 1877, which I find in this office the quantity is placed as follows:

| | |
|---|---:|
| Iron Rail 56 pounds per yard | 500 tons |
| Fish Plates - number of | 4000 |
| Track bolts - number of | 11,250 |
| Track Spikes (150 lbs. per keg) | 200 kegs |

Of this, 145 tons of iron rails were laid in the main track of the Dutchess and Columbia RR using 1080 fish plates and 2160 track bolts in doing so. The remainder of the material was used in building the line from Sylvan Lake east, a spur track at Millerton, storage tracks for NYB&M cars or stored at Clove Junction and Dutchess Junction.

In February 1877 we were called upon to account for this rail and could only do so by measuring the iron and estimating it's weight, and the fastenings used with it. In the spring of 1877 you decided to complete the line from Sylvan Lake to Clove Valley and all this material was ordered sent to Sylvan Lake for the purpose of building the line from where the construction left off in 1873, some 5100 feet east of the end of the Clove Branch RR to Clove Valley.

I then had the spur track at Millerton (which had never been used) torn up as well as the storage tracks for cars and everything belonging to the trustees was sent to Sylvan Lake except the 145 tons of rail and it's [sic] fastenings that was in the main line of the ND&C RR Co. This not being enough to complete the line, you bought in June 1877 70 tons of the trustees rails from Port Morris and it was also sent to Clove Valley.

In 1878, in July I think, the ND&C bought from Crocker Bros. 141 tons iron rail, 4650 fish plates and 1154 lbs. track bolts and turned them over to the trustees to offset the 145 tons rails and fastenings used in the main track of that road. Of this lot 70 tons was sent to Pt. Morris to replace the 70 tons that you borrowed from that place in 1877 and the balance, 71 tons, with the fish plates and bolts bought from Crocker Bros. was all sent to Clove Valley thus clearing the ND&C RR Co. of responsibility for any of the property.

I have had the track and sidings carefully measured from the end of the old Clove Branch RR to Clove Valley and find the length of track to be 25,831 Ft. to which add 483 Ft. of scale track at Sylvan Lake makes 26,314 Ft. of track to lay, which, with iron at 56 lbs. per yard, would require as follow:

| | |
|---|---|
| Iron Rail | 438-6/10 tons |
| Fish Plates | 3508 |
| Track Bolts | 7016 |
| Track Spikes | 187 kegs (kegs 150 lbs. each) |
| Ties | 13,574 |

There is now stored at Clove Valley 233 iron Rails each 30 Ft. long which would make 58 2/10 tons, 520 Fish Plates and 900 track Bolts. This added to what is above shown as in scale track, main track and sidings would show as below:

| In Track | Stored | Total | Original | Short |
|---|---|---|---|---|
| Tons of Rail | | | | |
| 438-6/10 | 58-2/10 | 496-8/10 | 500 | 3-2/10 |
| Fish Plates | | | | |
| 3508 | 520 | 4028 | 4000 | 28 over |
| Track Bolts | | | | |
| 7016 | 900 | 7916 | 11,250 | 3,334 |
| Kegs Spikes | | | | |
| 187 | | 187 | 200 | 13 |
| Ties | | | | |
| 13,574 | | 13,574 | unknown | |

I further find that we shipped to you at Keyport NJ July 1st 1873 400 fish plates and 950 track bolts.

The small quantity of rails apparently short probably accounted for by the difference between scale and estimated weight. The fish plate over I can only account for by supposing that some were sent from the ND&C though we have no account of them.

The track bolts and the spikes short were presumably used in laying the storage tracks and were bent, broken or lost in removing these tracks to Sylvan Lake. For further information or to corroborate this, I would refer you to my letter of Feb 5th 1877 and Apr 4th 1878 to you upon this matter.

Yours Truly  C. L. Kimball Supt

### Volume 21, Pages 247-256, 3 December 1885
*Complete inventory of trustees rolling stock (includes builder and disposition):*

4 locomotives:
- No. 2   Now known as   ND&CRR No. 5   Brooks Loco. Works
- No. 4   Now known as   ND&CRR No. 7   Brooks Loco. Works
- No. 6   Now known as   ND&CRR No. 6   Brooks Loco. Works
- No. 15 Now known as   ND&CRR No. 8   Danforth Loco. Works

- 10    Hay Cars
- 15    ox Cars
- 152   Gondolas  (by builders)

List of trustees rolling stock stored at Arthursburgh:
50 Box Cars

List of trustees rolling stock received at Dutchess Junction in 1873 and afterwards sent elsewhere:
Locomotives
No. 5 Sent to High Bridge 25 Sept 1875. I think this locomotive was afterwards sent to the Freehold & NY RR but am not positive.
No. 7 Sent to the Freehold & NY RR 13 August 1877.
11 Passenger coaches (with builders and recipients)
11 Hay Cars  27 Box Cars
10 Gondolas

The foregoing is all the information I am able to give you in regard to the rolling stock belonging to the trustees of the NY&BM Ry. Co. All my records of this property having been destroyed by fire in April 1876, all the records I have, is a book, copied from another book then in Mr. J. Q. Hoyts office by Mr. J. E. Ralph, in 1876 after the fire. I presume this book is correct but I could not attest to it's [sic] correctness.

Yours Truly  C. L. Kimball

Kimball's nostalgic description gives us a pretty good idea of what happened to most of the NYB&M property after the failure. In February 1888, there is mention of the deteriorating condition of trustees box cars stored on a siding at Arthursburgh. Over the years these box cars were sold to other railroads.

### Volume 28, Page 394, 3 October 1889
*Kimball tells Holmes:*

Mr. Giness has directed that 10 more of the old NYB&M box cars be got ready to ship to the Ohio & North Western RR Co. He wants these lettered the same as the lot of 15 that went to the same party in May, and numbered 516 to 526 inclusive.

**Volume 29, page 280, 5 March 1890**
*Letter to trustees complaining about their box cars taking up space on the ND&C tracks:*

They are terribly in our way and have been since they were taken from storage track at Arthursburgh.

As late as 1896, a full twenty-three years after the failure, the ghost of the NYB&M still haunted Dutchess County rails.

**Volume 41, Page 518, 15 May 1896**

The 4.1 miles of track used by the Clove Branch RR are actually owned by the NY Boston & Montreal RR which was never completed. That road is now in the hands of a trustee under the direction of the court.

# The End of the D&C Railroad

AFTER THE NYB&M FAILED, the line across Dutchess County became the D&C Railroad once again. The D&C struggled to stay afloat, but within a year, the mortgage was foreclosed in 1874, only five years after the first run. A sale was held on 5 August 1876, and John Crosby Brown bought the assets of the D&C Railroad for less than half of the original price. Rolling stock was stenciled "Jno. Crosby Trustee." The D&C operated under the direction of a court receiver for three years and competition was growing. Those three years, from 1874 to 1877, must have been discouraging indeed for everyone involved.

By that time, there were two other east-west railroads across Dutchess competing for business. The Rhinebeck & Connecticut Railroad ran across the northern part of Dutchess to connect with the D&C and the CW Railroad near Millerton. The Rhinebeck & Connecticut Railroad used the D&C Millerton to State Line connection until 1875, when they opened their own direct connection. Later, in 1881, the CW Railroad became the Hartford & Connecticut Western Railroad (H&CW). By 1882, the H&CW Railroad took over the R&C completely, and large shipments of D&H coal were routed through Rhinebeck instead of through Dutchess Junction. The D&H barges had a much shorter trip from Rondout across the river to Rhinebeck instead of sailing thirty miles south to Dutchess Junction. And besides, the rail mileage to State Line was also much shorter from Rhinebeck. We will get back to the coal business competition in more detail in a later section of this book.

By 1872, a railroad from Poughkeepsie through Pleasant Valley to connect to the D&C at Stissing was completed. This line was called the Poughkeepsie & Eastern Railroad, but they went bankrupt in a year and a half. The line was sold and renamed the Poughkeepsie, Hartford & Boston Railroad.

### The Beginning of the ND&C Railroad

On 8 January 1877, a new corporation was formed and a charter was granted for the railroad line. It was to be called the Newburgh, Dutchess & Connecticut Railroad, the ND&C. This new corporation took possession of the old D&C railroad line on 1 February 1877. The ND&C did not own any rolling stock. It was all rented from the trustees of the D&C. Later, as business improved, the equipment was to be purchased. This was not exactly a flying start, but things were looking up.

The ND&C Railroad began operations with a collection of well-used rented equipment. Coaches used link and pin couplers and relied on hand-operated brakes. Three of their locomotives were wood burners that had been in service for over twenty years. The ND&C had a total of fifty-eight miles of track, all in Dutchess County. Stations along the line had been built from the same set of plans and looked alike. Standard station colors were ochre yellow with brown trim around the windows and doors. Station roofs were made of slate to combat the ever-present danger of fire from sparks from locomotive smokestacks. Many of the streams and ravines were bridged with wooden trestles not suitable for any heavy trains. There was certainly a lot of room for improvement, but at least they were up and running. Loads of iron ore were coming out of the CB Railroad at Sylvan Lake. Coal and freight were moving across the Hudson River at Dutchess Junction. Milk shipments from local dairy farms were on the increase. With a little bit of luck, the ND&C Railroad might make it yet.

In less than ten years, the Dutchess & Columbia Railroad (D&C) had seen a series of financial failures resulting in several name changes. You can be sure that this period of chaos and failure was also a period of learning. Many of the people who lived through those ten years were still there working for the management of the new ND&C Railroad. The new owners and management of the ND&C Railroad were not the flamboyant empire builders that George H. Brown had been, but they proved to be much more stable and successful. The ND&C was to survive through good times and bad for more than twenty-five years until it was absorbed into the CNE Railway and later, the New Haven Railroad (NH) system in the early years of the twentieth century.

# ND&C Letterbooks

So what are letterbooks anyway? The short definition might say that they are bound copies of letters or business records commonly used before the invention of copiers, FAX machines, and computers. Indeed, the early volumes of the ND&C letterbooks were written by hand even before typewriters came into use. This conjures up an image of a Dickens-type office clerk hunched over an oak desk carefully writing out business correspondence. Before mailing the letters he would use a water, chemical, and wet cloth method to make a copy of each one on thin onion skin paper. The copies were then bound into an eleven by seventeen size hardcover book to form permanent records. The thin onion skin

**ND&C RR letterbooks at the Beacon Historical Society, Beacon, NY.**
Photo by author.

translucent paper allowed seven hundred or more pages in each volume. One of the later ND&C volumes actually has one thousand pages.

The ND&C letterbooks do not have an index. However, there is a type of table of contents in the front of each volume. Standard paper pages in the front list subjects alphabetically. The listing is primarily the names of the persons who were to receive the original letters. You can easily locate a letter to a specific person, but there is no index for any of the letter contents.

Reading the handwritten script can sometimes be a challenge. The translucent pages are easier to read if you slip a sheet of white paper behind them.

The copy process also caused problems when the wet cloth was moved sideways, smudging the lettering. Despite these problems, most of the pages are readable. With practice, you even get to know the handwriting quirks of the individual clerks, and commonly repeated word sequences begin to stand out. Later, volumes were typed, which made reading easier.

Forty-eight volumes of the ND&C letterbooks have survived. The old ND&C headquarters building was renovated into stores and apartments. Workers found the letterbooks, and Beacon Historical Society member Larry Way donated the books to the society archives. The earliest dated book is from 1879, when the ND&C was only two years old. The last book is dated 1904, less than one year before the ND&C was absorbed into the CNE Railway. Some of the volumes in between are missing and probably will never be found, but the existing ones give us a rich insight into the business of running a railroad in the late 1800s. More than just running the business, the books also paint a vivid picture of the people who made it all happen.

**Sample page from the ND&C RR letterbooks, Volume 33, page 179.**
Collection of the Beacon Historical Society.

Now that we know what a letterbook is, let's sample the contents of the ND&C records.

# The ND&C Gets Started

WHEN THE LINE was operated as the Dutchess & Columbia Railroad, the headquarters were in a brick building in Millbrook. This was centrally located and also close to the home of President George Brown. After the change to Newburgh, Dutchess & Connecticut Railroad, the headquarters were moved to Dutchess Junction and later to Matteawan, which is now part of Beacon, New York. The new president of the ND&C Railroad, General John L. Schultze, had an office at 59 Wall Street in New York City. The superintendent who ran the ND&C was a veteran railroader named Charles Kimball who lived in Matteawan. It was logical to have the superintendent's office close to where most of the action happened at Dutchess Junction. Many of the letters are from Kimball to Schultze reporting on events on the line or asking for management decisions about major plans. Because General Schultze was relatively new to the ND&C, he asked Kimball for some information about the history of Dutchess Junction. Below is Charles Kimball's response.

**Volume 18, Pages 230-231, 21 March 1884**
*(Some words are not readable but most of it follows.)*

To Gen. Jno. L. Schultze,
59 Wall St. NY

**Postcard view of ND&C (later CNE and NH) railroad station in Millbrook, NY.**
Collection of Heyward Cohen.

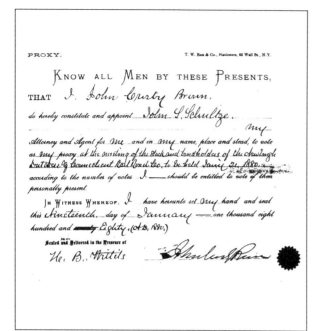

**Proxy for an ND&C RR stockholders meeting.**
Collection of the Beacon Historical Society.

**General Manager Charles L. Kimball, 1890.
Photo from the R&LHS Bulletin #34 in 1934.**
Courtesy of Leroy Beaujon.

Replying to your favor of the 20th instant I have to say that in 1872 our facilities at Dutchess Junction for doing business consisted of one large passenger depot with roof exiting over the NYC&HR double track, our main track and one siding and also covering our local freight depot. This building was owned jointly by the D&C and NYC&HR.

The D&C owned a dock 702 feet long fronting the above Main depot and Hudson River 2/3 of which was used handling coarse freights. There were two tracks on the part of the dock, one of which was used to reach the ferry bridge when coal was loaded in cars from two floats or scows which was controlled by the company. 400 tons coal per day could be loaded here from Penn. Coal Co. dock, Newburgh by these scows and 300 tons coal per day has been hoisted from canal boats to cars on the 2nd track referred to on the dock, by two hoist engines and derricks, besides the lumber and other freight which was handled by hand.

On the other 1/3 of the dock our passenger and merchandise freight business was handled, which came to us by barge from NY and by steamer Fanny Garner which plied between Dutchess Junction and Newburgh connecting with all D&C and NYC&HR trains at the time. This boat (F. G.) would make the trip one way in about 15 minutes and 100 tons of freight could have been handled daily on this boat if the same had been offered. From 200 to 300 tons was handled per day on this portion of the dock and track that passed over and beyond it out on a pile trestle that extended at the time some 300 feet north west beyond the dock.

Besides the sidings on the dock the D&C owned one long siding on the west side of the NYC&H main track connecting with same at both ends, and on the east side of said main track the D&C owned five shorter sidings averaging about 500 feet in length each. At this time the rolling stock in use on the road was owned by other parties and

**Joint NYC&HR RR and D&C RR station at Dutchess Junction, 1873. Looking north, with Beacon in the distance and Dennings Point to the left. Abandoned bridge and pilings are from the failed BH&E RR to Dennings Point. The D&C tracks go off to the right, up the hill to Tioronda and Wicopee Junction.**
Collection of the Hudson Northern Model Train Club of Hopewell Junction, NY.

consisted of seven locomotives, 3 coaches, 2 baggage, Ex. and mail cars, 2 eight wheel caboose cars, 1 combination bag. and pas., 27 box frt., 9 platform cars, 124 gondola cars, (100 of which belonged to the Penn. Coal Co.), and 4 stock cars.

I find that the distance from the iron bridge in NYC&HR track north of Dutchess Junction to our south line of river front is 2300 feet. On this property could be laid a dock extending from the stone pier in over head bridge just north of Dutchess Junction to the channel bank, 3300 feet in length, as shown in a plan now at your office, that would when covered with RR tracks furnish a storage for 1500 freight cars. Take away half these cars and we could handle a business equal to 700 cars each way per day, but to do this would require a double track RR.

With improved terminal facilities, additional sidings and rolling stock, the D&C with her single track could have handled 400 freight cars each way per day. If I have not touched up all the points advise me and I will explain further.

Yours Truly   C. L. Kimball

This description gives us quite a bit of information about the facilities that the ND&C had. However, the station that Kimball mentioned burned to the ground and all the previous records were lost in 1876, before the ND&C took over.

The illustration above shows a view along the Hudson River Railroad (HR) tracks looking north from Dutchess Junction station in 1873. The bridge in the distance is left from the failed BH&E Railroad plan to reach the Hudson River. You can see the row of pilings to the left leading out to Dennings Point. No tracks were ever built on these pilings. To the right of the tracks is the D&C or ND&C main line

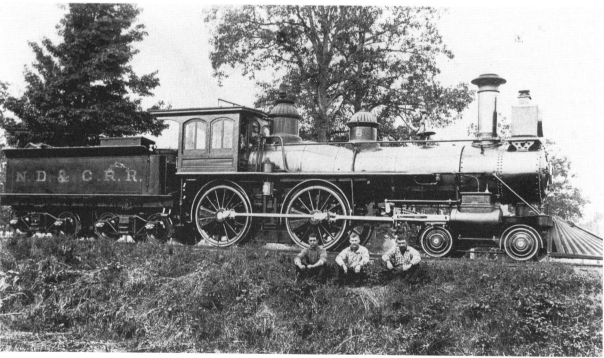

# RAILROAD TIME TABLES

## Of All Railroads in the Hudson Valley.

Above: RR timetables from the collection of the Beacon Historical Society.
Facing page, top: ND&C RR locomotive Millbrook at Bangall Mills, 1882.
Author's collection.
Facing page, bottom: ND&C RR locomotive #6.
Collection of J. W. Swanberg.

going up the hill to Wicopee Junction. Overhead is the extension of the station, which burned in 1876.

The first two volumes of the ND&C letterbooks cover most of 1879, and the predominant message you get in reading them is the problem of trying to run a railroad with equipment somebody else owned. In several places in these volumes, there are lists of locomotives and cars that the ND&C used but the Trustees owned. A few months later, another list shows a different roster of equipment in use. Maintenance could be a problem, too. There is a copy of a letter, dated 9 April 1879, to James Lawry who was the attorney for the Trustees at 61 Wall Street in New York. The purpose of the letter is to make arrangements for needed repairs to engine #6 before putting her into service. Putting an engine in the shop goes a bit slower when you have to clear it with a lawyer in New York first.

The letter to the Trustees lawyer about repairs to #6 must have been approved to have the job done by the Harlem Railroad. On 27 May (a month and a half later), there is another note to the lawyer:

> Will forward engine six tomorrow morning to Millerton. Will Robert's man receive her there or should I send man to Brewster & deliver and get receipt there?
> Signed    C. L. Kimball

On the following day, 28 May 1879, there is an unsigned copy of the receipt for the delivery of engine #6.

> Received from the Newburgh, Dutchess and Connecticut Railroad Co. One (1) locomotive - being NYC&HR Ry No. 6 - In good order together with the following tools belonging to said engine.
>
> *(List of over 30 items including coal scoop, coal pick, jacks, wrenches, flags, etc.)*

> I to pay freight charge on the same from Millerton to Brewster.
>
> [space for a signature]

This seems to be one of the engines left over from George H. Brown's failed Canadian venture. Two months later, in July, there is a follow-up letter inquiring if engine #6 can be repaired at the Harlem Railroad or does it need to be sent to Schenectady? Freight to Schenectady would be expensive. After four months, they have not even decided where the job will be done. Don't count on using #6 for any revenue runs just yet.

Some of the equipment assignments seemed to be fairly stable and permanent. For example, the 1856 wood burning locomotive called Washington was assigned to the Clove Branch Railroad to haul passengers, freight, and iron ore. The old Washington toiled on the eight miles of Clove Branch track for a number of years until she was replaced by a new engine called the General Schultze in 1883. Maybe she stayed there because nobody else wanted a twenty-year-old wood burner.

The engine Washington was offered for sale for two thousand five hundred dollars as early as April 1881 in a letter to the Freehold & New York Railroad.

### Volume 12, page 3, 18 April 1881
*Two-page letter to J. Ralph (in reply to a previous letter) Supt. & C. F&NY Railroad:*

> Making a statement of what repairs the engine would require which I will send to you as soon as prepared. I think the engine would answer for a light train on your road very nicely - She is smart and doing good work on the C.B. Road but is not heavy or powerful enough for the business of that road when both furnaces are in blast. She ought in my judgement to be worth $3000 as she stands. Come up and look at her and we

will talk the matter up fully - what is your maximum grade?

[The rest of the letter is personal regarding buying a house, who got married, and who died. It seems that they are old friends. Also Kimball owned property in Monmouth County, New Jersey.]
    signed  C. L. Kimball

**Volume 12, page 52, 29 April 1881**
*Two-page Letter to J. Ralph Supt.
F&NY Railroad Keyport, New Jersey:*

In reply to your favor of the 12th. We will sell you the engine Washington of the C. B. RR just as she stands for $2500 provided we can procure another engine to take her place within a reasonable time. I make this proviso for the reason that the shops are busy and if we had to rent an engine for several months before a new one could be procured we might better keep the Washington. I will see at once what can be done in the way of getting another machine and advise you. In case you wish to take the Washington at the above price, which I think is fair for both companies, Mr. Van Buskirk advises that main valves need facing, etc. etc, [list of needed repairs] These repairs he estimates would cost from $50 to $75 and with them the engine should run years on a light train with ordinary roundhouse repairs that any engine might need. Her tires are in fairly good condition and would probably last years without turning. The rear tires are worn the most as we have had to Back her one way on the C.B. extension but as you would probably only run her ahead this would do no harm. Please let me hear from you soon in the matter.
    Your Truly  C. L. Kimball

Does Kimball sound like a used car salesman when he talks about the worn tires and says they will be fine for what you want to do with them? A copy of a letter dated 15 April 1879 is a good example of the exchanges of cars and engines over a period of several years. It lists a number of equipment transfers:

 25 Sept. 1875 Engine #5 and a list of cars were sent to High Bridge
 May 1876, four passenger coaches were sent to the NJ Southern.
 8 May 1876 Engine #15 was sent to the NJ Midland.
 28 June 1877 six box cars and ten gondolas were sent to the Freehold and NY
 13 Aug 1877 Engine #7 was sent to the Freehold and NY
 13 June 1878 twenty box cars were sent to the Greenwood Lake Ice Co.

Even as late as 23 December 1880, there were still more equipment transfers. There is a copy of a bill for eighty-four dollars to J. C. Davis of Cold Spring "For transferring the last lot of cars to West Point. Engines were taken down November 19."

There is no indication of the numbers or ownership. It must have been a bookkeeping nightmare trying to keep track of what went where and who was supposed to pay. The ND&C used the equipment owned by the trustees. Whenever the ND&C did repair work, they sent a bill to the trustees. In Volume 12, starting on 2 May 1881, there is a fifteen-page listing of bills sent to the trustees over the period of June 1877 to March 1881.

The list includes a wide variety of items from travel expenses and labor to parts, material, and paint.

Superintendent Kimball began shopping for a new locomotive to replace the lightweight and aging Washington. This turned out to be more of a problem than he had expected. He wrote another letter to Ralph explaining the delay.

**Volume 12, 3 May 1881**
*Short letter to J. E. Ralph
Supt. & C. F&NY Railroad:*

Replying to your favor of yesterday I have to say that I have asked the Baldwin Locomotive works, The Rogers Locomotive and Machine Works and the Danforth Locomotive and Machine Company to name prices and earliest date of delivery possible for such a locomotive as we want and asked them to answer at once. As soon as I hear from them I will advise by telegraph to save time stating whether or not we will part with the Washington. There are two Westinghouse brakes on fixtures for them here. [?]
    Yours Truly C. L. Kimball

### Volume 12, 5 May 1881
*Short letter to J. E. Ralph*
*Supt. F&NY Railroad Keyport, New Jersey:*

Dear Sir [Why so formal now?]

 Todays mail brings word for these locomotive builders - Grant cannot deliver an engine before February 1882. - Danforth Locomotive and Machine Co. will not name a date - Rogers Locomotive and Machine Works named March 1882. None of these will name a price now. Have not heard from Baldwin. It does not look like we could spare the Washington.
    Yours Truly C. L. Kimball

It sounds like all the locomotive builders were very busy in the spring of 1881. By that time the Washington was twenty-five years old and too light to handle the ore trains coming out of Sylvan Lake. There was not much choice in the matter. The Washington was repaired and patched and continued to struggle with the ore trains.

### Volume 12, Page 562, 26 September 1881
*Letter to Schultze explaining*
*the condition of Washington:*

 Replaced some flues and more on order. We will need another engine to take her place and keep her here until the new flues have been put in and her valves put in order. H. Lasher either by carelessness or ignorance twisted one of the steam pipes in the engine that was sent up to take the place of the Washington, rendering it necessary to retain the engine to fix the joint. We are short of power at present and have been for several days but will be alright in a day or two. Lasher is inclined not to give the Washington a fair chance I fear. In fact I don't think much of his ability anyway.

In reading further in the ND&C records, the check to cover the delayed sale of the Washington did not arrive until April 1884. In a later section, we will see more about the process of finding a replacement engine.

Another wood-burning locomotive that was just about as old as the Washington was the Tioronda.

By September 1881, the Tioronda also was up for sale.

### Volume 12, page 471, 1 September 1881
*Letter to Jno. P. Muldoon, Hudson, New York:*

Dear sir, I will sell you the locomotive Tioronda which you saw yesterday just as she stands (minus the tender) for three hundred & fifty dollars ($350.00) cash. I will also give room somewhere in our yard to cut her up if you wish provided you do it within a reasonable length of time.
    Yours Truly C. L. Kimball

### Volume 12, Page 537, 19 September 1881
*Letter to Gen. Jno. Schultze, pres.:*

 I enclose check for $350.00 on Marine Nat. bank drawn by Marnie [?] Briggs of 128 Pearl St NY and endorsed by H. C. Briggs which is the proceeds of sale of the worn out locomotive Tioronda which was the property of the estate of James Brown. This check had better be presented at the bank tomorrow and if there is anything wrong about it please telegraph me at once as the engine will remain here until the day after tomor-

row and could be held if the check is found to be worthless.
                    Yours Truly  C. L. Kimball

It seems that Kimball was not favorably impressed by Mr. Muldoon the scrap dealer. The check must have been good because there are no further letters about it. We can only assume that poor old Tioronda met her fate in the fall of 1881.

Finding a shop to do major repair work seemed to be a perpetual problem. Either the shops were too busy or they charged too much. There are many letters in the ND&C books on this subject. Here are some samples:

**Volume 13, Page 454, 21 February 1882**
*Letter to James Cook, Danforth Locomotive and Machine Company, Paterson, New Jersey, inquiring if they can overhaul a Mogul (#8) they built for the Dutchess & Columbia Railroad in 1872.*

**Volume 13, Page 564, 14 March 1882**
*Letter to Schultze stating that Danforth cannot overhaul the engine and return it until July 1883. Other builders have about the same workload.*

**Volume 13, Page 597, 23 March 1882**
*Letter to Charles G. Ellis, superintendent, Schenectady Locomotive Works:*

We accept your proposition of March 16th and will forward the engine to you at once. [signed by  C. L. Kimball]

It sounds like Kimball had found a shop to do the work and was wasting no time in getting the job done. There were no letters to the lawyers to arrange this repair job. It was possible that the ND&C had purchased the engine from the trustees and permission was no longer required.

Throughout the years of ND&C operation, there are many references to equipment belonging to the trustees. For example, in 1882, a letter discusses estimated value.

**Volume 15, Page 9, 14 September 1882**

Estimated value of James Brown rolling stock  Locomotives
  No. 1  In good repair. Will need at the end of 12 months new flues, piston rods and packing. $4750.00
  No. 2  In good repair. Will need next year new crosshead, pistons and packing. $4750.00
  No. 3  Needs general overhaul. Wants new tires, crank pins, pistons and packing. $2750.00
  No. 4  Now in shop undergoing repair. Is to have new tubes, flues, body patched and will then be worth $5000.00
[long list of other rolling stock]

By 1883, the ND&C had been in operation for six years, but they still did not own much of their equipment.

**Volume 15, Page 677, 2 February 1883**

Listing of rolling stock belonging to trustees NYB&M Railway
  4 locomotives #5, #6, #7 and #8
  [long list of cars]

**Volume 15, Page 678, 3 February 1883**

Valuation of trustees rolling stock.
Engines #5, #6 and #7  $5000 each
Engine #8  $8000 (#8 was rebuilt in 1882)
[list of other rolling stock for a total of $56,850]

Confusion can be catching as evidenced from a letter written to the master mechanic in 1883. Superintendent Kimball chewed out Van Buskirk for swapping tenders between engines so the numbers did not match. It was confusing the crews. Even the people who were in charge of the railroad did not always know the ownership of properties.

**Volume 18, Page 399, 9 May 1884**
*Letter to Schultze about history of the ND&C:*

**List of materials to paint the ND&C RR Hopewell Junction depot, 1884.**
ND&C RR letterbooks, Volume 18, Page 88.
Collection of the Beacon Historical Society.

D&C bought two mogul engines and sold one to P&E in October of seventy two. The other is property of trustees and is in service here. [engine #8?]

I don't know how this engine came to be in the hands of NYB&W RR. Engine #8 sent to NJ Midland RR 8 May 1876 and returned to Dutchess Junction 14 Apr 1880 rebuilt last year in Schenectady.

Another letter to Van Buskirk in June 1884 asked a question.

**Volume 18, Page 556, 21 June 1884**
*Question to W. Van Buskirk:*

When do you propose to lay up the trustees engines #6 and #7 and put the ND&C engines #3 and #4 in service and pay the company the rent? Something must be done to reduce expenses.

In 1884 and 1888, there are notations about locomotives and other equipment being purchased from the estate of James Brown or from the NYB&M Railroad Company. Despite the turmoil and shortages of rolling stock plus competition from other lines, the ND&C survived and continued serving the farms and towns of central Dutchess County.

Of course other railroad property had to be kept in good condition. Early in 1884, Charles Kimball sent out a letter with instructions and a list of materials to paint the Hopewell Junction depot. There was no premixed paint on the list. It included white lead, turpentine, raw oil, and several color pigments. Hopewell Junction depot looked as good as new in the spring of 1884, with a fresh coat of paint on ochre yellow walls and chocolate brown trim. With paint being mixed for each job, it was doubtful that all ND&C stations looked exactly alike.

One of the major factors that kept the ND&C in business was ownership of tracks and right of way. The monthly rental checks for track rights from other railroads often spelled the difference between solvency and bankruptcy for the ND&C. This was particularly true in the case of the NY&NE Railroad, which paid the ND&C thousands of dollars per month for using the tracks between Hopewell Junction and Wicopee Junction.

# Dutchess Junction

OVER THE YEARS, Dutchess Junction was the center of ND&C Railroad activity. At the peak of operations, Dutchess Junction was a thriving town with a train station that served two railroads, the ND&C Railroad and the New York Central & Hudson River Railroad (NYC&HR). There was also the busy ferry and freight dock for Hudson River boat traffic. The ND&C Railroad repair shops were located at Dutchess Junction as well. The railroad owned the tenement houses in which the workers lived. Descriptions of the ND&C facilities include a locomotive repair shop, a carpenter shop, brass foundry, paint shop, car repair and build shop, coal and water facilities, plus a turntable with a roundhouse and train yard. A brick manufacturing company was adjacent to the railroad property. Dutchess Junction was a bustling, active community.

Today, there is very little evidence that Dutchess Junction ever existed. When you ask where Dutchess Junction is, most local residents respond with only a puzzled look. The nearest passable road is more than a mile away, but if you hike through the trees to Dutchess Junction, all you are likely to find are a few overgrown foundations and some scattered bricks. Metro-North and Amtrak trains thunder past what seems only to be woodland along the banks of the Hudson River.

Before this location was called Dutchess Junction, it was a surveyor's marker called a plumb point. The name originated from the plumb bob, a pointed weight on a string that surveyors and carpenters used. Through a slip of the pen on an old map, the letter 'b' was lost and it became Plum Point even though there was no point and not one plum tree anywhere

**View of Dutchess Junction, NY, c. 1880. Long freight dock and depot at left. Ferry slip in the center.**
Collection of J. W. Swanberg.

near. In 1849, tracks for the Hudson River Railroad line were built along the river bank past Plum Point. Then, in 1868, Plum Point was chosen as the starting point for a new railroad eastward across Dutchess County. It was called the Dutchess and Columbia Railroad. Since this new railroad connected to the NYC&HR Railroad Hudson line, the area was named Dutchess Junction.

By 1872, the D&C Railroad facilities at Dutchess Junction included a passenger station with a roof extending over the D&C track and two tracks of the Hudson line. The station also covered the local freight depot. The D&C Railroad and the NYC&HR Railroad co-owned the building. There was a dock 702 feet long on the river side of the station that was with steam powered hoist engines and derricks to handle freight and coal from river barges. Coal barges from the D&H Canal terminal near Kingston came down the river to Dutchess Junction. These river barges handled up to three hundred tons of coal per day. The D&C Railroad used two scows or floats to carry train cars of Pennsylvania coal across the river from an Erie Railroad connection in Newburgh. The Penn Coal Company owned these car floats. The train cars on floats carried as much as four hundred tons of coal per day across the river.

Part of the dock was used for merchandise and passenger service from Newburgh and New York City. A ferry named the *Fanny Garner* shuttled back and forth across the river to Newburgh handling as much as one hundred tons of freight per day plus passengers. In four short years, Plum Point had gone from woodland to Dutchess Junction, a bustling freight-and-passenger-handling community with rail and water connections to the world.

In April 1876, a disastrous fire destroyed the station. The fire also destroyed the records of the D&C Railroad. The probable cause of the fire that destroyed the station was noted in a letter eleven years later in August 1887:

> In fact the fire that destroyed our station buildings at Dutchess Junction originated in the corner of the building where the lamps were cleaned and filled.

After the fire, Superintendent Kimball specified that all lamp facilities must be built in separate buildings away from other structures. As a result of the fire, records for the first ten years of the D&C Railroad were lost. In later years, the company had to rely on the memory of men like Charles Kimball when there were questions about the early times.

Most of what we know about that old Dutchess Junction station comes from a description written by Charles Kimball years after the fire, and from a drawing dated 1873. The photo on page 27 is a view looking north along the tracks with the station roof arching overhead. In the distance, you can see Dennings Point and the bridge and pilings for the trestle that was never completed when the BH&E Railroad went bankrupt in 1870. The D&C Railroad main track curves off to the right up the hill, across the Fishkill Creek Bridge to Matteawan.

While looking at that 1873 station drawing, questions come to mind. Why was a wooden station structure built over the tracks where steam locomotives spouted clouds of smoke and sparks? Other stations along the line were built with slate roofing material to prevent fires. Was there any protection under the arch roof? We will probably never know the answers, but later stations at Dutchess Junction were built with only a pedestrian bridge over the tracks instead of a roof structure.

After several name changes and financial failures, the D&C Railroad was reorganized as the Newburgh Dutchess & Connecticut Railroad. Beginning in 1877, the ND&C Railroad was the owner and manager of Dutchess Junction. The ND&C Railroad proved to be much more stable than the D&C Railroad and endured more than twenty five years into the early part of the twentieth century.

One of the problems at Dutchess Junction was getting access to the Hudson River dock, which was on the west side of the NYC&HR Railroad tracks. There was only a narrow strip of land between the tracks and the river. Passengers could walk up and over a bridge, but freight was a different problem. Carloads of coal and freight had to be moved across the NYC&HR double main line to and from the dock. A diagram in the ND&C letterbooks, dated October 1881, shows proposed changes to the switches the ND&C Railroad used to move trains across the NYC&HR Railroad double main line. From the looks of the diagram, it seems that the ND&C trains would move onto the northbound NYC&HR main then back up moving north. The next move was forward at a shallow angle across the southbound NYC&HR main into the dock area. All this would be done in reverse sequence to get out again. This must have involved careful management to prevent accidents.

In 1881, there were major changes in the ND&C operations at Dutchess Junction, when the New York & New England (NY&NE) Railroad opened a larger freight and ferry service about a mile or so north along the river at Fishkill Landing. This ferry service hauled train cars to and from the Erie Railroad terminal in Newburgh. A connecting track was built from the Fishkill Landing ferry up the hill to the ND&C at a point called Wicopee Junction. The NY&NE Railroad paid the ND&C Railroad for the right to run trains eleven miles from Wicopee Junction to Hopewell Junction on ND&C rails. At Hopewell, the NY&NE turned east on their own tracks toward Connecticut. The two railroads were then running

ND&C RR letter with a diagram of proposed changes to the track layout crossing the NYC&HRR double main line for access to the Dutchess Junction dock area, October 1881. The ND&C RR depot is at the lower left. Hudson River is at the top. North is to the right. ND&C trains would come down the hill from Wicopee at the lower right onto the track adjacent to the depot. To get to the dock, they had to back up on the northbound side of the NYC&HRR main line, then move forward across the southbound side of the NYC&HRR main. These moves were done in reverse order to get back out again.

freight and passenger trains in both directions on the eleven-mile stretch of single track main between Wicopee and Hopewell.

The NY&NE ferry operation at Fishkill Landing had a brand new, larger, and more powerful car ferry named the *William T. Hart*. This ferry was much more efficient compared to the car floats that the the ND&C at Dutchess Junction used. At that time, the *Hart* was the second largest ferry in the world. It had two complete steam engines and required a crew of twenty-four men. The Fishkill Landing facility had another big advantage over Dutchess Junction. It did not cross the NYC&HR tracks

**Left: Former ND&C RR station at Matteawan which is now part of Beacon, NY. The ND&C RR letterbooks were found while renovating this building. Main Street is on the upper level at the left.** Photo by author, March 2002.

**Right: Original Matteawan station built by the D&C RR in 1873 on Main Street. First floor was at track level and waiting rooms were on the second floor. It later became the headquarters of the ND&C RR, and a third floor was added. This building is still in use for business and apartments in Beacon, NY. 1870s.** Collection of the Beacon Historical Society.

at grade. The line up the hill to Wicopee Junction and Matteawan crossed over the Hudson line on an overhead bridge, so there were no traffic conflicts. ND&C Railroad management saw the advantages of the NY&NE operation and struck a deal.

By January 1883, all ND&C carload freight that crossed the river traveled on the NY&NE ferry at Fishkill Landing and was transferred at Wicopee Junction for a fixed transfer charge. This arrangement lasted more than twenty years. The ND&C no longer needed the car floats, and the pace of business on the Dutchess Junction dock slowed considerably. Barge and ferry traffic at Dutchess Junction continued, but the volume of business was much smaller without the car floats.

ND&C Railroad superintendent Charles Kimball decided to move his office from Dutchess Junction to Matteawan in May 1882. There is no stated reason for this in the books. Perhaps he felt that an office on Main Street was better for business. Or maybe he just wanted his office closer to home. There were very few telephones in Matteawan in 1880, but Charles Kimball had one in his home. His new office was equipped with telegraph and telephone lines to communicate with ND&C stations to control train movements. This included NY&NE trains that ran on the ND&C line between Wicopee Junction and Hopewell Junction. Telegraph lines were also connected to the NYC&HR Railroad and New York City.

By early 1890, both the ND&C and the NY&NE were feeling the competition from the newly opened Poughkeepsie Railroad Bridge. The bridge route was much faster and more efficient than the system of breaking a train apart and hauling the sections across the river on a ferry. Dutchess Junction and Fishkill Landing continued to fight for business for a number of years, but it was a losing battle. Regardless of the competition, the business of keeping a railroad running continued at

Dutchess Junction. Despite the competition from the bridge route, there seemed to be plenty of traffic on the ND&C in the spring of 1890.

### Volume 29, Page 574, 23 May 1890

Yesterday we handled in the 24 hours, midnight to midnight, in all, regular and special trains, 53 trains between Wiccopee Junction and Hopewell Junction.

That is an average of more than two trains per hour for the whole twenty-four hours. How many more trains could be handled on a single track main line? It is no wonder that the repair shops were busy.

One of the problems at Dutchess Junction and Fishkill Landing was keeping the river access deep enough for steamboats and barges. Periodically, the dock area would have to be dredged, which was an additional expense with which the bridge route did not have to contend.

### Volume 30, Page 233, 15 September 1890

At high tide we have scant nine feet in channel across flats to the dock. At dock not as much but bottom is soft mud and safe.

### Volume 30, Page 239, 17 September 1890

Yours of the 15th at hand. You can unload at the NY&NE RR dock at Fishkill Landing where they have from 10 to 12 feet of water at low tide, but the track is 15 or 20 feet from the edge of the dock. Ties would have to be carried to the cars.

Although the car floats were no longer carrying freight cars to the Dutchess Junction dock, the dock was still used for barges and steamboats. In May 1896, eight dollars each was the quoted price for forty foot white oak pilings to act as dock fenders. That same summer, Brakeman Frank Bloomer fell between cars and suffered a broken leg and bruises while backing cars onto the Dutchess Dock.

Statements of tonnage moved on the dock were still included in management reports. In the summer of 1898, the river channel to the Dutchess Junction dock was dredged again, and engine #3 ran off the points of a switch in the yard.

In June 1899, the Dutchess Junction station was painted. The ND&C Railroad and the NYC&HR Railroad split the cost. Because of an accident and court case, the ND&C Railroad decided to build a fence around the Dutchess Junction yard in 1899. Settlement of the court case cost the ND&C $1,775.04 plus the cost of the new fence. In November 1899, more changes were made to the Dutchess Junction yard. Two of the yard tracks used for parking the wrecking crane and passenger coaches were upgraded to eliminate water accumulation. A new coach storage track was added. The following year, the Dutchess Junction platforms were reconstructed.

The ND&C turntable at Millerton collapsed under a heavy locomotive in April 1903. During the repairs, the mechanics found out that there were new, upgraded parts available from William Sellers & Company of Philadelphia. After finishing the Millerton turntable upgrade, similar parts were used to improve the Dutchess Junction turntable. From these bits and pieces of information we can see that Dutchess Junction was indeed a thriving community. It also included tenement houses for the workers. On several occasions in the ND&C letterbooks, the tenements are mentioned when a tenant is behind in rent payments. On 1 February 1888, there was a notice of delinquent rents for four names. One wonders if they were evicted in time for the great blizzard of 1888 a month later. During that blizzard, work trains were assembled and sent out from Dutchess Junction with men and shovels to fight the drifts along the line.

The tenement houses also needed occasional maintenance work. On 9 March 1900, Vice President G. Hunter Brown wrote a letter to Kernahan and Patterson at 80 Front Street, in New York. That company had installed the roofs of the tenements in 1884, and sixteen years later they were in need of attention again. The letter requested that a representative come to Dutchess Junction and meet with Master Mechanic Holmes to plan the repair job.

The pace of activity at Dutchess Junction slowed to a crawl when winter ice on the river halted boat traffic. This was the time to catch up on deferred maintenance projects. The ND&C used two of the smaller locomotives on the dock and in the yard area. When the river was frozen, these engines could be put into the shop for items such as firebox repairs, new flues, and tires. Most ordinary repair work was done in the ND&C shops at Dutchess Junction, but major items required a trip to a locomotive overhaul facility. A locomotive manufacturer generally took care of the major work. Putting the dock engines in any shop was not a simple task because the engines did not actually belong to the ND&C Railroad, as the following letter illustrates. The road had been in operation as the ND&C Railroad for seven years, yet almost all of their rolling stock belonged to somebody else. These engines were the property of the trustees of the NYB&M Railway that had gone bankrupt ten years earlier.

### Volume 15, Page 600, 10 January 1883
*Letter to ND&C president, Gen. Schultze from Superintendent Charles Kimball:*

I enclose herewith W. G. Van Buskirks report of the condition of the two engines #6 and #7, property of the trustees. I agree with Mr. Van B. fully that these engines should be sent away to be repaired, and in view of the large rent paid for their use, and the fact that they were for a long time in service at High Bridge by the NYC&HR RR, I think it is more than right that the trustees should foot the bill.

Will you place the matter before Mr. [ ? ] soon as possible so the repairs may be made this winter as the engines will be required next spring and they are useless as they are now.   Signed C. L. Kimball

Some of the maintenance procedures didn't always work out as planned. In a letter dated 3 February 1883, Superintendent Charles Kimball is chewing out Master Mechanic Van Buskirk for swapping tenders between engines so the numbers did not match. It was confusing the crews. In another letter, Kimball asked Van Buskirk why there were nineteen gondolas waiting on the shop track when they were needed out on the line. Apparently, the friction between Kimball and Van Buskirk came to a breaking point in the fall of 1885.

### Volume 21, Pages 164-165, 4 November 1885

Kimball asked for the resignation of Van Buskirk, master mechanic. The last straw was allowing a coach with a bent axle to be used on a train to Hopewell. He will officially leave on 1 January 1886, but Kimball wants to pay him for November and December and let him go right away.

Kimball accepted Van Buskirk's resignation on 13 November 1885, but he was to be paid to the end of the year. In view of Van Buskirk's seventeen years of service, Kimball agreed to help Van Buskirk find a new position. Kimball wrote to a long list of railroads requesting free passes for a job hunting tour through Virginia, South Carolina, Tennessee, Illinois, and Louisiana. There is no mention of where Van Buskirk eventually moved to. A man named Holmes replaced Van Buskirk as master mechanic of the ND&C Railroad at Dutchess Junction.

During that same winter of 1885-86, Kimball was engaged in making arrangements for a new depot at Dutchess Junction. In the ND&C letterbooks, it is not clear whether this new station is to replace the one that burned ten years earlier or what facilities may have been used during that time. Kimball and ND&C lawyer Eno went to a railroad commissioners meeting in Albany. They made the decision to build a new depot at Dutchess Junction not costing more than one thousand, five hundred dollars. The cost would be split between the ND&C and the NYC&HR Railroad. To make room for the new depot, some of the sidings and the ND&C main track had to be moved. A letter on 7 January 1886 requested bids for construction of a new depot to be a forty by twenty frame building. Five construction bids came in, and the lowest one was for $1,450 from B. T. Hall, which was accepted. Three years later, Kimball was writing letters of complaint about the defects and weak points in the roof of the new depot.

In addition to building a new depot, Kimball also was involved in expanding the Dutchess Junction machine shop and purchasing more tools. He sent out a letter on 11 January 1886 looking for a good used thirty-six-inch lathe for car axles and wheels. A month later, on 12 February, Kimball reported to President Schultze on the purchase of a lathe, a planer, and a drill press from the Prentice Tool Supply Company in New York City. The total cost for all three tools was $1,215. That same day Kimball asked Holmes, the new master mechanic, for a complete cost accounting of the machine shop addition and all the tools purchased.

### Volume 24, Page 67, 17 May 1887
*Letter to Cayuta Wheel and Foundry Company, Sayre, Pennsylvania:*

We are now buying our wheels bored as we have facilities for fitting axles and pressing wheels on. Can you bore them to our order and if so what is your charge?

The summer of 1887 must have been a busy one for the ND&C shop crew. In early June, Kimball informed ND&C Railroad president Schultze that he had assembled all the materials and was ready to begin construction of a new car repair building at Dutchess Junction. The plan was to put it on a strip of land that the NYC&HR Railroad claimed. He asked Schultze if he should start work. The following day, Kimball was told to begin construction of the new car repair shop. There was no indication of whether Schultze had actually consulted the NYC&HR Railroad about the disputed location.

In addition to building a new car repair shop, Kimball also went shopping for a used passenger coach. On 6 August 1887, a second hand Erie Railroad coach #427 was delivered to the ND&C at Dutchess Junction. That same day it was put into service on train #56.

In August 1887, the ND&C purchased a used driver wheel lathe to be delivered in October from a railroad in Ohio. They also had purchased a one hundred ton, hand-powered wheel press that they later traded for a 150 ton press. It seems that the ND&C had a fairly complete and busy shop operation at Dutchess Junction. They even took in some contract repair work for other small railroads in the area. We can get a few more clues about the extent of the ND&C operations at Dutchess Junction from a series of letters to their insurance agent in October 1887.

### Volume 24, Page 592, 14 October 1887
*Letter to Melville Brown, 22 Pine Street, New York:*

Cannot we insure the Engine House, Machine Shop & Blacksmith Shop together at fourteen hundred and fifty dollars as they are connected and virtually one building, and save dividing the tools located in those departments named.

C. L. Kimball   Supt.

### Volume 24, Pages 609-612

*These four pages were an inventory list of tools and equipment in the Dutchess Junction shops*

### Volume 24, Page 627, 19 October 1887

*Letter to insurance agent:*

There is no woodwork done in the engine house, machine shop & blacksmith shop building or any of the buildings insured, except the carpenter shop.

The carpenter shop is a new building and is located west of the engine house machine and blacksmith shop. The building south of it is an old one and is to be torn down.

Letters to metal distributors give us further information about ND&C Railroad shop operations:

### Volume 28, Page 167, 9 July 1889

We use all our brass and copper scrap in our own brass foundry and at present need no journal bearings. At what price will you sell us one cask, about 1200 lbs. of Lake Ingot copper delivered F.O.B.?

### Volume 28, Page 635, 16 December 1889

We make our own car journal bearings hence use all old bearings. All purchases are made through my office. When in need of new metal we buy of Phelps Dodge & Co. as a rule.

### Volume 29, Pages 144 and 145, 29 January 1890

*Letter to President Schultze outlining equipment status. (This letter is blurred and the numbers are very hard to read.):*

During the year engines 6 & 7 have been rebuilt and made as good as new at a cost for labor and materials $6159.29 [very blurred] Both engines have new tenders and trucks complete, are furnished with Westinghouse automatic air brakes and the first named had a new steel boiler all of which is included in the above mentioned cost of repairs.

Engines 4 & 8 received general repairs. All of our engines are now in good condition, except Nos, 3 & 9, which are becoming pretty near worn out.

Passenger coaches, freight cars, buildings, fences, and track held a similar status.

### Volume 29, Page 173, 4 February 1890

*Letter to Baker Heater Company saying that the weather has not been cold enough to really test the car heaters, but they seem to work:*

The waste pipe is defective. It will freeze up when the mercury stands at 20 degrees above. We have had great trouble with your fittings. Nearly all the joints proved to be leaky after a week or so in service.

### Volume 29, Page 188 and 195, 8 and 11 February 1890

The new wheel press has been installed and is working. The old press is being returned for a credit of three hundred dollars.

### Volume 29, Page 479, 29 April 1890

*ND&C superintendent Charles Kimball instructed Master Mechanic Holmes to take down the worn brass lamps in the coaches and have them nickel plated for five dollars each.*

### Volume 29, Page 266, 3 March 1890

*Requisition for March included axles, arch bars, blank bolts and nuts for ten pairs of trucks to take the place of the old style Lake Trucks that were giving out:*

The building of our engine house has reduced our supply of lumber so that we must replenish it to the extent called for in the req-

**ND&C RR #4 "Millbrook."**
Collection of J. W. Swanberg.

uisition which is needed at once.

C. L. Kimball

It seems that Dutchess Junction yard was modified many times during its lifetime.

**Volume 29, Page 231, 22 February 1890**
*Instructions to support ND&C chief engineer Everett Garrison on trestle work:*

Garrison will be at Dutchess Junction about 9:20 AM next Monday to set the stakes on new line and to stake out the culvert foundation under Bay Trestle. Have the stakes made and a man on hand, with a sledge to drive them, to meet Mr. Garrison as above.

**Volume 29, Page 301, 11 March 1890**
*Chief Engineer Everett Garrison was planning to have work done at Dutchess Junction Kimball wrote to him and asked:*

I am in receipt of your two letters also the map showing proposed changes in line at Dutchess Junction. Did you compute the number of yards it would take to make the embankment for the proposed main track independent of the filling in of the trestle or filling for new sidings?

The new engine house was completed on 6 March 1890. The cost of labor was $646.33, and the total of materials was $1,377.38, for a grand total of $2,023.41. A new water tank was built out of yellow pine timbers in the spring of 1891.

**Volume 29, Page 312, 17 March 1890**
*Letter to Melville Brown,
Wall Street, New York:*

This Co. has recently erected a six stall Round House at Dutchess Junction located just east of the turntable and north east of the engine house and machine shop, but entirely detached from that and other buildings. It forms the segment of a circle of which the turntable is the center and the fronts of the stalls are each 12 Ft. center to center, four stalls being 65 feet deep and two of them 75 Ft. deep. The building is of wood covered with 3 ply standard roofing which is said to be fireproof. Heated by steam.

This building has cost us a trifle less than $2500.00 and we wish you to insure it for $2000.00 making the policy from now until Oct. 17th 1890 at noon, that being the time when our other insurance expires and we can then include this building with others in our next policy.

The Dutchess Junction Paint Shop which is on our policy of Oct 17/89 for $100.00 has been torn down and is no longer in existence.

Please advise as to insurance on the Round House as soon as possible.

Yours Truly   C.L. Kimball

### Volume 29, Page 393, 12 April 1890

We shall be ready to commence work finishing the foundation for the scale at Dutchess Junction on Wednesday Morning next.

As a follow up to installing the new scale, there were two more letters in the spring of 1891.

### Volume 31, Page 341, 1 April 1891

*Kimball wrote to Page Harris & Company, New York:*

I find the second hand track scale belonging to you-the one you took in exchange for the new scale we put in at Dutchess Junction about a year ago-is still standing at Dutchess Junction.

### Volume 31, Page 345, 4 April 1891

*Instructions to ship the old track scale to Howe Scale Company, Rutland, Vermont. With that much activity, even repair shops needed a bit of maintenance.*

### Volume 30, Page 626, 24 December 1890

*Letter to Green, Tweed & Company, 83 Chambers Street, NY:*

The main belt that we want tightened at our Dutchess Junction shops is 14 inches wide and 44 feet long. We have no clamps or in fact any of the necessary tools to tighten it.

The ND&C Railroad made at least two ventures into building their own rolling stock. A combination baggage, mail, and smoking car was built in the Dutchess Junction shops, as well as a number of ballast handling work cars.

### Volume 30, Page 309, 6 October 1890

During the coming winter we hope to build a baggage mail & smoking car in our shops at Dutchess Junction NY.

The next mention of the car-building project was not until May 1891. The project apparently had been started but progress was slower than planned. A year later, on 13 April 1892, Kimball wrote to Schultze that he wanted to contract with the Gilbert Car Manufacturing Company in Green Island, New York, to finish the baggage/smoking/mail combination car. The work force had been short over the winter and they could not get skilled men to finish the car. The cost estimate from Gilbert was too high, so they decided to finish the car in the ND&C shops. In August 1892, they were buying fixtures for the handling of mail on the new car. It took about two years, but the car was eventually completed. Finally, in November 1892, Kimball sent a letter to the local newspaper editor inviting him to come and see the new combination baggage and mail car that had been built at the Dutchess Junction shops.

During the winter months, deferred maintenance projects and occasionally building new equipment kept the shop crews busy. A number of ballast cars were built in the Dutchess Junction shops over the winters, but the jobs did not always get finished on time.

**Volume 76, Page 626, 8 June 1903**

Our shops have been overcrowded in turning out ballast cars to take care of this work. We will not be through with our car construction until probably the middle of July.

When practical working electrical systems became available, the ND&C Railroad at Dutchess Junction was one of the earliest customers. An electrician named Wright installed an electric light plant at the Dutchess Junction shops in March 1892. Kimball wrote a letter inviting the public to come and see the new installation.

We shall be pleased to exhibit the same to any one who is thinking of adopting such a light.

**Volume 33, Page 353, 1 April 1892**
*The electric light plant at Dutchess Junction was built under a contract with Judson and Hancock.*

75 - 16 candle power lamp dynamo.
40 - 16 candle power lamps located as we require.
whole system insulated from contact with wood.

**Volume 34, Page 608, 2 December 1892**
*The electric lights at Dutchess Junction did not work properly. Kimball wrote to Judson and Hancock::*

We look to you to put the plant in order at once to perform the work satisfactorily and trust that you will lose no time in doing so for we need the lights and must have it.

In November 1893, another fire disaster struck Dutchess Junction. This time the roundhouse, lumber shed, storehouse, and timbers supporting the water tank burned. Some of the structures that burned were less than three years old. Years later, a story written by Inglis Stuart relates some of the events of that Thursday night in November.

Nearing the end of my chapter it seems one incident should be narrated and that relates to the roundhouse fire alluded to in the earlier part. There was a colored man named George Washington, who after his emancipation in Virginia, came here and became coachman for a well known family. In 1873 this family was lost when their steamer went down. George then got employment on the N. D. & C. at Dutchess Jct. In 1893 when the fire broke out, he was advanced in years and by no means as agile as formerly but he had quick perception and, despite the rapidity with which the flames spread, he managed to run No. 1 to a place of safety. The other housed locomotives were reduced to hulks and it took a long time to restore them. I often talked with George but his modesty was such that he never referred to his deed.

In the following weeks, the ND&C struggled to keep the trains running and rebuild the lost buildings and the water tank. Replacing the tools and other contents of the shops took additional time and money. Here are some sample letters from that effort.

**Volume 36, Page 596, 27 November 1893**
*Letter to Willard Lumber Company,
New Hamburgh, New York:*
Our roundhouse, Lumber Shed and storehouse were entirely destroyed by fire last Thursday night and I enclose an order for some lumber to rebuild the same. Under the circumstances, I trust you will get this stuff to us at the very earliest moment you can, as we can do but little toward rebuilding until it arrives.

**Volume 36, Pages 600-601**
*Inventory of supplies in the tin shop at Dutchess Junction on 1 July 1893.*

**Volume 36, Page 623, 7 December 1893**
*Request for price on forty-seven windows and three doors from two lumber yards.*

**Volume 36, Page 631, 14 December 1893**
*Sending an order to Niagara Stamping and Tool Company for tinsmith tools to replace the ones destroyed in the fire.*

**Volume 36, Page 661, 1 January 1894**
*Urgent letter to Crosby Steam Gauge & Valve Company, Boston:*

We have received the 1 brass vacuum gauge and 6 brass coil syphons ordered Dec 20th but the 6 6 3/4 inch iron case Crosby steam gauges on same order have not arrived. We need them badly [underlined] a recent fire having destroyed our roundhouse and storehouse, ruining the gauges on three locomotives and burning all spare gauges.

**Volume 36, Page 665, 3 January 1894**
*List of materials bought since the fire with a request for usage information from Holmes. The list includes tools, stock, paint, furniture, lumber, and portable machinery. A new water tank and supporting frame are included. There is also a section for repairs to locomotives #3, #4, and #7.*

The heroic efforts of George Washington had saved engine #1, but at least three ND&C engines were severely damaged. By early 1894, the trains were back to a "normal" schedule, and the shops were again in operation.

The year 1895 saw major changes in ND&C Railroad management. J. Crosby Brown replaced President "General" Schultze. Our old friend Charles Kimball died that year and a much younger man named G. Hunter Brown Jr., who was the son of George H. Brown from the D&C Railroad days, replaced him. Brown Jr. also just happened to be the nephew of the new president. Both these men were part of the Brown family, which owned the ND&C Railroad.

G. Hunter Brown Jr. was a college man with little experience in railroading. He was more like a business manager, and he did not seem to have much interest in the actual workings of the railroad. Starting in 1895, the ND&C Railroad letterbooks, written mostly by G. Hunter Brown Jr., have a completely different style. Emphasis shifted from daily railroading to business dealings. G. Hunter Brown Jr. attended to railroad internal matters when he had to, but his main interest was business relations and the "Club" in New York City or murals for the office walls. He also sprinkled in a few mentions of sporting events such as football games, rowing competitions, and golf tournaments. One of the more interesting tales about G. Hunter Brown Jr. was that he occasionally wore pink shirts instead of the traditional starched white.

G. Hunter Brown Jr. did get involved in some of the maintenance and repairs at Dutchess Junction on 30 March 1896. Brown wrote to D. Budd at the Dutchess Junction Brick Company, which was adjacent to the ND&C Railroad shops. The iron chimney on the Dutchess Junction boiler had blown down over the winter. It had a brick base, and Brown wanted to build a new chimney of bricks that would not rust out from the steam engine gasses. The Budd brick Company owed money to the ND&C for past brick shipments. Brown proposed taking the price of new bricks off their bill. He wanted the bricks delivered to the boiler house by the "usual method," (by wheelbarrow) because the boiler was so close to the brick Company. This deal sounded like a very practical business approach to a set of problems. The ND&C collected on a back debt and at the same time obtained a new, more durable chimney for the boiler with minimal cost for transporting the bricks. The ND&C Railroad did have to pay for labor and scaffolding to build the new fifty-foot chimney. Total cost was $143.

In January 1901, ND&C locomotive engineers and firemen had completed a correspondence course on better management of locomotives. G. Hunter Brown planned an evening meeting to distribute prizes. The affair was held on 16 Mar 1901 to announce the results of the Railway Educational Associations locomotive fuel economy class. A list of class standings and the prize-winning engineer and fireman were presented. Engineer Robert Mateer was top man and won fifteen dollars in gold. Fireman S. B. Schoonmaker was top fireman, and he won ten dollars in gold. At that time this represented more than a weeks pay. Copies of the notice were posted in the Roundhouse, the Machine Shop, and the office bulletin board.

G. Hunter Brown Jr. seemed to be very careful about safety issues. In May 1901, he wrote a letter inquiring about Ellis Track Bumper Posts. It seems that one of the ND&C tracks ended right up against the north wall of the Dutchess Junction station. He was interested in preventing any unscheduled entries into the station.

Later, in the summer of 1901, Brown sent a letter to the William Mann Company in New York City to order new business cards. He explained that his father had recently died and to drop the Jr. from his name on the new cards.

The dates in the last volume of the ND&C letterbooks cover the summer and fall of 1904. Even near the end of the ND&C Railroad, there were projects underway for major improvements at Dutchess Junction. The largest of these projects was a new station that the ND&C Railroad and the NYC&HR Railroad would own jointly. On 25 July 1904, G. Hunter Brown wrote a letter to Mr. H. Fernstrom, chief engineer of the NYC&HR Railroad, acknowledging the agreement to build the new station. There were to be two waiting rooms, one for the ladies and one for the gentlemen, with a ticket office in the center. A coal furnace would provide heating. The NYC&HR main line was to be on the west side of the building, and the ND&C main was to be on the east side. Brown made some suggestions about improving the planned signs on the building and also suggested making a hatch in the side wall of the coal bin so that coal could be dumped down a chute from a train car directly into the bin without extra handling.

By 1 August 1904, there were no acceptable bids for construction of the new station, so the NYC&HR Railroad decided to build it using their own manpower. Brown agreed with this plan and suggested that when the new station was completed, the old station should be moved and used as a freight house. The last few entries in the last volume of the ND&C Railroad letterbooks were in October 1904, with no indication of whether the station was ever constructed. Since the NYC&HR Railroad planned to do the building, and Dutchess Junction continued to operate for some twelve more years as part of the CNE Railway, we can probably assume that the station was completed. Perhaps some research into the CNE and NH archives might settle the question.

The New York, New Haven & Hartford Railroad had taken over the NY&NE Railroad operation in 1898. This included all the facilities at Fishkill Landing. During the summer of 1904, the New Haven Railroad made major changes in the service at Fishkill Landing. Passenger service was discontinued, and car ferry service to and from Newburgh was abandoned. The New Haven Railroad maintained the freight connection with the NYC&HR Railroad at Fishkill Landing. This left the unprof-

**The ND&C RR sent a bill to the NYC&HR RR in September 1905 for the cost of building a new depot at Dutchess Junction. Note that Newburgh is spelled without the letter *h* at the end.**
Collection of the Beacon Historical Society.

itable passenger traffic to the ND&C Railroad at Dutchess Junction, and it also meant that the ND&C had no way to move train cars across the river. Train traffic across the Hudson River had to use the Poughkeepsie Bridge, which was controlled by the New Haven Railroad. ND&C business projections were looking pretty grim.

The last two months' entries in the ND&C letterbooks were for September and October 1904. Almost every phase of the operation was being cut back or halted completely. Track gangs and shop crews were cut to the bare minimum; no overtime was allowed. One of the last entries was instructions for the conductors to perform coach cleaning and maintenance while waiting for runs. Shortly after that, the ND&C Railroad was no more. In 1905, the New Haven Railroad purchased the ND&C Railroad and merged it into the CNE Railway. The CNE Railway was completely absorbed into the New Haven Railroad in 1927.

So ends the story of the ND&C Railroad at Dutchess Junction. Dutchess Junction continued to struggle on for a number of years as part of the CNE Railway but it was a losing battle. The Poughkeepsie Bridge took the rail traffic crossing the river. Automobiles and trucks took most of the passenger traffic and local freight. River barge freight was not enough to keep Dutchess Junction alive. By 1907, the CNE had sold the roundhouse, ice house, and machine shops to private parties, presumably for scrapping. Passenger connections with the NYC&HR Railroad continued, but the last passenger train chuffed up the hill to Wicopee Junction in 1916. The tracks to Wicopee Junction were sold for scrap as was the Tioronda Bridge over Fishkill Creek. By 1950, all that was left was a lonely passenger shelter by the NYC&HR Hudson line. If you look at today's map, you may find the name Dutchess Junction, but there is no town, no station, and no brick factory. The nearest passable road is more than a mile away. There are only trees and a few scattered bricks. As happens with so much of man's works, nature has reclaimed Plum Point, for there is no longer a junction there. Every day hundreds of AMTRAK and Metro-North riders may glance up from their newspapers as the train thunders past woodland that once was Dutchess Junction.

**Dutchess Junction, May 1950.**
Collection of Leroy Beaujon.

# The Clove Branch Railroad

A SHORT FOUR-MILE LINE called the Clove Branch Railroad (CB) was chartered in 1868 and opened in 1869. This was about the same time frame when the Dutchess and Columbia Railroad (D&C) was built from Dutchess Junction through Hopewell. The CB Railroad connected with the D&C Railroad about a mile northeast of present Hopewell Junction. At that time, Hopewell was not yet a junction. The connection point was near what is now the intersection of Route 82 and Clove Branch Road, which is near the old original Hopewell. In my collection I have a 1916 CNE Railway blueprint that clearly shows the Clove Branch Railroad junction embankment. In addition, there are aerial photographs taken in 1935 on file at the Dutchess County Soil and Water Conservation District in Millbrook, New York, that shows the line of the roadbed at Clove Branch Junction. The CB Railroad roadbed ran roughly parallel to Clove Branch and Beekman Roads, past the site of the Beekman golf course, then angled northeast across where the Taconic Parkway is now, to the iron ore mine at Sylvan Lake. The Clove Branch Railroad can be easily traced on the 1935 aerial photos.

The main purpose of the Clove Branch Railroad was to haul iron ore out of the mine at Sylvan Lake. The Clove Branch Railroad was essentially a short branch of the D&C Railroad. However, it was chartered and operated as a separate line that reported to the D&C management like a subsidiary. The president was the same George H. Brown who was president of the D&C Railroad. Maintenance work on CB Railroad rolling stock was done in the D&C Railroad shops at Dutchess Junction. D&C superintendent Charles Kimball was also the superintendent of the CB Railroad. This arrangement continued when the D&C Railroad became the ND&C Railroad in 1877 and the new president was "General" Schultze.

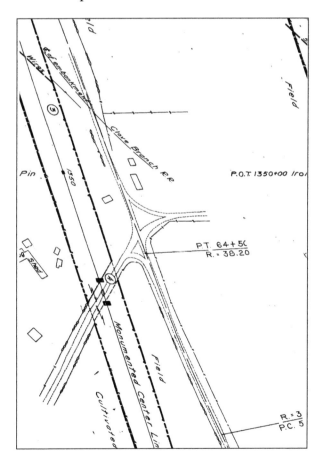

**1916 CNE Rwy blueprint showing Clove Branch Junction to Hopewell Junction at the bottom, to Arthursburg at the top. It clearly shows the curve of the CB RR connection just north of the intersection.** Author's collection.

**Part of an aerial photo from 1935 showing Rte. 82 and Clove Branch Rd. intersection (upper left). Former ND&C RR runs parallel to Rte. 82 (dark line far left). Faint dark triangle at that intersection was Clove Branch Junction. Clove Branch RR turned off north of Clove Branch Rd. (curved dark line center). You can trace the dark ROW line to the right of center toward Beekman Rd.**
Photo on file at Dutchess County Soil & Water Conservation District, Millbrook, NY.

Twenty years later, when the Clove Branch Railroad was abandoned, the ND&C Railroad claimed the assets.

When the CB Railroad was barely four years old, President Brown had grand plans to build a railroad from New York City to Montreal in Canada. Near the end of 1872 it was called the New York, Boston & Northern Railroad (NYB&N). That name lasted about a month into January 1873, when it was expanded to New York, Boston & Montreal Railway (NYB&M). The CB Railroad and the D&C Railroad were to be links in a chain of small lines connected together to reach from New York City to Montreal via Rutland, Vermont. The CB Railroad was to be extended eastward from Sylvan Lake to connect with a line to New York City. The NYB&M Railway was less than a year old when it went bankrupt in the financial panic of 1873. George Brown's dream of a Canadian American railroad empire died. Construction had been completed only about a mile east of Sylvan Lake, when the NYB&M Railway failed. The connecting line to New York City was never built. Each of the linked railroads reverted back to previous ownership. The D&C Railroad struggled but failed in 1874. Three years later, in 1877, it was reorganized and emerged as the Newburgh, Dutchess & Connecticut Railroad.

A series of freight bills from the CB Railroad illustrate the name changes. The first one is dated 16 July 1872. The form originated from the Sylvan Lake station and was being sent to the Dutchess & Columbia Railroad. The second form is dated 18 January 1873. This form also originated at the Sylvan Lake station but in the "to" section of the form, the D&C Railroad name had been stricken out and the name New York Boston & Northern Railroad had been stamped on the paper. That name lasted only a month or so. The third form, dated 18 June 1873, has the name New York, Boston & Montreal stamped on it. The NYB&M went bankrupt later in 1873. By 1880, the fourth form was printed with the name Newburgh, Dutchess & Connecticut Railroad. The ND&C name lasted beyond the abandonment of the CB Railroad.

In 1877, the new ND&C Railroad management under President Schultze decided to extend the CB Railroad from Sylvan Lake four miles eastward to Clove Valley using materials left over from the failed NYB&M Railway effort. The track extension to Clove Valley did not actually belong to the CB. The CB Railroad leased the extension from the trustees of the bankrupt NYB&M Railway. The record books do not actually make it clear who paid for construction of the Clove Valley extension. A notation states that G. Lapi hired E. Garrison who began the work. The extension allowed CB Railroad passenger and freight service to reach a few customers and an iron furnace in

**Freight bill from Sylvan Lake station dated 16 July 1872. Note that the heading on the form states the name as Dutchess & Columbia Railroad.**
Author's collection, courtesy of Thomas Hourican.

**Freight bill from the Sylvan Lake station dated January 1873. The name, Dutchess & Columbia Railroad has been blacked out. The new name New York, Boston & Northern is overprinted.**
Collection of Heyward Cohen.

**Freight bill from Sylvan Lake station dated 18 June 1873. The name Dutchess & Columbia Railroad has been blacked out. The overprinted name is now New York, Boston & Montreal.**
Author's collection, courtesy of Thomas Hourican.

**Freight bill dated February 1880. Name is now Newburgh, Dutchess & Connecticut Railroad.**
Author's collection, courtesy of Thomas Hourican.

Clove Valley. Passenger traffic was very light and in March 1884, Beekman station was designated a flag stop. CB Railroad handled local freight, mail, and passengers, but its main source of revenue was iron ore. When ore shipments were slow, the CB Railroad revenues barely covered expenses.

### Volume 15, Page 571, 5 January 1883
*Superintendent Kimball wanted to trim the track force on the CB Railroad.*

We are earning next to nothing on that road now.

The earliest surviving ND&C Railroad letterbook was written in the first half of 1879. In the first few pages of that book, there is mention of the locomotive Washington being used on the Clove Branch Railroad. The Washington was an 1856 vintage, wood burning, 4-4-0 that the D&C Railroad had purchased second hand for $4,000 in 1869. This engine was actually too light and not powerful enough for hauling heavy ore loads. In January 1882, there is a letter discussing who is to blame for the damage done by running poor old Washington into the ore trestle at Sylvan Lake. Despite the difficulties, Washington was repaired and labored on. It was not until a derailment wreck in March 1883 that the twenty-seven-year-old engine was finally replaced by a new and more powerful double ended engine named General Schultze.

In addition to loads of ore, the CB Railroad also hauled charcoal to fire the furnace at Clove Valley. The roster of equipment included several cars built especially to haul charcoal that was bulky but relatively lightweight. Charcoal cars had an annoying tendency to catch fire. This was generally caused by charcoal that was still warm and possibly smoldering when loaded. In February 1884, a load of charcoal from Bennington, Vermont, arrived at Clove Valley including the trucks from another CB Railroad charcoal car that had burned in Vermont. One would imagine that a wooden car with a load of charcoal could make a very hot fire. The trucks were returned to the ND&C Railroad shops at Dutchess Junction to be salvaged for useable parts. On 15 January 1888, the insurance for the CB Railroad charcoal cars expired. The management decided not to renew the insurance, and the charcoal cars were taken out of service.

### Volume 30, Page 311

Schedule of CB RR property to be insured.
- $ 500 on engine house
- $ 500 on building occupied as a depot and tenement.
- $ 200 on a building occupied as a shed and stable.
All situate at Sylvan Lake, Dutchess County NY.
- $ 5000 on one locomotive wherever it may be including all appurtenances and connections thereto, said locomotive being marked Gen Schultze CB RR No. 9

Starting in September 1887, some of the ore from Sylvan Lake was shipped to the iron furnace at Copake, New York. It went via the ND&C Railroad to Stissing where it was transferred to the New York & Massachusetts (NY&M) Railroad and routed through Boston Corners to Copake. The NY&M Railroad provided all cars used in this service. These shipments helped the revenue situation, but the CB Railroad was still barely surviving. To add to the problems, Freight Brakeman H. D. Austin was killed on Christmas eve 1887, while switching cars at Clove Valley.

During the 1880s, the CB Railroad barely survived. Notes in the record books refer to cutting expenses and reducing the labor force. On several occasions, there is mention of salvaging used track and switches from the CB Railroad sidings to be used on parts of the ND&C Railroad. On 31 October 1890, ND&C superintendent Charles Kimball sent word to the track crew to remove the track scale at Clove Branch siding and ship it to Dutchess Junction. The scale may not actually have been removed because it is mentioned as being in use again several years later.

### Volume 31, Page 424, 30 April 1891
*The agent at Clove Branch Junction writes:*

> The tin roof on the depot there is loose and the heavy wind is likely to tear it off, that it leaks in a number of places that were supposed to have been repaired last summer. In fact it has leaked since repairs were made just as badly as before.

Private parties began making offers to buy parts of the CB Railroad. J. Bryant of Hopewell Junction offered to buy the old railroad sheds at Sylvan Lake. On 25 July 1891, all mail service on the Clove Branch Railroad was discontinued. Despite the dismal financial conditions, a new fifty-foot steel bridge from the Phoenix Bridge Company was delivered to the CB Railroad in December 1891. On 11 April 1892, all service on the CB Railroad was suspended until the new bridge was installed.

### Volume 33, Page 411, 12 April 1892

> On Tuesday May 3rd at 10:15 AM Mr. T. W. Spencer, inspector for State Board of RR Commissioners, will be at Dutchess Junction for the purpose of inspecting this road and the CB RR. I want a special train ready at that time consisting of engine, coach #7 clean and in good order, with Fairchild as conductor, and one brakeman, to go over the road. Acknowledge receipt.

It seems that Superintendent Charles Kimball showed Spencer the new bridge on the CB Railroad.

Some of the passenger traffic on the CB Railroad was for pleasure excursions to Sylvan Lake. On 17 August 1892, the Fishkill Methodist Sunday School class rode to Sylvan Lake on the ND&C Railroad and the CB Railroad with a connection at Clove Branch Junction. The CB train made a special stop at the Sylvan Lake grove before attending to the usual switching at the Sylvan Lake mine.

The Tower brothers of Poughkeepsie owned the Sylvan Lake Mine. ND&C record books contain a number of letter copies discussing ore shipments. One such example is dated 26 August 1893. Charles Kimball wrote to A. E. Tower stating that the CB Railroad had lost about four thousand dollars in the past year and the losses were growing larger. Kimball had discussions with President Schultze who said that if the trend continued, they would have to close down the CB Railroad. The small iron mines and furnace operations in the eastern United States were losing the competitive battle with huge new mining operations in the Great Lakes region.

In 1895, Charles Kimball died, and that same year President John Schultze left the ND&C Railroad with no explanation in the record books. J. Crosby Brown was the new president, and his nephew G. Hunter Brown, who was the son of George H. Brown the first president of the original D&C Railroad, headed daily operations on the ND&C. Brown family members were the majority owners of the ND&C and CB railroads.

G. Hunter Brown was a college man, and his official title was not superintendent. He was called vice president and general manager. He changed ND&C management emphasis from "veteran railroaders" to "business managers." He would preside over the abandonment of the Clove Branch Railroad.

After only a few months in his new position, G. Hunter Brown began writing letters to iron ore customers such as W. A. Miles of the Copake Iron Works. In a letter to Miles dated 4 March 1896, he stated:

> Unless a marked improvement in the volume of ore shipped from Clove Valley takes place immediately, the road will be closed.

This letter was probably prompted at least in part by events the previous day on the CB Railroad.

### Volume 41, Page 163, 3 March 1896
*Brown wrote to J. Crosby Brown, president, 59 Wall Street, New York.*

Clove Branch engine rendered useless this morning by burnt out fire box. Repairs will cost $600. Shall we put her into the shop to prepare for spring work?

With mounting expenses and falling revenues, the CB Railroad could not survive much longer. To add to the problems, the Board of Railroad Commissioners inspected the line and submitted a list of items to be fixed including removal of elm trees at Clove Branch Junction. Local residents threatened violence if the railroad tried to cut down their beloved elm trees. G. Hunter Brown probably had much to ponder in the spring of 1896.

A major blow to the CB Railroad came in April 1896. The Tower brothers notified G. Hunter Brown that they were closing down their Poughkeepsie iron furnace and did not know when it would be operational again. The Tower brothers also said that they were negotiating with another iron furnace company in Troy, New York, to sell them ore from the mine at Sylvan Lake. Brown wrote back to the Tower brothers stating that the volume of ore shipments must be at least two thousand tons per month or the CB Railroad would be shut down.

### Volume 42, Page 44, 25 April 1896

It is a fact that steps are being taken to close the Clove Branch Railroad and the Clove Branch extension in the near future owing to the remarkable falling off in your ore shipments from Sylvan Lake, which it goes without saying was the main support of the road.

### Volume 42, Page 430, 29 June 1896

Application has been made by our management to the Board of Railroad Commissioners of this state with the view of getting the necessary authority to close the Clove Branch railroad and its Extension.

Apparently, the Tower Brothers were not successful in selling any ore to other furnace operations. A. E. Tower and Brothers notified the ND&C that they had decided to close the Sylvan Lake Mine. ND&C management asked if this was a permanent closing or did they think they might open it again in the future. The answer would have a bearing on the abandonment of the Clove Branch Railroad.

The final decision to begin closing down the Clove Branch Railroad must have been made in the early part of July 1896. On 14 July, G. Hunter Brown wrote letters to C. W. Bryant, the agent at Sylvan Lake, and to E. I. Miller the agent at Clove Branch Junction. Here is the text of those letters.

### Volume 43, Page 62, 14 July 1896

Dear Sirs:
Please take notice that on and after August 1st, 1896 the Clove Branch Railroad will cease to be operated as the Clove Branch Railroad, and that the services of all employees with the exception of a track foreman and one man will no longer be required after the above mentioned date. Please state to all concerned that the management of this Company regret exceedingly to be forced to take

these necessary steps and sever the connections of themselves with the Company, but as they themselves are aware the business of the Clove Branch Railroad has been nil for many months, and it hardly seems fair that the ND&C RR Co. should be obliged to pay all the expenses of the maintenance of this property without receiving any benefits from it. Special orders will be issued you at a later date covering the disposal and care of the different houses and property of the Company which have been under your charge.

Personally if there is anything that I can do to aid yourself and others in obtaining other situations, by means of letters of recommendation or otherwise issued from this office, I should be glad to do so. Yours truly [Signed] G. Hunter Brown
Vise. Pres. & Gen. Mngr.

During that same month of July 1896, a Poughkeepsie Baptist church group wanted to run an overnight camping excursion to Sylvan Lake via the ND&C Railroad and the CB Railroad. Here is part of G. Hunter Brown's response.

### Volume 42, Pages 552-554, 20 July 1896

You will note that we have but one train from Sylvan Lake to Clove Branch Junction and return per day, and this service is performed in the morning, hence you could not get out in the afternoon.

I would add in closing that it is fortunate that your party contemplate making this trip this early in the season from the fact, as you will notice by the enclosed poster, that the passenger business of the Clove Branch Railroad ceases at the close of business, July 31st hence your party in all probability will be the last one of that magnitude that will pass over these rails for some time.

A few days later, G. Hunter Brown sent out these notices.

### Volume 42, Page 592, 25 July 1896

After August 1, 1896 the Clove Branch Railroad will be simply an arm of the ND&C and not operated as a division.

### Volume 42, Page 600, 25 July 1896

After 31 July 1896 agents will no longer sell tickets to Sylvan Lake. Freight will still be accepted for Sylvan Lake, Beekman and Clove Valley.

### Volume 43, Page 98, 25 July 1896

It has been deemed advisable by the management of the ND&C RR, which operates the Clove Branch RR, to withdraw all passenger service over the said road. We will still keep the road open and retain the charter by delivering carload and less than carload freight on Saturdays only by running in a special train.

### Volume 42, Page 606, 27 July 1896

After 1 August 1896 freight service to Clove Valley will be weekly.

### Volume 43, Page 105, 30 July 1896

We do not expect at present to permanently abandon the operation of the Clove Branch Railroad.

The railroad that, at one time, was planned to be a main connection between New York City and Montreal was reduced to a weekly freight run that did not even cover expenses. They did, however, leave the door open for possible renewed business by keeping the charter active with weekly freight trains. In the late summer and fall of 1896, operations on the Clove Branch settled down into a weekly routine.

### Volume 43, Page 129, 7 August 1896

Engine #1 will be used for the Saturday special train to Clove Valley.

### Volume 44, Page 152, 9 September 1896

Beekman and Clove Valley while nominally unrepresented by a local agent, our agent at Clove Branch Junction takes care of the entire Clove Branch Railroad.

### Volume 43, Page 314, 6 October 1896
*Instructions not to couple engine #1 behind a passenger coach when going to Clove Branch Junction for the Saturday run.*

It is against the law.

Despite the major changes in service, the problem of trees along the right of way did not go away. On 15 December 1896, Brown wrote a two-page letter asking advice from the inspector of the State Railroad Commissioners regarding cutting trees along the right of way. The trees were close to the tracks but they were also the landmarks for deeds to the local farms. Some of the trees were near local homes at Clove Branch Junction, and the residents objected to the cutting. One resident named Peter Baldwin threatened violence if they cut the trees in front of his house.

By the following year, ND&C Railroad management was beginning to lose hope of any business renewal on the Clove Branch. Worse than that, they were losing money on the Clove Branch. In October 1897, the board of directors passed a resolution to cease operation of the Clove Branch as of 31 December 1897. G. Hunter Brown composed a letter to eighteen customers in Beekman, Clove Valley, Gardiner Hollow, and Poughkeepsie. The Tower brothers were included on that list. He stated that unless business increased dramatically, the Clove Branch would be closed at the end of 1897.

On 1 December 1897, G. Hunter Brown made an offer to the Tower brothers to buy a used boiler that was rusting away at their Sylvan Lake facility. He offered them twenty-five dollars for the boiler and stated that the ND&C Railroad could use such a boiler to replace one that was worn out at the dock in Dutchess Junction. They must have reached an agreement on the sale. Later in December, Brown instructed the Dutchess Junction shop crew to pick up the boiler. Apparently the Tower brothers had no serious plans to reactivate the Sylvan Lake operation.

**Ruins of the Clove Valley iron furnace on Furnace Rd., Clove Valley, NY.** Photo by author, May 2002.

### Volume 48, Page 338, 29 December 1897
*Letter to G. B. Holmes, Dutchess Junction:*

This is to legally inform you that the president of the ND&C RR Co. holds full bill of sale for one engine, one combination passenger and baggage car and 43 gondolas of the CB RR Co. in exchange for indebtedness due ND&C RR Co. by CB RR. Hereafter all this equipment will be the property of the ND&C RR and included in and added to its equipment.

G. Hunter Brown Jr.

The Clove Branch actually kept running for a short time in January 1898. On 10 January, G. Hunter Brown wrote a seven-page letter to the State Railroad Commissioners defending the decision to close the Clove Branch and refuting complaints by some of the customers. This lengthy letter outlined the financial losses and the lack of business volume, or any prospect of increased business in the future.

### Volume 48, Page 504, 19 February 1898
*Letter to the Board of Railroad Commissioners:*

The last weekly train to run on the Clove Branch was on 15 Jan 1898. Since then the only traffic was a work train to remove a boiler.

After nearly thirty years, this was the end of service on the Clove Branch. During the summer and fall of 1898, the rails of the Clove Branch were put up for sale as scrap. The scrap metal bid was awarded to E. H. Wilson and Company, Columbia, Pennsylvania. Removal of the rails was accelerated in October 1898.

### Volume 51, Page 502, 10 October 1898
*Brown wrote to Foreman Joseph Rico with instructions to go to New York and recruit*

a gang of 20 good Italians to take up the rails of the Clove Branch.

They want to be good, hardy, strong men who can put in a heavy day's work. I am willing to pay $1.30 per day of ten hours.

Brown made arrangements for rooms for the salvage crew at John D. Ukenas in Hopewell Junction. On 2 November, Brown made arrangements for a relief crew for the salvage engine crew so they could return to Matteawan to vote in the election and then return to work. Engine #9, the General Schultze, a fourteen-year veteran of Clove Branch service was being used for the salvage work. The work of removing the rails was completed about the end of November 1898.

Brown also wrote to the Phoenix Bridge Company and offered them the fifty-foot lattice span bridge removed from the Clove Branch, but they declined the offer. That bridge was barely six years old. By mid December 1898, the lattice bridge was on flat cars at Clove Branch Junction. The ND&C Railroad also had an extra turntable left over from the Clove Branch salvage work.

On 31 January 1899, the Railroad Commissioners granted permission to make the Clove Branch Station a flag stop only. Most trains would then not even have to slow down for Clove Branch. But this was not the end of the Clove Branch story.

In a series of letters dated 3 and 4 Apr 1899, the ND&C was considering a proposal to install new tracks on the Clove Branch to haul out forty thousand tons of ore per year from Sylvan Lake. The problem was that one landowner named Harpel refused to go along. They were considering condemning his land again, as they did thirty years before, but that would take time.

Less than six months after removing the rails from the Clove Branch, the ND&C Railroad was contemplating rebuilding it. It seemed to be a situation of too little, too late, for the land had reverted back to the previous owners who did not want the railroad running through their yard or cutting down their elm trees. Faced with this situation, but also wanting the ore shipment revenues, ND&C management looked for alternatives. G. Hunter Brown began making arrangements to haul ore out of the Sylvan Lake mine with wagons and teams of horses. At the same time, he was looking for an alternate route to build new tracks into Sylvan Lake.

In April 1899, there were a series of letters to George F. Terry, assistant general Frt. agent, New York Central Railroad, (NYC) on the subject of moving ore from Sylvan Lake to an iron furnace in Poughkeepsie, New York. The ND&C Railroad had arranged to have the ore hauled by teams from Sylvan Lake to Clove Branch Junction a distance of four miles. The ND&C Railroad would then haul it to Dutchess Junction and transfer it to the NYC to get to Poughkeepsie. A few days later, the ND&C learned that there was a move under way to team the ore to Hopewell Junction and load it onto Dutchess County Railroad trains going directly to Poughkeepsie. There was a discussion with Mr. Terry of the NYC about ways to prevent the switch in routes and keep the business for the ND&C and the NYC. The ND&C even extended credit to the Tower brothers for the shipment of supplies into the mining operation at Sylvan Lake.

By the middle of June 1899, the ore was coming out of Sylvan Lake mine again. The record books do not explain why, but the route did not go to Dutchess Junction and the NYC. Instead it went north on the ND&C to Stissing Junction where it was turned over to the P&E for delivery to Poughkeepsie via Pleasant Valley. Low sided gondolas were moved to Clove Branch Junction to be filled with ore from the wagons coming out of Sylvan Lake.

The ND&C had not been able to get consent of the property owners to lay new tracks into Sylvan Lake. They began negotiations with the Tower brothers to again condemn the properties. Apparently they had enough confidence in the future of the ore business to make long range plans. A new siding was built at Clove Branch Junction to handle deliveries of coal to the Tower brothers mining operation. The coal was carried in wagons to Sylvan Lake.

### Volume 58, Page 63, 22 July 1899
*A second three-page status letter to President Brown:*

We will have to extend the siding at Clove Branch some 3 cars. Business is quickening there, more teams are going on and I think before the month is out we will be running 100 tons per day out of that place.

### Volume 58, Pages 204 and 205, 14 August 1899

*Letter discussing the shortage of cars to haul ore from Clove Branch Junction:*

The ND&C is now using 47 cars in service to haul ore and will need more because demand is increasing. Tower Brothers are pushing for 1000 tons per week.

The ND&C did not have enough cars to handle the volume of ore. They wrote a letter to the P&E asking them to supply cars for the operation that was hauling ore via the P&E at Stissing to Poughkeepsie. Apparently, the P&E did not supply any cars. On 23 August, the ND&C made arrangements to get additional cars from the NYC. On 8 September, ore began moving via Dutchess Junction and the NYC.

### Volume 57, Page 527, 8 September 1899

The hill crew will take to Glenham spur today 20 old Fall Brook hopper bottom coal cars for use in the ore business between Dutchess Junction and Poughkeepsie.

Commencing Monday we will move this ore in Fall Brook cars via Dutchess Junction and New York Central to Poughkeepsie.

### Volume 57, Page 526, 8 September 1899

Train 50 will feed out 5 cars per day of old Fall Brook hopper bottom cars from east Glenham spur commencing Saturday morning to Clove Branch Junction switch for the use of the ore business between Clove Branch Junction and Poughkeepsie via Dutchess Junction.

Now that more cars were available to haul ore, the strain began to show on the teamsters.

### Volume 58, Pages 467-469, 2 October 1899
*General Freight Agent William Underhill wrote a 3-page letter to A. E. Tower of Poughkeepsie:*

The iron company has not provided facilities at Sylvan Lake to house the men and horses for hauling ore. They also have only one loading chute so some teams have to shovel the ore. This limits ore shipments to a fraction of what the RR agreed to handle. William Peattie, the boss of the teamsters has threatened to pull his men out if the situation does not improve.

### Volume 57, Page 688, 25 October 1899

There is a new contract with the teamsters hauling ore from Sylvan Lake.

Under this new system which called for a weigh master & operator at the Junction we now find 18 teams drawing ore daily.

An operator and a weigh master were hired for the Clove Branch Junction track scale. An office with a stove was set up for the weighing operations. The ND&C began accepting hopper cars loaded to as much as forty-six thousand pounds. A system of postcards was used to alert The Tower brothers of each shipment of ore. The US mail must have been more reliable in those days.

On 1 Dec 1899, ND&C vice president, G. Hunter Brown wrote a four-page letter to A. E. Tower about rebuilding the Clove Branch Railroad. Brown told the Tower brothers that they must obtain the required authority from the landowners and install the four and a half miles of rails on the Clove Branch, then agree to ship a minimum of sixty thousand tons of ore on the ND&C in the first year of operation. The Clove Branch Railroad (ND&C) would maintain and operate the four and a half miles of track. If the Tower company abandoned the operation, the ND&C would have the first option to purchase the tracks. A cost estimate of $26,099.56 for building the tracks was included. Brown seemed to be wary of the viability of the Tower brothers' business and was not going to risk anymore ND&C money in the venture.

For some unstated reason, the ore shipments must have halted. More than a year after starting, there was a note that team ore shipments from Sylvan Lake would resume on 17 November 1900. Then on 2 January 1901, the ND&C was considering reopening the Clove Branch station for the use of the weigh master for the ore loads coming out of Sylvan Lake, provided there would be enough volume to justify costs. In March 1901, the ND&C put thirty cars in service to haul the ore. A note on 20 May 1901 says that the Tower Brothers Iron Works was complaining about ore moving too slowly on the ND&C Railroad. General Freight Agent William Underhill suspected the accuracy of the Clove Branch track scale. He sent out a note on 21 June 1901 with instructions to carefully weigh a car at Clove Branch then weigh the same car at Dutchess Junction. More than a year later, in October 1902, there was mention of accumulating a string of ore cars from Sylvan Lake to test the hauling capacity of new 4-4-0 engine #9. This engine was not the General Schultze, which was being stored at Dutchess Junction awaiting sale.

There is no more mention of Clove Branch or the ore business and not one word about new tracks into Sylvan Lake. It seems that the iron ore business just sort of faded away without any fanfare or formal ending. As far as the ND&C Railroad was concerned, that was the last of Clove Branch. Three years later, the ND&C itself no longer existed and the CNE Railway operated the line.

On today's maps you can find Clove Branch, Sylvan Lake, Beekman, and Clove Valley but they are residential communities. A golf course covers part of the old right of way. The iron mine and furnace are long in the past and people drive to work or go shopping by car. A hundred years of underbrush and trees have hidden almost all traces of the Clove Branch Railroad.

# Buying and Selling Equipment

THE ND&C RAILROAD, like most other business ventures, bought, sold, or traded equipment. Among the larger items were locomotives and cars. There is more to buying a locomotive than just picking out a type and sending in a check. The letterbooks of the ND&C Railroad give us some insight into the process. Most of the ND&C equipment in the early years was inherited from the previous railroad, the D&C. The details in the ND&C books are mostly for buying replacements for old, worn out D&C equipment and then selling the older units, sometimes for only the scrap value. One of the earliest scrap victims was the 1856 Baldwin wood-burning locomotive named Tioronda.

### Volume 12, Page 471, 1 September 1881
*Letter to Jno. P. Muldoon, Hudson, NY:*

Dear sir, I will sell you the locomotive Tioronda which you saw yesterday just as she stands (minus the tender) for three hundred & fifty dollars ($350.00) cash. I will also give room somewhere in our yard to cut her up if you wish provided you do it within a reasonable length of time.
    Yours Truly C. L. Kimball

### Volume 12, Page 537, 19 September 1881
*Letter to General Jno. Schultze Pres:*

I enclose check for $350.00 on Marine Nat. bank drawn by Marnie (?) Briggs of 128 Pearl St. NY and endorsed by H. C. Briggs which is the proceeds of sale of the worn out locomotive Tioronda which was the property of the estate of James Brown. This check had better be presented at the bank tomorrow and if there is anything wrong about it please telegraph me at once as the engine will remain here until the day after tomorrow and could be held if the check is found to be worthless.
    Yours Truly C. L. Kimball

Probably the best example of the purchasing process is for the replacement of the old D&C locomotive Washington. This engine was an 1856 vintage wood-burning 4-4-0 that the D&C had purchased used in 1869. She was twenty-one years old when the ND&C Railroad was formed out of the bankrupt D&C Railroad. Washington was used almost exclusively on the Clove Branch Railroad to haul iron ore out of the mine at Sylvan Lake. She was actually too small and light for this service. Washington was up for sale at least as early as April 1881, when the ND&C Railroad was less than four years old.

### Volume 12, Page 3, 18 April 1881
*Two-page letter to J. Ralph, Superintendent, Freehold & NY (F&NY) Railroad:*

Making a statement of what repairs the engine would require which I will send to you as soon as prepared. I think the engine would answer for a light train on your road very nicely - She is smart and doing good work on the C.B. Road but is not heavy or powerful enough for the business of that road when both furnaces are in blast. She ought in my judgement to be worth $3000 as she stands. Come up and look at her and we will talk the matter up fully-what is your maximum grade?
    Signed  C. L. Kimball

### Volume 12, Page 52, 29 April 1881
*Two-page letter to J. Ralph superintendent Freehold & NY (F&NY) Railroad Keyport, New Jersey:*

In reply to your favor of the 12th. We will sell you the engine Washington of the C.B. RR just as she stands for $2500 provided we can procure another engine to take her place within a reasonable time. I make this proviso for the reason that the shops are busy and if we had to rent an engine for several months before a new one could be procured we might better keep the Washington. I will see at once what can be done in the way of getting another machine and advise you. In case you wish to take the Washington at the above price, which I think is fair for both companies, Mr. Van Buskirk advises that main valves need facing, etc. etc, [list of needed repairs] These repairs he estimates would cost from $50 to $75 and with them the engine should run years on a light train with ordinary roundhouse repairs that any engine might need. Her tires are in fairly good condition and would probably last years without turning. The rear tires are worn the most as we have had to back her one way on the C.B. extension but as you would probably only run her ahead this would do no harm. Please let me hear from you soon in the matter.
    Your Truly  C.L Kimball

### Volume 12, 3 May 1881
*Short letter to J. E. Ralph superintendent & Company F&NY Railroad:*

Replying to your favor of yesterday I have to say that I have asked the Baldwin Locomotive works, The Rogers Locomotive and Machine Works and the Danforth Locomotive and Machine Company to name prices and earliest date of delivery possible for such a locomotive as we want and asked them to answer at once. As soon as I hear from them I will advise by telegraph to save time stating whether or not we will part with the Washington. There are two Westinghouse brakes on fixtures for them here. (?)
    Yours Truly  C. L. Kimball

In the previous letters Kimball has been writing to his old friend J. E. Ralph and included comments about buying a house, who got married and who died. The tone changes in the next letter when Kimball addresses him as Dear Sir and tells him the bad news.

### Volume 12, 5 May 1881
*Short letter to J. E. Ralph superintendent F&NY Railroad Keyport, New Jersey:*

Dear Sir, Today's mail brings word for these locomotive builders - Grant cannot deliver an engine before February 1882. Danforth Locomotive and Machine Co. will not name a date - Rogers Locomotive and Machine Works named March 1882. None of these will name a price now. Have not heard from Baldwin. It does not look like we could spare the Washington.
    Yours Truly C. L. Kimball

Two months later Kimball was trying to sell the Washington to a used equipment dealer in New York.

### Volume 12, Page 374, 31 July 1881
*Letter to Messrs Fisk, Delafield and Chapman, 19 Nassau Street, New York:*

Gents, The Washington is still unsold, price the same, but sale must be contingent upon our being able to supply her place with a new double end engine of greater capacity.
In case you wish to purchase her advise me and I will see how soon we could get a new engine built.
    Yours Truly C. L. Kimball  Supt.

Meanwhile, the Washington was toiling away pulling ore cars out of Sylvan Lake mine. In a letter to ND&C Railroad president

Schultze, Kimball explained the condition of Washington and the reasons why she was in the shop for repairs.

### Volume 12, Page 562, 26 September 1881

>Replaced some flues and more on order. We will need another engine to take her place and keep her here until the new flues have been put in and her valves put in order. H. Lasher either by carelessness or ignorance twisted one of the steam pipes in the engine that was sent up to take the place of the Washington, rendering it necessary to retain the engine to fix the joint. We are short of power at present and have been for several days but will be alright in a day or two. Lasher is inclined not to give the Washington a fair chance I fear. In fact I don't think much of his ability anyway.

It seems that Kimball was not impressed with some of the mechanics in the Dutchess Junction shops. That sort of problem was not always confined to the repair shop crew. In January 1882, the Washington was in the shop again to repair damage done when she was run into the ore trestle at Sylvan Lake.

By August 1882, Kimball was sending out more serious inquiries about purchasing a replacement for the Washington. He sent a letter to the president of the Schenectady Locomotive Works inquiring about a blueprint.

### Volume 14, Page 542, 3 August 1882

>I write to ask what such a locomotive would haul up a 66 Ft. grade on a five degree curve at a speed of ten or twelve miles per hour? Our Clove Branch Road is about 8 1/2 miles long and has one curve on a level that is 16 degrees. The grades do not exceed 66 Ft. I take it for granted this engine is to be supplied with a pilot at both ends.
>    Yours Truly  C. L. Kimball

Two days later, Kimball and Van Buskirk were on a train to Philadelphia for a shopping trip to Baldwin Locomotive Works. Apparently, they did not close a deal for there was no more about the trip. The situation changed drastically in March 1883. Kimball wrote to ND&C Railroad president Schultze describing a major crunch while backing a line of Clove Branch cars at Sylvan Lake.

### Volume 16, Pages 113-114, 19 March 1883

>At 3:05 PM March 15th by the engine Washington leaving the main track between the two siding switches at Sylvan lake. The tender left the rails first and when the engine was stopped, not more than fifty [feet] from where it left the rails, the forward truck of the tender was under the rear pair of drivers of the engine and the whole of the tender and the rest of the drivers of the engine remained on the rail OK. The engine was backing at the time. The track at this point was perfect and I cannot account for the truck of the tender leaving the rail unless something from the truck may have dropped and obstructed the wheels.
>
>The engine is very badly wrecked both pumps being broken, ash pan demolished, engine frame bent, and I fear one driving axle bent, spring hangers all broken, tender truck demolished and otherwise there are many little things broken. I hardly think it will even pay us to repair her. There was no damage to the cars in the train.

Now the situation had become critical. There was no replacement engine on order and ore cars were waiting at Sylvan Lake mine. Within a few days, letters went out to other railroads and locomotive dealers looking for an engine available immediately. In another letter to President Schultze, Kimball and Van Buskirk had been to Philadelphia to Baldwin Locomotive Works and E. H. Wilson Company, agents for sale of old locomotives. They looked at E. H. Wilson's engines and decided that they were not worth three thousand, five hundred to four thousand.

### Volume 16, Page 272, 23 April 1883

The best we can do with the Baldwin Locomotive Works for such an engine as we want is $8250, delivery early in October at Philadelphia.

### Volume 16 Page 297, 27 April 1883
*Letter to Schultze:*

Will you be at your NY office next Tuesday or Wednesday AM?

I shall probably have the Rhode Island Locomotive Works bid by tomorrows mail and I want to submit the matter to you and decide and get an engine under way soon as possible.

Yours truly  C. L. Kimball

### Volume 16, Page 331, 4 May 1883
*Letter to Schultze:*

I closed with Rogers Locomotive Works for the Locomotive at $8000 and we shall get her about August 25th.

It looks like they had decided which engine to buy, but they still had the problem of getting ore out of the Sylvan Lake mine until the new engine was delivered.

### Volume 16, Page 332, 5 May 1883
*Letter to Schultze:*

It is not probable that the CBRR will ever require more than the one engine, and as the repairs will be done at the ND&C shop it will be better to give the new engine a name rather than a number, inasmuch as the ND&C engines are known only by numbers, and if a number was given to the CB engine we would then have two engines numbered "one" which might lead to trouble and confusion charging cost of repairs etc. Suppose we call this engine "Sylvan Lake" or "General Schultze". Please advise.

Yours Truly C. L. Kimball

The following day, on 5 May 1883, an acceptance letter went out to Rogers Locomotive Works for a double ended engine with an $8,000 price. Specifications in the letter stated that the engine must be capable of hauling a train of two hundred tons plus a caboose up a grade of sixty-five feet per mile on a sixteen degree curve at a speed of ten miles per hour. The tank must hold one thousand, two hundred gallons and the engine is to be equipped with two headlights and pilots for operation in either direction.

That same day, two more letters went out. A rejection letter went out to the Rhode Island Locomotive Works, and an inquiry went to the Illinois Central Railroad asking how their Rogers locomotive performed. Maybe Kimball was a bit nervous about the new engine.

### Volume 16, Page 345, 7 May 1883
*Letter to Burnham, Parry, and Williams of Baldwin Locomotive Works, Philadelphia:*

Replying to yours of April 20th offering to build an engine. We have just closed a contract with another party for the engine. Their offer being fully as low as yours and besides they could deliver some two months earlier than your contract enabled you to. This latter was quite an item as our branch is hiring an engine at $6.00 per day. Thanking you for the trouble you have been to in the matter I am Yours Truly C. L. Kimball

### Volume 16, Page 361, 8 May 1883
*Letter to Rogers Locomotive Works:*

When you forward the specifications please send me the Baldwin catalog that I left in your office a few days ago. We shall not number the new engine you are building as it will be the only one on the CBRR. In Painting, place the title of the road "CLOVE BRANCH RR" on the sides of the tank in letters of suitable size and tasteful arrangement and on the panel under the cab windows the

**Clove Branch RR locomotive General Schultze at Sylvan Lake, 1885. Collections of Stickels.**

name "GEN. SCHULTZE". The sides of the headlight should also be lettered "CBRR".

Yours Truly  C. L. Kimball

About a week later, they got a response from the Illinois Central Railroad outlining the weak points of their Rogers Locomotive. Kimball immediately sent Van Buskirk to the Rogers Locomotive Works in Patterson, New Jersey, to make sure that all of these problems were corrected in the new ND&C engine.

Unfortunately, Volume 17 of the ND&C letterbooks is missing, so we have no records from August 1883 until January 1884. The next mention of the new engine was on 2 February 1884, when the engine was in service. Kimball reported that the Clove Branch Railroad was having more broken rails that winter because the General Schultze was heavier on the driving wheels than the old Washington. The CB Railroad had suffered eight broken rails that winter up until 31 January 1884. During early 1884, the ND&C Railroad was in the middle of a program to replace all the brittle iron rails with stronger steel rails. The old iron rails were sold for scrap value.

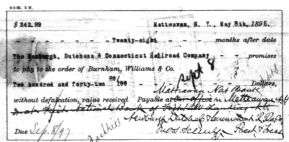

**Above: ND&C RR monthly note payment to Burnham Williams for locomotive #8.** Author's collection.

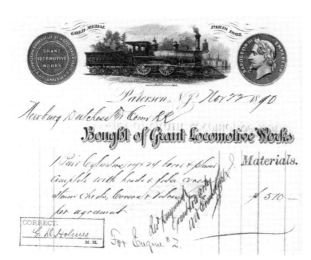

**Left: ND&C RR ordering parts from Grant Locomotive Works.** Beacon Historical Society.

Built by Baldwin Locomotive Works, Philadelphia, PA, April 1895. First owner was ND&C RR Engine Second #8. Changed to CNE RR # 226. Later Became CNE RR Engine Second #38. Scrapped in 1925. Collection of Leroy Beaujon.

The fate of the damaged Washington is not certain. In April 1884, the ND&C received a check for five hundred dollars from a John J. Hurley in payment for her. Stories say that she wound up at a construction company in Delaware, but that has never been verified.

### Volume 18, Page 296, 9 April 1884
*Letter to Schultze:*

I enclose John J. Hurley check for $500 payable to the ND&C railroad of Beacon. This check is in payment for the old locomotive Washington and belonged to the Clove Branch RR.

W. Moore

It is interesting to note that Moore said that the ND&C Railroad was in Beacon. The city of Beacon was formed by combining Matteawan and Fishkill Landing, but not until 1913.

Conditions outside of railroad control could alter the decisions to buy or sell equipment. In early 1895, the ND&C Railroad purchased a Baldwin 4-4-0 locomotive from Burnham Williams of Philadelphia. This engine was in service for almost three years when the battleship *Maine* was blown up in Havana Harbor in Cuba on 15 February 1898 and the Spanish American War was threatening. On 20 April 1898, the US Congress directed President McKinley to use the US military forces against Spain. Three days later, ND&C vice president G. Hunter Brown wrote a letter to Burnham Williams with an offer to sell the engine back to them.

### Volume 51, Page 18, 23 April 1898

We entered into a contract on 4 May 1895 with your firm for the purchase of a locomotive to be numbered #8 for the total price of $8,744.04 payment to be made in 36 notes of $242.89 each due on the 8th day of each month. I believe that the last note on account of this engine is to be paid on May 8th. I write to ask what offer, if any, you can make for the return of this engine. She is in daily service on our road and has been kept up in first class condition ever since put into service in 1895. You having all blueprints and drawings it is unnecessary for me to give you any further information about her.

I shall be glad to receive a prompt answer

to this letter as I should like to lay it before our board of directors who expect to meet on April 28th.

Your prompt attention will therefore oblige,

Yours truly    G. Hunter Brown
VP & Gen. Mgr.

Brown does not state a reason for wanting to sell the engine but a letter the following week gives a clue about the situation. You may recall that the Clove Branch had been abandoned only three months earlier.

### Volume 51, Page 23, 29 April 1898

Plans to paint the depots on the line have been delayed. Owing to the recommendation of our president to retrench in every possible direction and in all departments until it is definitely determined how the war will effect the general business of the country.

Apparently, Burnham Williams did not want the engine back, for she continued in service as ND&C Railroad #8. This engine later became part of the CNE Railway as #226. Later, the CNE number was changed to second #38 and she was condemned for scrap in March 1925.

The last new locomotive that the ND&C Railroad purchased was their second #9 in 1902. After the abandonment of the Clove Branch in 1898, the General Schultze had been designated ND&C #9. The General Schultze (as #9) was up for sale during the summer of 1902, so the new engine on order became the second ND&C Railroad #9. There were no buyers for the General Schultze and she became ND&C Railroad second #1 and was stored at Dutchess Junction. The CNE Railway finally sold her in 1906.

By 1902, newer locomotives were heavier and more powerful than older ones, and man-

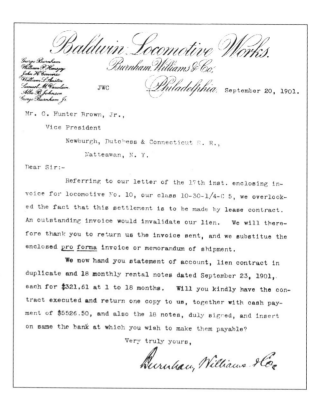

**Financial arrangements for the purchase of ND&C RR locomotive #10.**
Collection of the Beacon Historical Society.

agement was concerned about the weight on bridge structures.

### Volume 71, Page 222, 29 April 1902
*Letter to Burnham Williams Company, Philadelphia:*

Please refer to your letter of March 11th, 1902 and your proposal to deliver to us an American Wheel Engine the duplicate of our #6 constructed by your firm for this railroad company for the sum of $9,600. Delay has been occasioned in this matter due to the fact that we have been seriously discussing the question as to whether we would not be obliged to have a more powerful type of locomotive than the one shown in the lines of your proposal. We write to ask if it would not be possible for you to give us a figure on an American Wheel Locomotive very similar to engine #8 but providing her with 19" x 24" cylinders instead of 18" x 24" and accomplishing this without materially increasing weight on drivers and allowing us a 9 Ft. wheel base for drivers?

Please also advise what the cost of an engine of this increased cylinder power would be. I presume of course you would specify this machine would carry 185 lbs. of steam, which is a heavier pressure than that allowed for #8 now in service. Please also advise when a delivery of some such engine could be made. We would like to have you reply as far as delivery is concerned that some such engine could be sent us in the early fall.

A meeting of the Board of Directors is called for May 8th and I would like to submit this matter to them on that date.

Burnham Williams responded saying that if ND&C wanted bigger cylinders they would need a bigger boiler, which would weigh more. They quoted 114,000 pounds total weight with 74,000 pounds on driving wheels carrying 185 pounds pressure with a driver wheelbase of nine feet two inches The engine would be very similar to engine #8. ND&C vice president G. Hunter Brown asked ND&C chief engineer Everett Garrison if this heavier engine would be safe on ND&C bridges. Garrison responded that additional stringers must be added to the Tioronda Bridge.

### Volume 71, Pages 286-287, 8 May 1902
*Letter to Baldwin Locomotive Works, Philadelphia:*

Your proposal to furnish this company with an American type locomotive somewhat on the lines of Class 8-32-C as per circular #1 enclosed for the price of $10,250 fob our line:

I beg to advise that at a meeting of the Board of Directors held this day I was authorized to advise you that we will accept this price provided that you can arrange in some manner or other to give us fall delivery and that you will submit to us specifications covering a locomotive of this type.

We would advise that in submitting us specifications the weight of this locomotive be kept down as low as possible consistent with steam pressure which she should have in order to make her efficient, as some of our bridges are none too strong and the weights given on circular #1 for 8-32-C class are heavier than anything that we have on our road at present writing. I understand that those weights will strain our bridges nearly 10% more than the weights on drivers and trailers of Atlantic Type Engine #10 furnished us last fall by your firm. It is for this reason therefore that we want to keep the weight

**ND&C RR locomotive #10, Baldwin Locomotive Works, 1901.**
Collection of J. W. Swanberg.

down to the lowest possible point consistent with efficient tractive effort.

### Volume 71, Page 521, 3 June 1902
*Letter to Burnham Williams Company: ND&C wants a small change in the specification for the passenger locomotive now on order. ND&C wants the locomotive without the* fusible plug.

The locomotive was to be completed about 4 October and the price had increased from $10,250 to $10,365 with the addition of steam heat for eighty dollars and air signals for thirty-five dollars. ND&C would pay fifty percent when the locomotive passed ND&C inspection. The remainder was to be paid in eighteen monthly notes at an interest rate of six percent.

While the ND&C Railroad was in the process of buying their second #9 locomotive from Baldwin, there were problems with older units. Engine #8 was the one that the ND&C had tried to sell back to Burnham Williams in 1898. It seems that cracks had developed in the fireboxes of two Baldwin products, and G. Hunter Brown did not want the same problems in the new engine.

### Volume 71, Pages 567-568, 9 June 1902
*Brown writes to Burnham Williams Company:*

We write to ask if you can explain why it is that the firebox in engine #8 built by your firm for our company in 1895 should suddenly commence to develop a series of cracks? These cracks appear to run from the mud ring up to the swell of the firebox and they are 15 in number so far as we can see at this writing. We also find that the firebox of engine #10 recently delivered to us has a crack in the rear sheet through a rivet. We bring this matter to your attention in the hope that you can advise us as to why these cracks are developing when the engines have received the utmost care and attention and to avoid if possible anything that has been improperly done in the way of construction in these locomotives in our new machine ordered from you last week, which will probably bear #9. We have several locomotives that have been in service for from 15 to 18 years whose fireboxes are in much better condition than that of #8 which was built in 1895.

On 21 June 1902, G. Hunter Brown sent numbering and painting instructions to Baldwin for the new engine #9. He also instructed them to install the Consolidated Car Heating system. A few months later, in early October 1902, the ND&C Railroad was testing the new engine. They tested the hauling capacity by pulling a string of loaded ore and gravel cars from Clove Branch and Billings. The inspection and test must have gone well because a few days later they sent the first payment.

On 14 October 1902, the ND&C Railroad sent a draft for $5,182.50 which was fifty percent of the payment for the new engine #9 received on 10 October. The remainder was to be paid in eighteen monthly notes of $301.59 each. Three years later, the ND&C became part of the CNE Railway and engine #9 became CNE Railway #227. Later, she was changed to second #39 and was condemned for scrap in 1926.

In many ways, purchasing a passenger car was more complicated than buying a locomotive. In addition to the basic mechanical items such as wheels, brakes, and couplers, there was a host of decisions for things like wood, carpet, upholstery, window shades, lighting, heat, washrooms, doors, and cuspidors. In the winter of 1899-1900, the ND&C was engaged in rebuilding coaches #5 and #7 in the Dutchess Junction shops. Coach #5 was being lengthened and converted into a smoker and baggage car, then renumbered as #16. At the same time, they had a new sixty foot coach on order to be delivered in May 1900 from the

Jackson & Sharp Company in Wilmington, Delaware. The new coach would be the new #5 to replace the old #5.

The general specifications for Jackson & Sharp cars were changed a bit for the ND&C. On the order, G. Hunter Brown specified mahogany instead of quartered oak and double thick French plate glass windows at one hundred dollars additional cost. The order also specified straight back, medium height seats. On the mechanical side the order called for thirty-three-inch Lobdell best cast wheels in place of the Buffalo wheels. He also specified double iron bolsters with a spread of three feet six inches. Weight of the car was estimated at sixty thousand pounds. Total price including

**Right: Inventory of ND&C locomotives dated September 1902.** Collection of the Beacon Historical Society.

**Below: New ND&C RR coach #5 built by Jackson & Sharp of Wilmington, DE.** Collection of J. W. Swanberg.

the French plate glass was five thousand, eight hundred dollars. The ND&C agreed to pay three thousand dollars on delivery and split the rest into monthly payments over the following year at an interest rate of six percent.

During the months of January and February 1900, the companies wrote a series of letters to pin down decisions on a variety of items. On 15 January, a letter added end windows to the new coach and requested Tower couplers made by Malleable Castings Company. The ND&C ordered passenger car couplers from the Malleable Castings Company for their other rolling stock at a price of ten dollars each.

The number of center lamps was reduced from six to five because of spacing problems. Washroom plans called for double hoppers instead of a hopper and a urinal with a notation that urinals were going out entirely anyway. Brown specifically requested no partitions at the ends of the car. He wanted to reverse the end seats and have a clear view out the ends of the car for management road inspection trips.

On 19 January, a letter went out to Jackson & Sharp with approval for the floor plan and side decoration blueprints. Coat hooks on the sides were considered to be a nice touch. There was, however, a problem with the color and design of the pantasote material in the curtains. Instead of dull brown, they wanted something brighter and suggested terra cotta.

A 28 January letter to Jackson & Sharp requested a change in the coach number. The new coach would be numbered 5 to replace the old #5, which was being converted to a baggage and smoker car then renumbered 16. Two days later, the ND&C ordered a half dozen "self-righting, non-upsettable, porcelain lined, enameled iron cuspidors made of heavy cast iron."

Jackson & Sharp also were the suppliers for curtains and carpet. They were going to install the same curtains and carpet in ND&C coach #7 as they used in #5. The curtains were described as "pantasote with Hartshorn rollers but without Burrowes fixtures and clip which runs in the groove." The ND&C had decided to groove the windows of coach #7 and asked for dimensions and for the new curtains to be supplied with Burrowes fixtures and bottom clips. Brown directed the ND&C master mechanic to send all of the Hartshorn rollers from coach #7 to Jackson & Sharp along with samples of the pantasote to have the curtains added. Coach #7 had thirty-four side windows and two end windows. Included in the order was a strip of Brussels aisle carpet exactly fifty-two feet ten inches long for coach #7.

Jackson & Sharp completed the new coach #5 well ahead of schedule. On 26 April 1900, the new coach #5 was delivered from the shops in Wilmington, Delaware. After an inspection, Brown did not like the shoddy toolboxes and ordered the ND&C shops to build better ones. He also ordered spare dome lights and glass for the windows. Brown sent a check for three thousand dollars and arranged twelve monthly notes for the remaining two thousand, eight hundred dollars.

A letter on 8 May 1900 related one of the first runs using the new coach #5. After the Thursday board of directors meeting, they rode to Millerton in the new coach #5. Wooden boards covered with white paper were placed over some of the seat backs to form a lunch table. With a bit of imagination we can picture the board members riding and lunching their way along the ND&C line in a shiny new mahogany coach with Brussels carpet, terra cotta curtains, non-upsettable cuspidors, and double thick French plate glass windows. This was just a taste of luxury travel in 1900. If you had enough money you could own a palace car for the ultimate in personal travel luxury.

# The BH&E Returns As the NY&NE

THE GRAND PLAN of the Boston Hartford & Erie Railroad (BH&E) had failed in 1870. Their plan had been to connect southern New England with a shipping port and ferry on the Hudson River at Dennings Point. Tracks were to be built from Connecticut through the southern part of Dutchess County to connect with the D&C/ND&C at Hopewell. Hopewell was not yet a junction. Grading of this line was well under way but track laying at Hopewell had just begun when the failure came. After the failure of the BH&E, the assets were reformed and emerged as the New York & New England Railroad, the NY&NE. By 1880, the ND&C records begin to show signs that the old BH&E plan of reaching the Hudson River was not really dead. The NY&NE Railroad planned to build a ferry facility at Fishkill Landing about a mile north of the old BH&E site at Dennings Point.

In December 1880, there was a two page cost estimate for building a railroad from Hopewell to Wicopee with right of way to Glenham. It was actually an update to an estimate that had been done years earlier. This would be eleven and a half miles of track, bridges, and stations, plus three-quarters of a mile of side track. Since the ND&C Railroad was already operating from Dutchess Junction through Hopewell, these tracks would have been parallel to the existing tracks. The parallel tracks were never built. The NY&NE decided instead to buy trackage rights on the existing ND&C Railroad between Hopewell and Wicopee. From Wicopee, they planned to build a new section of tracks to connect with the ferry and the Hudson River Railroad at Fishkill Landing, now part of Beacon, New York.

In April 1881, there were more letters about installing switch connections and adding sidings on the east and west sides of the ND&C main track at Hopewell for the connections to the NY&NE Railroad. Construction at Hopewell began in earnest in May 1881. Before it had failed the BH&E had done much of the grading between Hopewell and Connecticut, but little track had been laid down. The BH&E Railroad had built some parts of the NY&NE tracks east of Hopewell with access to the ND&C main line during the construction work eleven years earlier. This would have been the section of track on which George Brown's midnight run trapped the BH&E engines in 1870. Now, after eleven years, the NY&NE resumed construction of the line.

On 11 May 1881, a NY&NE train from Connecticut arrived at Millerton and ran down the ND&C main line to Hopewell at twelve miles per hour. The engine was lettered NY&NE, and it pulled five flatcars and twenty dump cars. Three days later, on 14 May there was a letter stating that NY&NE engines could use the ND&C main track south of Hopewell as far as the brook to get water.

One of the changes in the Hopewell yard was to move the freight depot to the new siding. In the process, a new road crossing was needed. On 28 June 1881, ND&C superintendent Charles Kimball wrote a three page letter to L. B. Bidwell, chief engineer of the NY&NE, discussing the application to the Town of East

**NY&NE RR mogul locomotive.**
Collection of the Beacon Historical Society.

Fishkill and the exact placement of the road across ND&C tracks. Kimball also kept President Schultze informed of progress.

### Volume 12, Page 397, August 1881
*Letter to President Jno. Schultze:*

Before you take your proposed trip we must decide upon the arrangement of tracks and location of passenger and freight depots at Hopewell and also the question of moving the water tank to suit the NY&NE and its future maintenance.

I should have forgotten this had not Mr. Lois Supt. of construction asked me today if we had considered the matter. I showed you a map of the grounds then with tracks etc. as proposed by Mr. Bidwell some two or three weeks ago. When will you decide this matter?

Yours Truly  C. L. Kimball

A meeting was arranged for Wednesday, 17 August 1881.

### Volume 12, Page 409, 12 August 1881
*Letter to Gorham P. Lois, Esq. superintendent construction, NY&NE:*

Genl. Schultze & Myself will [meet] you at Hopewell next Wednesday AM to decide as to plan of [?] Hopewell Yard, location of freight house and any other matters in the same connection that may come up.

If you are not authorized to act in the matter please advise Mr. Bidwell, chief engineer, as Genl. Schultze will soon leave to be gone two or three weeks and I would like this matter disposed of before he leaves. Yours Truly C. L. Kimball Supt.

There is no record of what transpired at the meeting. We can only assume that the questions were settled and construction continued through the summer months.

Probably the biggest obstacle in the line from Brewster to Hopewell was Whaley Lake. There was not enough room between the lake and the rocky hills to build the line, so they elected to cross part of the water. Workers soon discovered that the lake was very deep and partly filled with peat. After driving pilings more than 110 feet into the peat, they decided to use fill. The fill promptly sank out of sight so they added more fill and the peat began to rise up alongside the construction. Faced with a tight schedule and few options, they continued to add train loads of fill through the summer of 1881. It took eighty thousand cubic yards of fill before the roadbed was finally stable enough to lay tracks.

On 26 September 1881, there was a letter stating that the NY&NE expected to open for business in Hopewell on 15 October 1881. They did not quite make that schedule. On 7 October, the NY&NE began running a daily gravel train from Hopewell to Wicopee on the ND&C main. This train seemed to be hauling material for the NY&NE construction between Wicopee and Fishkill Landing. ND&C management also gave permission for the NY&NE to install a switch between Fishkill and Glenham for access to their gravel pit. Between Wicopee Junction and Fishkill Landing, the NY&NE tracks had to cross the NYC Hudson River line, which ran along the river bank. The NY&NE built a bridge over the NYC&HR Railroad to avoid traffic conflicts. After crossing the HR Railroad, the NY&NE tracks curved north along the shore toward Fishkill Landing. This route is still in use as part of the Metro North Railroad.

Construction at Fishkill Landing included a long stretch of pilings driven into the east bank of the river to support the tracks from Wicopee Junction. A considerable amount of fill was required for the roadbed between the river and the Hudson River Railroad tracks. The new line ran north along the shore to where the ferry facilities were being built.

On 8 October, a short note stated that the frog to connect the NY&NE main to the ND&C main at Hopewell was ready for installation. A temporary crossover connection to the ND&C main line was installed on 17 October 1881. With the completion of this connection, Hopewell became Hopewell Junction. The new target date to begin operation was then 1 November 1881. They did not quite make that date either.

The first train from Boston used the temporary crossover connection at Hopewell Junction and arrived at Fishkill Landing on 21 October 1881. It was one passenger coach and a NY&NE office car. Twenty NY&NE officers and directors plus a reporter from the *Newburgh Journal* were on board. After inspecting the work at Fishkill Landing, and eating a hearty meal while conducting interviews, the reporter was dropped off at Matteawan as the train returned to Boston.

This must have been an uneasy time for ND&C management. Here was a much larger railroad operation moving in and building facilities in ND&C territory, including a new ferry service across the Hudson River. The NY&NE Railroad operated 478 miles of track, which crossed state lines, while the ND&C had only fifty-eight miles, all in Dutchess County, New York. The new Fishkill Landing ferry operation was within two miles of the ND&C ferry at Dutchess Junction. In October 1881, before the NY&NE service opened, ND&C management wrote a letter to the NY&NE inquiring about the new ferry service and also asking about arrangements for freight transfers between the two roads.

Kimball and Schultze had other concerns as well. In the Hopewell Junction yard, the NY&NE wanted to change the alignment of the ND&C original main line to make way for more sidings. Of course the ND&C objected to moving their main away from a straight line. The ND&C must have won out on this point.

Above: View of NY&NE ferry facilities at Fishkill Landing. NYC&HR RR main line is in the foreground. Steamship William T. Hart is near the ferry dock. City of Newburgh, NY, is across the river. Collection of the Beacon Historical Society.

Below: NY&NE RR locomotive #119 at Fishkill Landing, built in 1882. This engine did the yard switching and pushed heavy freights up the hill to Wicopee Junction. Collection of J. W. Swanberg.

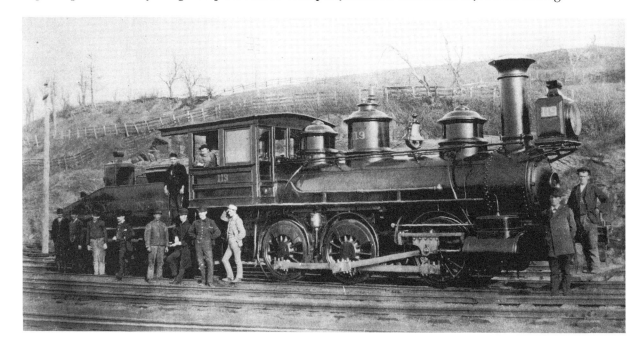

**Postcard view of NY&NE RR ferry docks at Fishkill Landing, now part of Beacon, NY. Erie RR ferry terminal is in the city of Newburgh, NY, across the river. Note the double smokestacks and tracks on the deck of the William T. Hart at right.** Collection of Heyward Cohen.

**Below: New Haven RR ferry *William T. Hart*. Used to carry train cars across the Hudson River between Newburgh and Fishkill Landing. Began service in December 1881 for the NY&NE RR. The New Haven RR took over the NY&NE RR in 1895. Service ended in 1904.** Collection of the Beacon Historical Society.

Later, photos and maps show the ND&C roadbed to be straight through Hopewell Junction.

By November 1881, the NY&NE was building a telegraph line along the ND&C right of way. Also in the plans was a telephone hookup between Dutchess Junction and Fishkill Landing to coordinate train movements on the shared trackage. In addition, a Western Union telegraph hookup was installed at Wicopee Junction where the two roads joined in what is now the city of Beacon, New York. In early December 1881, everything was ready.

On 5 December 1881, a letter went out to ND&C agents and conductors that the NY&NE would commence running trains 224 and 225 through to Fishkill on Thursday 8 December 1881. Additional letters to conductors and engineers explained that NY&NE trains had the same rights as ND&C trains on the tracks. For safety reasons, all trains from both roads were to be entered in the register books at both Hopewell Junction and Wicopee Junction. Of course dispatchers and agents along the line were in communication via telegraph. That is unless the wires were down or the batteries were dead or somebody did not listen to the sounder.

The main line connecting switch at Hopewell Junction was installed and traffic began moving on 8 December 1881. Four days later, on 12 December, the Fishkill Landing ferry began operations with a carload of New York State turkeys bound for Providence, Rhode Island. The tracks eastward from Fishkill Landing to Wicopee Junction (in Beacon, New York), as well as the section from Hopewell Junction into Connecticut were complete enough for traffic to begin flowing. Christmas turkeys for the tables of Providence, Rhode Island, passed over the ND&C tracks between Wicopee and Hopewell that cold December day in 1881.

In January 1882, there was an article in the *Fishkill Journal* about the new ferry named for William T. Hart, who was an early president of the NY&NE railroad. It had been built in Philadelphia for use in New York Harbor, but it was too high to fit under some of the bridges, so it was assigned to service between Fishkill Landing and Newburgh. At that time, it was the second largest ferry in the world, being three hundred feet long and eighty feet wide. The *Hart* carried a crew of twenty-four men. There was a paddle wheel on each side driven by independent steam engines that required three firemen each to shovel coal. By reversing one engine, the *Hart* could turn around in its own length. The *Hart* could carry up to twenty-seven freight cars or eighteen passenger cars and took about fifteen minutes to cross the Hudson River. At that rate, a fifty-car freight train took more than an hour to cross the river.

The next few weeks saw a flurry of letters to smooth out operating difficulties. Imagine the situation: here were two railroads trying to run scheduled trains, both passenger and freight, in both directions on one eleven-mile section of single track main line between Hopewell Junction and Wicopee Junction. Here is a sampling of the letters from the ND&C point of view.

> 13 December 1881: Orders for the NY&NE gravel train to stay out of the way of other trains.
>
> 14 December 1881: Letter to the NY&NE complaining that they had stated the wrong day for commencement of rental payments for trains on the ND&C tracks.
>
> 14 December 1881: Letter stating that no NY&NE train will do local freight business between Hopewell Junction and Wicopee Junction.
>
> 14 December 1881: Orders for the ND&C agent at Hopewell Junction to intercept any

NY&NE RR locomotive #100 at Fishkill Landing. This is the heavy (fifty-five tons) consolidation type that strained the ND&C bridges. In 1882, the ND&C had much lighter 4-4-0 types. After bridge rebuilding, the ND&C RR bought heavier engines. Collection of J. W. Swanberg.

ND&C RR speed limit bulletin aimed at the heavier consolidation engines used by the NY&NE. The ND&C RR did not have any consolidation engines. ND&C RR letterbooks, Volume 14, Page 329, June 1882. Collection of the Beacon Historical Society.

> ND&C or Clove Branch cars that arrive on the NY&NE from the East.
>
> 27 December 1881: Kimball wrote a letter to President Schultze asking who should pay for upgrading the Glenham Bridge to meet the requirements of heavier NY&NE consolidation engines.
>
> 2 January 1882: Kimball wrote to the NY&NE division superintendent. asking that extra trains be run during the day because the ND&C did not want to hire more switchmen for the night shift.
>
> 2 January 1882: A letter transferring a switch key to the NY&NE to be used when extra trains run at night.
>
> 21 January 1882: A letter to the NY&NE complaining that their trains were going too fast when passing the Matteawan station crossing.
>
> 23 January 1882: A letter allowing NY&NE dispatchers to control movements between Hopewell and Wicopee at night when no ND&C trains are running.
>
> 23 January 1882: Letter to all agents saying that ND&C tickets were no longer valid on NY&NE trains.
>
> 28 January 1882: A NY&NE extra train struck the rear of ND&C train #4 at North Glenham Bridge after making the run from Fishkill (one and three-quarter miles) in two minutes.

In reading the letterbooks you can almost feel the frustration of the ND&C management in trying to control the situation. Here was a conservative local railroad trying to deal with an invasion of "cowboy" style train crews while still maintaining safe operations. The NY&NE crews were moving freight as fast as possible for their company and dealing with a slow traffic bottleneck. There was a marked difference in style between the two roads. In 1882, neither side could know the future outcome, but the same conflicting relationship lasted for over twenty years.

Heavier NY&NE consolidation engines contributed to the problems. In addition to greater weight on track and bridges, the crews tended to run them faster. ND&C superintendent Kimball tried to limit the problems in June 1882 by posting a speed limit bulletin for all the conductors and engineers to see. There was no mistake about who the notice was directed to. It specified "consolidation engines" and the ND&C did not have any such engines, but NY&NE did.

The following day, on 21 June 1882, Kimball wrote to the NY&NE complaining that the consolidations were running at an unsafe speed of twenty-five to thirty miles per hour on the ND&C tracks. Complaints most often were ignored. On 19 July 1882, Kimball wrote a strong letter to the NY&NE requesting that NY&NE conductor Brigham and engineer Miller be suspended for running thirty-five miles per hour from Hopewell to Wicopee. The wear and tear on tracks and bridges forced the ND&C into an expensive bridge upgrade and replacement program. In October 1882, the ND&C actually banned NY&NE consolidation engines from running over the Glenham Bridge until it was strengthened. There was also a greater amount of breakage of the old iron rails, particularly in cold weather. Heavier steel rails eventually replaced iron rails.

High speed was not always the problem. On 22 July 1882, it was the opposite situation. NY&NE train #54 with two engines and twenty-eight cars stalled several times on ND&C tracks causing ND&C train #3 to be fifty-nine minutes late. This brings up the question of why would a train with two engines and only twenty-eight cars keep stalling? What was in those twenty-eight cars? There is no reason given. Charles Kimball must have been frustrated that day. It was only three days after he had written to the NY&NE to complain about Conductor Brigham and Engineer Miller speeding at thirty-five miles per hour on those same rails. Was the stalling purely accidental?

Besides the traffic and safety problems, the ND&C had to make adjustments in other ways also. Because both roads used the depots and other facilities along the line, they shared the expenses. Salaries for the agents and switchmen at Hopewell and Wicopee were split between the two roads. The telegraph and dispatching workload increased as well. On 2 February 1882, Kimball wrote a letter to President Schultze asking permission to hire more men. His request must have been approved because eleven days later a letter went out recruiting night operators and switchmen for Wicopee.

Additional facilities were needed too. In February 1882, Kimball wrote a letter to L. B. Bidwell inquiring about the specifications for the new freight house that the NY&NE was building in Hopewell. His stated reason for asking was "to govern the quality of workmanship." That same week, President Schultze wrote to J. H. Wilson of the NY&NE Railroad with an agreement to sell land at Hopewell Junction to the NY&NE for one hundred dollars for the construction of a turntable. In November 1882, the ND&C sent an itemized bill to the NY&NE for $44,631.56 for improvements to the right of way in the years ending 30 September 1881 and 1882.

Relations between the two roads were not always cordial. On 18 February 1882, a letter went to the NY&NE Railroad complaining about the delay in payment for damages to ND&C train #4 that had been struck by one of their trains on January 28. It was not until 12 October 1882 that the NY&NE even admitted responsibility for the January 28 accident. The slow payment theme is repeated over and over in the letterbooks during the next twenty years. In one case, the NY&NE sent a bill to the ND&C for car repairs and the ND&C replied that they have no such cars.

As far back as during the NY&NE construction there had been complaints that the NY&NE were stealing workers away by offering more pay. By April 1882, ND&C track crews were demanding more money. The NYC&HR Railroad track crews were already on strike, and ND&C crews were threatening to walk out. NYC track crews were being paid the rate of $1.20 per day, and the company had offered $1.35 per day, but they were holding out for $1.50 per day. ND&C crews were still at the $1.20 rate, and the foremen were paid forty dollars per month. ND&C superintendent Kimball wrote to President Schultze saying that the ND&C had no alternative but to raise workers' pay. He suggested $1.35 per day for the laborers and forty-five dollars per month for the foremen. He also stated that if the other railroads in the area are forced to the $1.50 rate, the ND&C would have to match it or lose the crews. On 22 April 1882, track crew pay was increased to $1.35 per day, and foremen's salary was increased to forty-five dollars per month.

Beyond the operational difficulties, there was another side to the friction between the two roads, the business competition aspect. As far as the ND&C was concerned, the NY&NE was paying rental to run trains through ND&C territory, but this did not include doing any local business. The NY&NE began handling freight at Hopewell Junction just across the yard from the ND&C operation, and at the same time they began clogging the ND&C sidings with disabled NY&NE cars.

One case of business poaching is outlined in a long letter dated 19 April 1882 complaining to G. Williams, general freight agent of the NY&NE Railroad. It seems that a druggist named Greene had a shop across the street from the ND&C station at Matteawan. Greene had ordered a soda fountain weighing six hundred pounds to be shipped from Boston. The soda fountain arrived via the NY&NE through Connecticut. Instead of transferring the shipment to the ND&C at Hopewell Junction, the NY&NE carried the unit to Fishkill Landing (right past the Matteawan station) and then charged the druggist to cart the soda fountain back to Matteawan. This routing cut the ND&C completely out of the deal and forced the druggist to pay higher shipping costs. Needless to say, Kimball was not happy with the situation and neither was Mr. Greene for that matter.

In Volume 15 on pages 241-260, there is a twenty page copy of the agreement between the ND&C and the NY&NE. It includes all the legal language of the lease contract. The question is, why was this copy in the letterbooks in October 1882 almost two years after it was signed? Was somebody considering legal action?

Of all the freight carried by railroads, there was probably more coal than any other item. Homes, businesses, industry, steamboats, and railroads were all heated or powered by coal. Every small town had at least one coal dealer and sometimes several. In many situations, different railroads supplied dealers in an area. This sometimes involved intense competition or some sort of "gentleman's agreement" to maintain prices. Since railroads did not always trust each other or honor the "agreements", there was considerable friction and sometimes open hostility in the coal business. This was particularly true after the opening of the Poughkeepsie Railroad Bridge in 1888, which opened a direct rail route to the coal fields without slow and expensive ferry service across the Hudson River.

**Volume 15, Pages 514 and 540, 18 December and 28 December 1882**
*NY&NE wanted to open a coal yard at Wicopee and charge thirty cents a ton for hauling from Newburgh. ND&C rate for the same haul was seventy cents a ton. Kimball said that such a yard would seriously interfere with our business. He wanted NY&NE to reconsider their price.*

Is this price fixing or is NY&NE just undercutting ND&C? In several places in the letterbooks there are sections dealing with different railroads making deals and agreements not to undercut each others rates, or to split up the business in a particular area. Apparently, the rules of business conduct were a bit more open and had less concern for the customer in the 1800s. At that time, the railroads were the only practical means of land transportation, and they got away with being arrogant and demanding. They had no real competition outside their own ranks. As long as the roads could agree on what they would charge, the customers had to pay. A later section will discuss the coal business in greater detail.

Still another phase of the friction between the roads involved equipment. NY&NE crews were not particularly careful with equipment that did not belong to their company. The NY&NE would return cars to the ND&C after use with wheels flattened from braking. They also sent ND&C cars off to other lines and they did not come back until they needed repairs. In one case, ND&C cars were found in Canada, and they needed new wheels when they were finally returned.

In June 1882, Kimball discovered that empty ND&C cars were being used as switching buffers for the Newburgh side of the NY&NE/Erie Railroad ferry service. A constant source of complaints was the NY&NE crews leaving switches unlocked, causing derailments and accidents. At one point, Kimball sent a strong letter to the NY&NE requesting the return of all switch keys held by their crews. Occasionally, an NY&NE engine would back through an improperly lined switch and smash the switch rods.

**Volume 15, Page 274, 28 October 1882**
*Kimball sent messages to all agents stating:*

Do not allow NY&NE trains to leave cars on crossing or local sidings at your station. If the crew insists or has orders from officers of the NY&NE you will drop your red stop signal and report to me by telegraph at once. You will hold the train until you get orders from me.

He also sent a copy to the NY&NE.

**Volume 15, Page 285, 30 October 1882**

NY&NE trains left 30 cars on Brinckerhoff siding, 30 on Fishkill siding and 8 at Glenham siding. How can we dispatch trains without sidings? When are you going to move them?

**Volume 15, Page 289, 30 October 1882**
*ND&C was detaining three NY&NE trains because there was no more room on the ND&C.*

**Volume 15, Page 294, 1 November 1882**
*NY&NE crew took a partially unloaded car from Brinckerhoff. ND&C wanted it back.*

Kimball was complaining that the NY&NE was interfering with ND&C business by clogging sidings, and he might take steps to break the blockade. Meanwhile the links and coupling pins would be missing from ND&C cars in the yards. The ND&C would send bills to the NY&NE for repairs to damaged or missing equipment, but collecting those bills was always a struggle. The number of incidents makes you wonder how much of it was actually from carelessness.

**Volume 15, Page 367, 16 November 1882**
*Erie Railroad was pressuring NY&NE to return the empty cars that were clogging up the ND&C sidings. They had loaded cars and need more empties. NY&NE was dragging their feet in moving them.*

**Volume 15, Page 393, 21 November 1882**
*Kimball was arranging a personal meeting with E. Holbrook, superintendent of NY&NE.*

**Volume 15, Page 441, 30 November 1882**
*Kimball said they are now handling about 230 to 250 cars per day.*

It would seem that Charles Kimball's meeting with Mr. Holbrook resolved some of the problems between the two roads. I certainly would like to have been a fly on the wall at that meeting. This was not the end of the story, however. Over the years, NY&NE cars would continue to clog ND&C sidings and yards. It seems that the ND&C was a convenient place for the NY&NE to park rolling stock.

Sparks from engine smokestacks were always a problem, but poor maintenance of the stacks and screens made things worse. In the summer of 1882, there were many grass fires along the line. Kimball wrote to the NY&NE master mechanic in Hartford saying

> Fix your engines. Number 42 started 5 fires in Matteawan today.

Two days later, on 7 August, he wrote to G. M. Felton, the NY&NE general manager in Boston:

> Your engines started fires in about twenty places yesterday between Wicopee and Hopewell and in two places destroyed a long piece of RR fencing besides burning over about sixty acres of farm land and considerable farm fence.

Apparently, his letters were ignored. On 9 August he wrote to W. T. Keenan, the NY&NE superintendent at Hartford:

> Yesterday one of your engines on train #2 started a fire that destroyed eight stacks of hay near Brinckerhoff. Engine of train #54 started a fire at Brinckerhoff Station yesterday.

The following day, Kimball instructed the ND&C master mechanic to see if he could find the trouble with the NY&NE engine stacks. He also instructed all the ND&C section foremen to report and record all fires. On 15 August, Kimball wrote a formal letter to G. M. Felton, the NY&NE general manager in Boston. He explained that all the fires were caused by NY&NE engines and that the ND&C had consulted local judges and legal counsel regarding the problem.

The rash of fires stopped. Perhaps Kimball's letter got some attention. Or maybe it just rained. The problem of NY&NE engines starting fires did not go away for very long. There are many letters of complaint to the NY&NE over the years.

After a year of joint operations, the relationship between the ND&C and NY&NE began to settle down. It was never a really friendly match. It was more a matter of each road needing the other and being stuck with the situation. The NY&NE needed access to their Fishkill Landing facility via the ND&C tracks. The ND&C needed the monthly rental checks to keep the red ink out of the books. They had to live together but they did not have to like it.

Gradually, the economic situation began to change the thinking of ND&C management. On 30 December 1882, Charles Kimball wrote a letter to the NY&NE with a proposal. His suggested plan would have the NY&NE take over moving ND&C local freight to and from Newburgh via their Fishkill Landing facilities for a standard handling charge. That same month, there was a note explaining that the ND&C did not have any car floats in operation that season. The Penn Coal Company owned the car floats that were in use. The duplication of services between Dutchess Junction and Fishkill Landing did not really make much sense from a business point of view. Even so, the ND&C maintained the Dutchess Junction operations for many more years. Was it just pride, or was it for a feeling of independence? Whatever the reasons the facilities at Dutchess Junction lasted well into the twentieth century, several years after the ND&C no longer existed. The last train out of Dutchess Junction to Wicopee and Matteawan did not leave until June 1916.

During early 1883, the love-hate relationship between the two railroads continued. In February 1883, a few modifications to the contract were made allowing the NY&NE Railroad to handle the night dispatching between Hopewell and Wicopee. From an operational point of view, this made sense. The ND&C did not have any trains scheduled for nights anyway. The disadvantage was the NY&NE gaining a greater foothold in ND&C operations. It was one more small step in a series that eventually saw the complete absorption of the ND&C. It took more than twenty years of struggling, but by 1905, the ND&C was no more.

During those twenty years of struggling, the track and tonnage rental that the NY&NE paid often was the difference between red and black ink in the ND&C ledgers. In the first three months of 1883, the rental numbers were: January $2437.05, February $2418.22, and March $2968.89. The NY&NE probably considered it highway robbery. This was a significant portion of the ND&C income when you consider that their total profit for the year 1882 was only $367.74. By 1887, the NY&NE was pressuring the ND&C for a new contract to reduce the track rental payments. Meanwhile, the ND&C continued sending letters to the NY&NE complaining about their locomotives starting fires and about the overdue payments for damage to ND&C equipment.

The financial situation was not all that great on the NY&NE side of the fence. On 7 August 1883, Charles Kimball wrote a letter to ND&C president Schultze saying that

> It is reported among some of the employees of the NY&NE Railroad that there is every prospect of a receiver being appointed to take charge of that property very soon.

There is no further mention of this in the ND&C books.

By mid 1882, the ND&C was becoming dependent on the NY&NE for local freight service back and forth across the river to Newburgh. The two roads agreed on rates. From their Fishkill Landing facilities, the NY&NE actually carried the ND&C's local freight business across the Hudson River. Three years later, in 1885, the NY&NE began undercutting the ND&C milk business by shipping milk from Hopewell Junction to New York City. The ND&C was being squeezed by the much larger NY&NE operation. Even so, they continued to survive on revenues from passenger service, milk shipments, ore shipments out of Sylvan Lake, plus coal and freight along the line between Hopewell and Millerton.

Before air brakes came into general use on trains, the crews could often be found walking on top of the freight cars to reach the hand brake wheels while trains were in motion. This of course was a safety hazard, especially around bridges and tunnels. One safety measure was called bridge "tell tales." This was actually a very simple set of ropes hanging down over the tracks a distance before the bridge or tunnel. Anyone on top of a car would be brushed by the ropes as a warning that an obstruction was close at hand. These tell tales became another sore point between the NY&NE and the ND&C. This all came to a head in the spring of 1886 when the NY&NE brakemen were tampering with the ropes while riding on the tops of the cars. Many of the ropes were completely missing, and the ND&C management made numerous complaints to the NY&NE.

Even after years of joint operation on one set of rails, the NY&NE crews had a tendency to bend the rules. On 10 June 1889, two NY&NE freight trains collided at Glenham. One was eastbound and the other westbound, and they had orders to cross at the Glenham siding, but the eastbound did not pull into the siding and met the westbound head on. They were moving at a slow speed so no major damage was done.

The NY&NE style of bending the rules often resulted in more serious problems. January 1891 was a particularly disastrous time for the NY&NE on its own rails.

### Volume 31, Page 35, 20 January 1891

The NY&NE had two quite bad wrecks yesterday, one at Reynoldsville and one at Bristol, a big slide of rock in one of the cuts East of Hawleyville that blocked the road some hours and the big Frt. house at Hartford was destroyed by fire. Quite a list of catastrophes for one 24 hours.

Meanwhile the war of letters continued over the ND&C rails.

### Volume 32, Pages 29-30, 17 July 1891
*Kimball wrote to the NY&NE RR superintendent:*

Two eastbound NY&NE trains passed Matteawan at the reckless speed of 15 miles per hour and the engine of the second train was less than 150 feet from the caboose of the first train.

NY&NE RR engine #125 passing Matteawan station. This engine was built in November 1882. Note that the station does not yet have the third story added. Collection of the Beacon Historical Society.

### Volume 32, Page 651, 14 December 1891
*Kimball wrote to Williams, superintendent of the NY&NE, to complain that they had been sending trains through with over one hundred cars. Kimball said that was unsafe. Trains should not be longer than sixty cars.*

With the opening of the Poughkeepsie Railroad Bridge in December 1888, the NY&NE ferry at Fishkill Landing began to feel the pinch of competition from coal trains rolling across the river into Dutchess County. Ferry service would sometimes come to a halt when the Hudson River ice became too thick in the winter. The bridge did not have this problem. The bridge route also was faster without the handling required to get train cars on and off a ferry boat.

In 1893, the NY&NE faced another problem. They lost a court case brought by the Rumsey family, who were the previous owners of the Fishkill Landing property. On 24 July 1893, Charles Kimball wrote a three-page letter to ND&C president John Schultze in which he described the situation. Kimball had met the

Rumsey's lawyer and was told that the NY&NE must pay the court award of twenty-five thousand dollars for the property and an additional twelve thousand dollars for the use of the property since it was occupied by the NY&NE. The NY&NE agreed to pay the twelve thousand dollars but asked for a delay on the twenty-five thousand dollars. They were negotiating with the Erie Railroad to forward all their river crossing freight via Campbell Hall and the Poughkeepsie Railroad Bridge, then to Hopewell Junction via the newly opened Dutchess County Railroad. The NY&NE was already handling about fifty cars per day in each direction on the bridge route and expected to increase that rate to one hundred cars per day. If these negotiations proved successful, then the NY&NE proposed to give up the Fishkill Landing property and return it to the Rumsey's and, therefore, pay only the twelve thousand dollar rental. The ND&C letterbooks do not say whether the Rumseys were ever paid for the property, but the Fishkill Landing site remained an active railroad facility for years afterward.

The NY&NE faced an even greater challenge in the form of J. P. Morgan and the New Haven Railroad. The two roads were in direct competition in the New England area, and the New Haven began cutting off access to NY&NE business. NY&NE revenues dropped, and J. P. Morgan began acquiring NY&NE stock at low prices. By 1895, he had control of the NY&NE and, along with it, the Fishkill Landing ferry terminal. The ND&C books began to refer to the NY&NE as the New England Railroad (NE). The change of name and management did not seem to improve their safety record.

### Volume 41, Page 248, 21 March 1896

The NE RR had an eight car wreck at Brinckerhoff yesterday. ND&C crew is working with the NE people but the line will not be clear till Monday night.

### Volume 41, Pages 270-272, 26 March 1896

*The ND&C Railroad and the NE Railroad disagreed about the cause of the wreck. NE said it was a defective switch point and ND&C said it was a rotten car sill that broke. The argument was over who would pay for the cleanup.*

The influence of New Haven Railroad control began to show early in 1896. The NE Railroad was making a concerted effort to capture the milk hauling business in Dutchess County. With the change in control of the NY&NE Railroad to the NE Railroad, the track rights contract was being renegotiated. Part of this discussion was the expansion of the Fishkill Landing facility to handle more traffic. Responding to this, the ND&C asked for forty thousand dollar rental for use of their road. Clearly, the New Haven Railroad had plans to increase traffic over the ferry, and the ND&C wanted part of the action.

The name New England Railroad did not last long. Within three years, in July 1898, the name again was changed. The ND&C line from Hopewell Junction to Wicopee Junction was then traveled by trains of the New York, New Haven & Hartford Railroad, Highland Division. Fishkill Landing operated as part of the New Haven Railroad. A few years later, in June 1904, the NHRR withdrew all passenger service on the line but continued to handle freight. Later that same summer, the train car ferry was discontinued, leaving only the connection with the NYC Hudson line.

After years of a stormy relationship, the NY&NE was no more, and the ND&C survived. But then the ND&C had the giant New Haven Railroad at their door with J. P. Morgan running the show.

# Bridges of the ND&C

MOST OF THE BRIDGES on the ND&C were inherited from the bankrupt Dutchess and Columbia Railroad. Almost all of them were light duty, wooden structures that could not stand the strain of heavier locomotives and trains. Over the twenty-five years of ND&C operation, many of these bridges were replaced with iron and steel structures. This became an important issue when the NY&NE Railroad began running heavy, fast trains over the ND&C line between Hopewell Junction and Wicopee Junction in December 1881. Within a few months, by October 1882, two bridges at Glenham were in dire need of strengthening. The ND&C forbade the running of NY&NE heavy consolidation engines over these bridges until they could be rebuilt.

Even though heavy NY&NE traffic did not use that route, the bridge painting crew began reporting that nuts and bolts were either loose or completely missing from the Tioronda trestle, which ran high over Fishkill Creek in what is now Beacon, New York. There were many bridges and culverts along the ND&C, but the Tioronda Bridge was by far the largest. It crossed Fishkill Creek ravine from high rocky abutments. Problems on this bridge could make a spectacular splash.

**Tioronda Bridge over Fishkill Creek in Beacon, NY. This line was abandoned and scrapped in 1916.**
Collection of the Beacon Historical Society.

**Above: Abutment from the ND&C RR Tioronda Bridge. This abutment is now part of Madam Brett Park on Fishkill Creek in Beacon, NY.** Photo by author, March 2002.

**Left: East Glenham Bridge, still in service, March 2002.** Photo by author.

Stronger brace rods and more bolts were added to the bridges. So called "fireproof paint" was used to prevent blazes on the wooden ties and pilings. Bridge painters were paid a higher wage than the track force. A good bridge painter could earn as much as two dollars per day. These measures worked for a period of time, but trains were getting heavier, faster, and more frequent.

Within a few years, the ND&C was forced into a bridge replacement program which began with letters to the Phoenix Bridge Company at 410 Walnut Street in Philadelphia. The first new purchase was a fifty-foot deck bridge for the Clove Branch Railroad in November 1891. The new bridge arrived at the Clove Branch on two flat cars on 24 March 1892. Service on the Clove Branch was suspended while a crew from the Phoenix Bridge Company installed it. Clove Branch Railroad service resumed on 15 April 1892.

Work started on iron and steel replacements for the Glenham bridges in January 1893. A temporary track was built with a speed restriction of four miles per hour while the work was in progress. The East Glenham Bridge was completed on 14 February 1893. Two locomotives, with a total weight of 150 tons, were used to test the new span. At 8:30 AM on 1 March 1893, a special inspection train left Matteawan station. On board, in a well-heated coach, were President General Schultze, Superintendent Charles Kimball, and Chief Engineer Everett Garrison of the ND&C. One would guess that they did not spend very much time outside of that well-heated coach that day.

The rebuilt West Glenham Bridge was completed a year later in early 1894 while plans were underway to rebuild the large Tioronda trestle previously mentioned. Tioronda was the largest bridge on the ND&C Railroad. It was 155 feet long resting on massive stone abutments high over Fishkill Creek. Bids and blueprints arrived, and a contract was awarded to the Phoenix Bridge Company on 30 January 1896. As part of the planning, the weight and wheelbase of ND&C Railroad's heaviest engine, #8, was needed to calculate strain and centrifugal force. The weight on drivers was 62,400 pounds and the weight on the forward truck was 38,700 pounds for a total of 101,100 pounds. In April 1896, ND&C vice president G. Hunter Brown offered the company derrick car for use in the construction. The new bridge was nearing completion when Brown ordered yellow pine planks for the guard rails on 18 May 1896.

A week after ordering the yellow pine, Brown got a message from the Phoenix Bridge Company that they wanted to borrow an engine and crew for work on the bridge. That was not in the contract, so Brown asked Chief Engineer Everett Garrison his opinion on whether to charge rent for the engine, and if so, what was the going rate.

Since the Tioronda Bridge was a rather large project, the ND&C asked the Phoenix Bridge Company to accept a ninety-day note in place of the payment due on completion. The bridge was on schedule to be completed at the end of May 1896. Phoenix agreed to accept the note as part payment on 2 June.

Brown asked the NY&NE Railroad about borrowing a heavy locomotive to test the Tioronda Bridge, but they refused. Much lighter ND&C engines would have to do for the test. They used engine #8 and Mogul #3 then filled them with water and coal. In addition, they loaded on pig iron and the test was performed at 3:30 PM on 11 June 1896. The grand total weight was 165,700 pounds. On 19 June 1896, Chief Engineer Everett Garrison signed the certificate saying that Tioronda Viaduct had passed all tests and was officially accepted. The ND&C sent a ninety-day payment note to the Phoenix Bridge Company. Meanwhile, the pilings of the Sprout Creek Bridge were being replaced, and all trains

**Railroad bridge at West Glenham, also called Rocky Glen. There is now a large concrete arch bridge at this location.** Collection of the Beacon Historical Society.

were restricted to six miles per hour while the work was in progress. It must have seemed like bridge construction would never end.

A few months after completion of the Tioronda Bridge, ND&C vice president Brown discovered that the Phoenix Bridge Company had not done such a great job. The bridge had been built with undersize anchor bolts. The bolts were less than half the size called for in the specifications. Brown was not happy. Volumes forty-five, forty-six, and forty-seven of the record books are missing. There is no indication of how the situation was resolved. We may never know if the Phoenix Bridge Company fixed the problem or if the specifications were changed. At least we know the Tioronda Bridge did not collapse, and it remained in service.

In the early days of railroading, most

bridges and tunnels had a safety feature called *tell tales*. Before the invention of air brakes, the job of a brakeman involved climbing on top of freight cars to operate the manual brake wheels. Walking on top of a moving train could be hazardous to your health if the train happened to pass through a tunnel or low bridge structure. To solve this problem the railroads devised a warning system which was a frame high over the tracks with several ropes hanging down over the trains. These tell tales were placed well back from the tunnel or bridge and acted as a warning to any brakeman that low clearance was just ahead. Even if he was not looking forward, the slap of a rope would get his attention. In the ND&C letterbooks there are several mentions of tell tales being involved in accident investigations and in some cases for vandalism or tampering problems.

During the summer of 1898, the tracks of the abandoned Clove Branch Railroad were removed. This included the fifty-foot deck bridge that had been installed in 1892. Brown offered to sell the six-year-old bridge back to the Phoenix Bridge Company, but they refused. By December 1898, the bridge was on flat cars at Clove Branch Junction. There is a notation in the record books, "we will let it go at a very reasonable figure."

The next bridge project was already underway. This was a thirty-one-foot deck plate bridge from the Phoenix Bridge Company for the Matteawan Raceway, which ran under the ND&C tracks to supply water power to Carroll Straw Hat Works. This was actually a water spillway and had nothing to do with a race track, but the ND&C books use the word *raceway*. Because of the late bridge shipment, work on the raceway was postponed until the spring of 1899. Meanwhile, there were discussions about the estimate for reconstruction of the Bangall trestle and work to be done on the Sprout Creek Bridge.

The Sprout Creek Bridge was located between Brinckerhoff and Hopewell Junction and represented a bit more of an engineering challenge than some of the other bridges. The old wooden piling structure in a swampy area was to be replaced by a steel span supported on large stone abutments. A board of directors meeting on 15 November

**Engineering analysis of ND&C RR bridge structures.** Author's collection.

**Sprout Creek Bridge, still in service.**
Photo by author, , April 2001.

1900 authorized the contract with the Phoenix Bridge Company to replace the old trestle with a one hundred-foot steel bridge at a price of $39.60 per foot. That same day, work began to obtain 160 cubic yards of stone from the ND&C Railroad quarry at Winchells in the northern part of Dutchess County near Millerton. One of the major concerns in designing the bridge was clearance for springtime high water and ice build up. Plans called for the bridge structure to be eight feet above the previous high water mark.

Preparations for the bridge construction continued into the spring of 1901. Plans for the deck area became simpler when the Board of Railroad Commissioners withdrew their recommendation regarding guard rails on all ND&C bridges. In February 1901, Vice President Brown wrote to Chief Engineer Garrison with a suggestion to shop around for a lower price for carved stone bridge seats for the abutments. The price was twenty-five dollars each and eight stones were required for a total of two hundred dollars, which he thought was too expensive. Actual building of the abutments did not begin until May 1901.

In a letter on 26 April 1901 to John Sterling Deans of the Phoenix Bridge Company in Phoenixville, Pennsylvania, Brown agreed to the use of #32 graphite paint from the National Paint Works of Williamsport, Pennsylvania, on the Sprout Creek Bridge. Heavy rains through March and April had caused high water and delays in the Sprout Creek bridge abutment construction. For financial reasons the ND&C wanted to complete the bridge within the fiscal year, which ended on 30 June. The water level finally dropped enough to start work on 2 May 1901.

Just as work was getting under way at Sprout Creek, another problem arose. Even though Tioronda had a new bridge, the approaches were found to be too weak for newer, heavy locomotives. As a precaution, conductors were advised to watch out for particularly heavy cars and not couple them close to the engine. This would distribute the weight when crossing the Tioronda approaches. During the spring and summer of 1901, the ND&C crews would be working on both Sprout Creek and the Tioronda approaches.

Brown wrote a two-page letter to Chief Engineer Garrison on 4 May 1901. He made arrangements for a management inspection of the line on May 18 and gave instructions to look over the Tioronda Bridge approaches. They were too weak for new heavier locomotives planned to handle increased coal traffic. The ND&C was planning to purchase a much heavier, new Atlantic type locomotive from Burnham Williams.

### Volume 67, Page 88, 4 May 1901

It will weigh on the forward truck 31,850 pounds, front drivers 29,102 pounds, rear drivers 31,104, on the trailing truck 22,150 pounds for a total of 113,206 pounds. With the tender added at 71,000 pounds the total wheelbase is 50 feet 4 inches.

Storms and high water were still a problem at the Sprout Creek work site. Brown wrote to John Sterling Deans of the Phoenix Bridge Company. A storm on the night of 17 May had flooded the Sprout Creek construction site. They now had a steam pump on the site. All the materials and the mason gang were on hand waiting for the rain to stop. Brown offered to accept sections of the bridge and store them either at the site or on ND&C sidings to unclog the Phoenix Bridge Company yard. Train 59 was allowed to stop at Sprout Creek Bridge to drop off or pick up workmen.

In another letter on 24 May 1901, Brown told the Phoenix Bridge Company that the Sprout Creek Bridge foundation work was progressing and the erection crew should be scheduled for 15 June. However, water conditions at Sprout Creek seemed to be getting worse. Brown told Stanton to get another water pump as soon as possible. The stone bridge seats for Sprout Creek arrived at Dutchess Junction, but rain was still hampering work at the bridge site. Brown instructed Roadmaster Stanton to inspect the stones to make sure they were correct.

In the midst of all this activity, there was a letter discussing plans to replace yet another wooden trestle just south of the station in Verbank. It was to be replaced with a steel structure, and the ND&C asked the local landowner for permission to relocate about one hundred feet of the stream.

Work did not always go smoothly on the Sprout Creek job. Through a mix up in orders, the workers for the Sprout Creek Bridge were dropped at Brinckerhoff and were delayed in getting to work on 7 June. The yellow pine guard rails for the Sprout Creek Bridge had not arrived. Brown wrote a letter of complaint saying that he had found out that the guard rails were still on the dock in Jacksonville. An emergency shipment of guard rails came from a yard in Albany, New York. Only one car of bridge iron had arrived at Wicopee Junction and had been forwarded to Brinckerhoff. The west abutment was completed on 7 June and they began pumping water out of the east cofferdam. One of the mason's helpers at the Sprout Creek work was injured in the foot. He was given a free pass home to Bangall. The eight stone bridge seats for Sprout Creek were inspected. Two of them were only eleven inches when the specifications called for twelve inches. The abutments would be adjusted one inch to compensate. The stones came from the Breakneck Quarry along the Hudson River near Cold Spring, but the billing was from Warwick, New York.

By 12 June, Chief Engineer Garrison was still working on calculations for the Tioronda Bridge approaches. Two courses of foundation stone had been laid for the east abutment of the Sprout Creek Bridge. They expected to be ready for the Phoenix Bridge Company crew by the 15th as scheduled. Superintendent Milliken from the bridge erection crew had visited the site. Brown wrote to the Phoenix Bridge Company that the Sprout Creek Bridge abutments would be ready on 19 June but so far only two cars of the bridge iron had arrived.

A status report on 25 June outlined progress. The decision had been made by the president and the board of directors to proceed with upgrading the Tioronda Bridge approaches by adding yellow pine bents in cement foundations. The superintendent of the Phoenix Bridge Company erection crew was now at Sprout Creek with all the tools and false work in place. Bridge iron had arrived and construction had started.

Unfortunately, this is where the story of the Sprout Creek bridge construction ends. The next three volumes of the ND&C letterbooks are missing. The next bridge entry appears in

Volume seventy-one in April 1902, when the ND&C wrote to the Phoenix Bridge Company to order another bridge similar to the Sprout Creek Bridge to be used at "opening #37 on our line."

In early 1902, the ND&C Railroad management wanted to replace the Tioronda Bridge with a stronger structure and asked the Phoenix Bridge Company to quote a price for a new 155-foot-long bridge similar to the one already at Tioronda. When the quote arrived, G. Hunter Brown wrote back to the Phoenix Bridge Company..

### Volume 71, Page 246, 1 May 1902

Some three or four years ago we received some figures on a similar structure for this same opening which came to about $8,500.00 and the difference between $8,500 and $12,000 is so very much that it prompts this inquiry.

Apparently, the ND&C Railroad management decided not to pursue the matter. A letter on 8 May 1902 rejected the offer, and there was no further mention of it. Brown wrote to Chief Engineer Garrison that the board had decided to buy a used span from the Pennsylvania Railroad Rockville Bridge for use at Tioronda. They planned to hire a bridge contractor to do some modifications and set it up at Tioronda. This was to be done to handle heavier locomotives that were planned for the coal business.

A Board of Railroad Commissioners inspection report in May 1902 added more work for the ND&C Railroad bridge crews. The report called for the addition of inside guard rails on all bridges. The ND&C agreed to comply and started adding inside guard rails to bridges from Dutchess Junction to Millerton.

During that same month of May 1902, Chief Engineer Garrison examined the Tioronda Bridge and said that current traffic was putting an unsafe strain on the structure. Additional stringers had to be added immediately. Even though the bridge was only about six years old, it was not strong enough to handle the increase in train tonnage. A new bridge from Phoenix Bridge Company would be an expensive proposition.

The Pennsylvania Railroad sent word that it had reserved one span of the double track Rockville Bridge to be sold to the ND&C. This sounded like a possible answer, but there were problems.

The Rockville Bridge was for double tracks and had three trusses, so the ND&C began looking for a buyer for the extra truss. In addition, the Rockville Bridge was a skewed design made to cross a gap at an angle. The ND&C began trying to find a bridge company to modify the Rockville skewed double track span into a right angle single track span and install it at Tioronda. Meanwhile, the heavy trains were straining the existing bridge.

In the first week of June 1902, G. Hunter Brown wrote to the Pennsylvania Railroad and asked to be released from the purchase of the Rockville Bridge span because no bridge company would agree to modify or install it. Five different companies had refused the contract: Phoenix Bridge Company, Penn Steel, Columbia Bridge Company, Penn Bridge Company, and Beaver Falls and Fort Pitt Bridge Company. The Pennsylvania Railroad released the ND&C from sale of the Rockville Bridge. Because a replacement bridge was not immediately available, stringers were added to the existing Tioronda Bridge. After that operation, the passenger train speed limit was lifted, but all other trains were restricted to four miles per hour.

A few months later, in October 1902, the ND&C board of directors authorized proposed improvements for the Bangall trestle. The wooden trestle was to be replaced by a new steel viaduct. The never-ending saga of bridge rebuilding continued. Less than a month later, the ND&C decided to contract for the Tioronda Bridge before doing the Bangall viaduct. ND&C president Brown authorized placing an order with the Phoenix Bridge Company for a new span at Tioronda for twelve thousand dollars. With no alternatives available, the ND&C was forced to pay the high price of twelve thousand dollars for a new Tioronda Bridge, even though the existing bridge was only six years old.

Through the winter of 1902-03 preparations continued for a new Tioronda Bridge. The ND&C requested blueprints to make sure they ordered the correct size ties. Letters were exchanged over a disagreement about strength specifications. In March 1903, the Phoenix Bridge Company agreed to increase the strength of the design for an additional $648 over the original twelve thousand dollar price.

In May 1903, Brown wrote to the Phoenix Bridge Company asking them if when they take the scrap metal from the Tioronda Bridge would they also take other scrap. ND&C management wanted them to take old Tioronda approach spans and the fifty-foot deck girder bridge that had been stored at Clove Branch. There is no indication in the letterbooks about whether the Phoenix Bridge Company actually took the scrap.

**One of the smaller bridge projects made from scrap rails, near Rte. 82 in Arthursburgh.**
Photo by author, May 2002.

In the spring of 1903, the ND&C was building a very large abutment for the new Bangall trestle. It contained 480 cubic yards of stone and was twenty-five feet high. Their derrick would not reach that high, so they asked to borrow a derrick from Mead and Taft of Cornwall Landing, New York. The derrick they wanted to borrow was actually very near to the ND&C tracks at the Dieterich estate in Millbrook. You may recall that in later days, this estate was the home of Timothy Leary and his LSD drug cult.

At the suggestion of Mr. Allison Hicks of Bangall, New York, the design of the abutment was altered. The west wing wall was moved back four feet two inches to allow more room for overflow from the dam in the spring floods.

**Steam train passing over the west Glenham Bridge. Photo undated. Note what appears to be bridge construction materials at lower left.**
Collection of the Beacon Historical Society.

A variety of bridge projects continued through 1903 and 1904, up until the last few entries in the ND&C books.

### Volume X, Page 250, 2 August 1904
*The ND&C will provide an engine and derrick car for the use of the Phoenix Bridge Company They will be setting up a new bridge at Verbank.*

### Volume X, Page 400, 16 August 1904
*The ND&C will pay Stephen E. Ladne one hundred dollars for the privilege of building an arch culvert on his land at Brinckerhoff.*

### Volume X, Pages 441 and 481, 19 and 25 August 1904
*Hams Bridge near Verbank has been completed by the Phoenix Bridge Company.*

In the summer of 1904, the ND&C Railroad was very nearly at an end. The New Haven Railroad had abandoned all passenger service on ND&C leased rails. A short time later the New Haven Railroad abandoned Hudson River car ferry service between Newburgh and Fishkill Landing. These actions meant a big cut in the ND&C revenue from trackage rights. The CNE Railway decided to abandon the connection from Millerton to State line, which would cut the ND&C off from all Connecticut traffic. The ND&C still had a shared station with the NYC Railroad at Dutchess Junction and connections with the Harlem line of the NYC at Millerton, but that was not enough business to survive. Almost all east-west rail traffic traveled over the Poughkeepsie Bridge and the Maybrook line. And those early automobiles were beginning to show up on dusty local roads. An agency in Poughkeepsie was selling Oldsmobiles. Cars imported from Europe had been available since 1895, and early Ford Model A cars were available starting in 1903. Automobile production in the United States was a total of four in 1895. By 1905, the total number was twenty-five thousand per year. Mass production and affordable cars came a few years later with the Ford Model T in 1909.

### Volume X, Page 521, 31 August 1904
*Letter to E. W. Bullinger, publisher of Bullingers Postal and Shippers Guide, New York:*

This notes your letter of Aug 30th addressed to our Mr. Brown, Vice Pres. & Ge. Manager.

There is no truth whatever in the report that the New York Central has purchased the ND&C RR or that the latter road will be operated by the New York Central.

The letter made no mention of the CNE Railway or the New Haven Railroad.

### Volume X, Page 719, 21 September 1904
*G. Hunter Brown wrote a letter to R. P. Stanton, road master:*

In pursuance of a vigorous policy of retrenchment instituted upon the direction of our President, you are directed, effective October 1st, 1904, to reduce the labor expenditures allotted to Maintenance of Way, or what is commonly known as roll No.1, to a figure within $1400.00 per month, of 27 working days. This amount includes the compensation of the Road Master.

The intention is to reduce the number of men and the number of hours worked. Masons, carpenters and painters will no longer be needed when current jobs are finished.

### Volume X, Page 730, 21 September 1904
*Improvement work on Mary Ann's Bridge is deferred because of high cost.*

That was the last mention of any bridge building activity in the ND&C Railroad letterbooks.

# More Rails into Hopewell Junction

DURING THE 1880s, there was intense competition between Poughkeepsie and Newburgh. Both cities wanted to be the business leaders of the Hudson Valley. The NY&NE Railroad ferry connection from Fishkill Landing to Newburgh was a boost to the Newburgh business interests. However, the Poughkeepsie Railroad Bridge, which would benefit Poughkeepsie, was under construction. Several years before the bridge was completed there were proposals to build a railroad from Poughkeepsie to Hopewell Junction and connect with the NY&NE Railroad, which would bypass the slower Fishkill Landing ferry. Completion of the bridge, in 1888, was added incentive to build this connecting railroad.

When the Poughkeepsie Railroad Bridge first opened in December 1888, the rail connection into Connecticut was the Poughkeepsie and Eastern (P&E) Railroad (renamed New York & Massachusetts Railroad or NY&M) which ran northeast from Poughkeepsie through Pleasant Valley and Pine Plains. The route connected to the ND&C Railroad at Stissing. It ran on ND&C rails to Pine Plains then on NY&M rails again to Millerton and State Line Junction. This route was never satisfactory for a number of reasons. It connected to Hartford but was not very convenient for southern Connecticut cities. In addition, the people who owned the line refused to sell it to the bridge company. The bridge company built a twenty-eight-mile line, called the Poughkeepsie and Connecticut (P&C) parallel to the old P&E (NY&M) through Pleasant Valley and Pine Plains to Silvernails in Columbia County. At Silvernails it connected with the R&C for access to New England.

In May 1889, the tracks from the west end of the bridge were completed to Campbell Hall, where they connected to the coal railroads of Pennsylvania and opened up rail connections to the west. All of this only emphasized the need for a direct rail connection from Poughkeepsie to Hopewell Junction, and thus to the markets of southern New England via the NY&NE Railroad. A line directly to Hopewell Junction would be shorter than the route through Pleasant Valley and Pine Plains, particularly for traffic to southern Connecticut and Rhode Island.

Even before the Poughkeepsie Railroad Bridge was completed, a new railroad was chartered to connect directly with Hopewell Junction. It was called the Poughkeepsie & South Eastern Railroad, and it was chartered on 31 August 1886. The stated purpose was to construct a line at or near the Hudson River in the City of Poughkeepsie and running thence through the city and through the townships of Poughkeepsie, LaGrange, Wappingers and East Fishkill to Hopewell Junction, a distance of thirteen miles. There were three Poughkeepsie residents listed on the application: Jacob A. Perkins, Robert F. Wilkinson, and Homer A. Nelson. The E. L. Dwyer was the president and George S. Bowen was general manager. Other names listed were from Brooklyn, New York. Construction began in 1889, but just how much was completed is unclear. The trail ends at that point. Perhaps further research will establish the fate of the P&SE Railroad.

The following year, in 1890, the Dutchess County Railroad was being built on what appears to be the same plan as the P&SE Railroad. In the ND&C Railroad letterbooks, Jacob A. Perkins, who was listed on the P&SE Railroad charter, had moved on and was referred to as superintendent of the New York & Massachusetts Railroad which was the reorganized name of what had been the Poughkeepsie & Eastern Railroad.

The Dutchess County Railroad spanned the twelve miles between Poughkeepsie and Hopewell Junction. It was also the last new railroad to be built in Dutchess County. As with most projects, things did not go as smoothly as planned. There were already two railroads in Hopewell Junction, and this would be the third. The ND&C and the NY&NE were ten years into their strained relationship when news of the Dutchess County Railroad began to filter into the ND&C letterbooks.

Right from the first mention of the Dutchess County Railroad, there seemed to be problems.

**Volume 30, Page 310, 6 October 1890**
*ND&C superintendent Kimball
wrote to President Schultze:*

> While in Poughkeepsie this AM I saw J. A. Perkins Supt. NY&M Ry. and learned from him that Mr. Stanton has run short of money & that work on the Dutchess Co. RR is at a standstill which is also confirmed by Milton A. Fowler and others.

The investors must have come up with more money. A few months later, in August 1891, there was a note stating that the Dutchess County Railroad wanted to connect with the NY&NE at Hopewell Junction east of the station so that they could extend their line to Clove Valley and get the Sylvan Lake ore

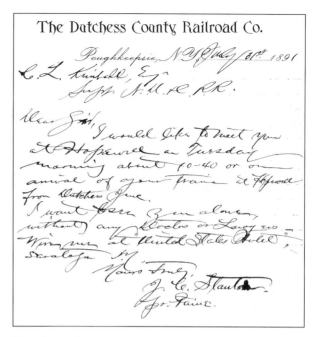

**Dutchess County RR Mr. Stanton asks for an urgent meeting with ND&C RR Mr. Kimball, "Without any doctors or lawyers."** Author's collection.

business for the bridge line. ND&C of course wanted to keep the ore business and told the Dutchess County Railroad to connect west of the station to make the ore business more difficult. The Dutchess County Railroad eventually did connect to the NY&NE east of the Hopewell Junction station, but there never was a direct link to the ore business at Sylvan Lake or Clove Valley.

On 6 August 1891, the Dutchess County Railroad requested a switch connection at Hopewell Junction to haul material for their line construction. Charles Kimball, superintendent of the ND&C Railroad, was concerned about setting a precedent in locating the switch. He felt that once the switch was in place it would be difficult to change the location.

Three weeks later, on 29 August, a shipment of five thousand railroad ties for the

Dutchess County Railroad arrived by steamship on the Hudson River. As it turned out, the water was not deep enough at the ND&C dock at Dutchess Junction, and the shipment was diverted to the NY&NE dock at Fishkill Landing. This cut the ND&C out of the hauling revenue and put the ties on a NY&NE train to Hopewell Junction.

The next mention of the Dutchess County Railroad was on 23 September 1891. This was a rate quotation of eight cents per hundred pounds for hauling a locomotive and tender (on wheels), plus one dollar for each platform car consigned to the Dutchess County Railroad at Hopewell Junction. Six days, later on 29 September, four cars of steel rails arrived for the Dutchess County Railroad at Hopewell Junction. By that time, things were getting crowded around the Hopewell yard, prompting ND&C superintendent Kimball to write a strong letter to the chief engineer of the Dutchess County Railroad.

In the letter, Kimball stated that the ND&C had thirty-two carloads of rails for the Dutchess County Railroad for which they had advanced $868.21 to the Erie Railroad. The DC Railroad did not have any track laid to receive the carloads of rails because they did not have angle bars, bolts, and spikes. To make matters worse, the Erie Railroad wanted their cars back. At that point, Kimball was not happy with Mr. Patterson's planning. Two weeks later, on 14 October, a note stated that the ND&C accepted at Wicopee Junction one locomotive, one tender and twelve empty cars, all consigned to the DC Railroad at Hopewell Junction.

In reading the letterbooks, you can almost feel the frustration building between the two railroads. The ND&C Railroad was trying to maintain order in the yard at Hopewell while running both passenger and freight operations for the two railroads already there. The Dutchess County Railroad was trying to build a new railroad while running out of money.

## Volume 32, Pages 412 and 413, 22 October 1891

*Kimball wrote a strong three-page letter to the Dutchess County Railroad.*

Your engine and cars arrived at the Hopewell yard on Oct 7th using the ND&C facilities for switching, coal and water. You said that when your track fastenings came you would install your own track. The fastenings came on Oct 14th. No work is being done on your tracks. Our sidings are clogged with 75 cars of your materials and other roads want their cars back.

We expect you to do your work on your own tracks by 31 Oct.

The last line of the letter was underlined to emphasize the ultimatum.

At that time, the DC Railroad must have built the temporary tracks to haul construction materials. The exact location of this connection has remained a small mystery for many years. According to the ND&C letterbooks, it was somewhere west of the Hopewell Junction depot, but that area is a swamp and is the streambed of Whortlekill Creek. In studying the question, I looked at a current map of that stretch and noticed that there is a likely spot about half a mile west of the depot beyond the Whortlekill Creek Bridge. Near that point there is a residential street named Terra Nova Drive, which seems to be just where a rail connection could have been. In addition, there is another street called Vicki Lane, which is about a quarter mile north through the woods toward Lake Walton from the end of Terra Nova. The alignment looked like a logical layout for the rail connection to haul construction materials.

There is further evidence in a CNE Railway blueprint in my collection. The blueprint is of

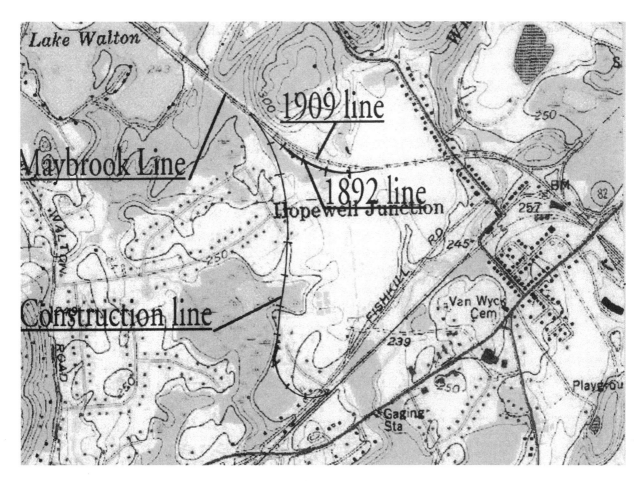

**Above:** DC RR temporary construction ROW between Lake Walton and Hopewell Junction. Maybrook Line goes through Hopewell Junction at right. Construction ROW branches off to the south in the center. Part of a USGS map modified by the author.

**Right:** Trees grow by stone abutments from the original 1892 alignment of the Maybrook Line. Concrete bridge in the background is from a 1909 realignment and double tracking. Maybrook Line between Hopewell Junction and Lake Walton, NY. Photo by author.

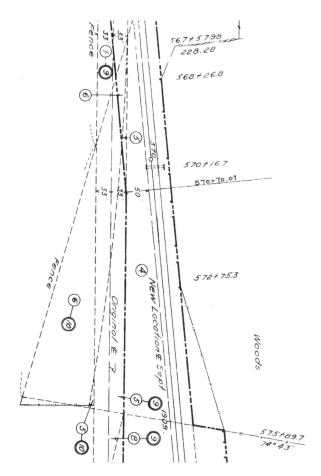

**CNE Rwy 1916 blueprint showing an unused switch connection. It points left into the woods just east of Lake Walton on the Maybrook Line. This seems to be the temporary construction line used by the DC RR in 1891. The railroads bought the property in 1890 and sold it in 1915.** Author's collection.

the track between Lake Walton and Hopewell Junction and is dated 1916. It shows the original 1892 alignment of the Dutchess County Railroad with a fairly sharp curve going into Hopewell Junction. The blueprint also shows the new CNE alignment when the curve was straightened and the line was double tracked. On the print this is marked New Location and Center Line Sept 1909. The interesting part is what looks like a switch turnout just east of Lake Walton. It curves off the old DC Railroad line to the southeast into the woods with "fence" marked on the print. Notes on the print indicate that this area was acquired by the DC Railroad in July 1890, which was almost two years before their line was opened into Hopewell Junction. The switch on the print is located at just about the correct point to pass through the backyards of the houses on Vicki Lane and connect with a line through the woods from Terra Nova Drive. The CNE Railway sold the property in 1915, after the Maybrook line was realigned and double tracked.

I decided to investigate the area on foot for a closer look. After several mapping hikes through the woods using a GPS satellite receiver, it seems very likely that this is the old construction roadbed. The trees have grown over the area in the last hundred years, but there is still evidence of a roadbed embankment at just about the correct location. Aerial photographs of that section also show a faint line through the trees. Of course, parts of the route have been graded over to build houses and streets. The next step was to hike back through with a metal detector and look for any old scrap metal that may still be there in the wooded sections. A few spikes or a rusty rail section would prove the point. Thus far, after three trips, I have not found any spikes or rails. There is, however, ample evidence of barbed wire fence along the old roadbed embankment.

On 4 November 1891, the DC Railroad still had not installed their siding at Fishkill Plains and continued to use ND&C tracks and sidings at Hopewell Junction for switching gravel and construction material. Kimball issued another ultimatum stating that "after tomorrow the ND&C will no longer allow such switching." Apparently, the construction connection was in operation in early November 1891, several months before the permanent

**Part of an aerial photo of the Lake Walton and Hopewell Junction area in 1935. Lake Walton at the upper left and Hopewell Junction at the lower right. New Haven RR Maybrook line is the dark line in the center. Faint line of the original 1892 alignment is visible in the center. The DC RR temporary construction ROW is the dark line branching south in the center.** Photo from Dutchess County Soil and Water Conservation District, Millbrook, NY.

connection was completed at Hopewell Junction.

On that same day, a letter records the fact that Kimball had talked to the Board of Railroad Commissioners regarding the exact location of the permanent DC Railroad crossing to be built at Hopewell Junction. This would be the planned crossing of the ND&C tracks to connect with the NY&NE tracks and is not the temporary connection used to haul construction materials.

There was also a cost estimate for protecting and maintaining the DC Railroad crossing at grade. Items on the estimate include the cost of starting and stopping engines, a flagman for day and night, lamps and oil, and track frog maintenance. The total estimated cost for the crossing was $1403.25 per year. This was a substantial sum of money in the 1890s when many railroad men worked for less than five hundred dollars per year. An additional letter went to the NY&NE asking for a map of their Hopewell Junction property to help locate the crossing and access point to the ND&C depot.

In the continuing battles between the two railroads, Kimball sent instructions to Charles Underhill, the ND&C Hopewell Junction agent, regarding consignments for the DC Railroad.

As soon as the freight charges are paid

place the cars on their tracks. All cars left on ND&C tracks will be charged regular demurrage.

Behind the flurry of construction activity there were also business concerns. Kimball wrote a letter to ND&C president Schultze discussing the situation. It seems that the NY&NE Railroad had been negotiating with the DC Railroad and the Poughkeepsie Bridge people. That combination could carry rail traffic over the bridge and directly to the NY&NE at Hopewell Junction, and thereby cut the ND&C completely out of that market. If that happened, the NY&NE would no longer need the Fishkill Landing ferry or the ND&C trackage rights to Hopewell Junction. Kimball suggested fighting back by making a deal with the Ontario and Western (O&W) Railway for a ferry transfer at Newburgh and extending the northeast end of the ND&C into Massachusetts. This was never implemented.

In January 1892, the DC Railroad was granted permission to install a grade crossing at Hopewell Junction. This was probably the grade crossing at Bridge Street, Route 376. Dutchess County Railroad construction was approaching the proposed Hopewell Junction crossing point.

### Volume 33, Page 14, 8 January 1892

> The piece of land that the Dutchess Co. RR proposes to cross on the south side of our track is two hundred feet in width exclusive of our right of way and we have a strip of twenty feet in width on the north side of our track exclusive of our right of way that they will cross in reaching our track.

On that same day, Charles Kimball happened to be in Hopewell Junction. He found DC Railroad men grading the two hundred-foot strip without permission, and he ordered them off the property. Kimball immediately notified President Schultze and asked a question: "If I find them working again should I use force or get an injunction?"

Apparently neither force nor an injunction were required. A week later the ND&C lawyer Mr. Eno sent a wire.

### Volume 33, Page 47, 15 January 1892

> I got stipulations today containing all that we ask for.
>
> Have agreed that they might go on tomorrow and grade their track between our road and the New England.

On 16 January, Kimball wrote back to Eno with some concerns about the agreement.

### Volume 33, Pages 48 and 49, 16 January 1892

> I thought that the General authorized you to settle the right of way across the 20 foot strip and the 200 foot strip giving them a right of way strip 50 feet wide across the two pieces outside of our right of way for $500.
>
> I note that we have nothing to say about the selecting of the man who is to operate the signals and crossing.

ND&C chief engineer Everett Garrison had written to the Union Switch and Signal Company to ask for blueprints and specifications of their crossing signal system. He wanted a Union Switch and Signal representative to go with him to Albany and explain the system to the Board of Railroad Commissioners. Kimball decided to go to Albany with Garrison and Mr. Goodman from the Union Switch and Signal Company. Meanwhile the DC Railroad contractors were back grading the two hundred-foot strip in Hopewell Junction. Kimball was not happy with the turn of events.

> I don't like the situation of things one bit. We have no voice in the matter of appointing or dismissing the man who is to take care of the

crossing except through the DC RR and I learn that Fowler is to appear with us before the RR commissioners today, which I don't like.

The ND&C letterbooks do not record what happened at the meeting in Albany. We can only assume that the questions were settled to the satisfaction of the Commissioners and that construction continued. During the first week of February 1892, there was a series of letters between Charles Kimball and Mr. O. Erlandson, the assistant chief engineer of construction for the Dutchess County Railroad. The subject was the difference in height between the DC Railroad rails and the ND&C rails. They did not match correctly at the crossing frog, and adjustments had to be made.

On 3 February, Kimball stated that he was going to Hopewell the following day to look over the situation. He also stated that the connection should be done with "step chairs" rather than try to make the joint with angle bars. On 5 February, the ND&C roadmaster, Mr. Smith, measured the rails so that "step chairs" could be made the following day. The DC Railroad supplied four sections of their rail for use in building the frog connections. By 8 February, there was a letter to ND&C president Schultze stating that the crossing was put in Saturday PM. That letter further said that the alignment and gauge were okay for the ND&C but for the DC Railroad the frog was slightly out of alignment and gauge.

After the crossing frog was installed, Kimball wrote a letter to the DC Railroad stating that a competent flagman was needed to guard the new crossing. On 23 February, he also sent out a notice that all trains must come to a complete stop and wait for the flagman's signal at the DC Railroad crossing at Hopewell Junction. A month later, on 23 March, Kimball sent out a notice to all shippers saying that the ND&C had no arrangements with the DC Railroad for transferring freight. He told the shippers to wait until the DC Railroad formally opened for business or take all responsibility. Even though the crossing had been installed, the DC Railroad did not open for business until the last week of May 1892.

Construction of the Dutchess County Railroad was not yet completed. One of the cars of material that the ND&C had delivered to the DC Railroad several months earlier belonged to the Central New England and Western (CNE&W) Railroad. The ND&C had inquired about the car, but it was not returned. As the story turned out, the DC Railroad contractor had been using the boxcar as a caboose and tool car. But then the car met with an accident, and the DC Railroad did not have facilities to repair it. The contractor asked the ND&C Railroad to repair the car and send the bill to the DC Railroad. A repair crew from the ND&C shop at Dutchess Junction went to Hopewell Junction with a spare truck and hauled the car to the shop. Repair charges totaled $106, and the car was sent home to the CNE&W. The bill went to the DC Railroad on 12 March, but as of 7 April there had been no payment. Considering the financial situation, it was probably a long time before the ND&C was paid for that repair job.

All was not well in the final stages of construction on the Dutchess County Railroad.

### Volume 33, Page 325, 26 March 1892

It is reported that J. C. Stanton, contractor DC RR, has made an assignment & his men have all quit work.

In a letter on 2 April 1892, Kimball instructed Charles Underhill, the ND&C Hopewell agent, to hold any DC Railroad materials until they paid for shipment of rails. On 13 April Kimball wrote to the DC Railroad asking for

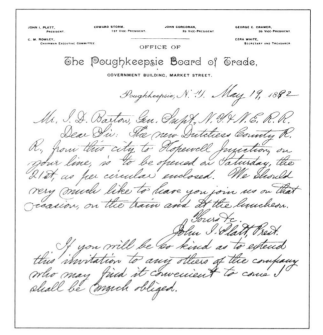

Above: Invitation to the opening ceremonies of the Dutchess County RR, May 1892. Author's collection.

Left: Poster for the opening of the Dutchess County RR, May 1892. Collection of the Beacon Historical Society.

back payment for the flagman at the Hopewell Junction crossing. Kimball decided to report the whole situation to ND&C president Schultze.

**Volume 33, Pages 429 & 430, 15 April 1892**
*Kimball wrote a three-page letter to Schultze regarding the status of dealings with the Dutchess County Railroad and its contractor Mr. Stanton:*

> DC RR has not paid a freight bill of $215.60 for a shipment of rails. This was advanced by Hopewell agent Underhill so he will be held for the money. DC RR has not paid for 2 months of flagman service at the Hopewell crossing. The flagman has been withdrawn and the DC RR warned about protection. I understand that Mr. Campbell, a contractor from Philadelphia, is to finish the work and that he was the original contractor and that Mr. Stanton subbed the work from Mr. Campbell.
>
> Matters are badly mixed and if I had to tell who is who, I believe they are all a lot of thieves.
>
> Had we not better employ council and if so who? Mr Eno is too busy to give the matter attention.

Since there was no flagman to protect the crossing at Hopewell, the ND&C had blocked the tracks so that no DC Railroad trains could cross. However, this did not stop the DC Railroad crew. On 4 May 1892, a DC Railroad train and crew with officials on board removed the pile of ties and connected the derail points,

**Above: ND&C depot at Hopewell Junction in it's original location , c. 1905.** Collection of the East Fishkill Historical Society.

**Below: Postcard view of Hopewell Junction depot and crossing signal tower, dated 1908. Looking west along the Maybrook Line toward Poughkeepsie, NY. Note that in this picture the depot has two chimneys. Later pictures of the depot show only one chimney.** Collection of Heyward Cohen.

then posed as a NY&NE train to cross the ND&C tracks at Hopewell without permission.

### Volume 33, Page 550, 21 May 1892
*Kimball wrote to Schultze:*

> The Dutchess Co. RR commences running regular trains next Monday. They ran a free excursion train to Poughkeepsie today. I was at Hopewell when they were getting ready to leave & should say that about 200 people took the train.

Kimball asked Schultze for a meeting to decide what the ND&C would do about exchange of passengers and baggage with the DC Railroad (renamed CNE&W Railroad) at the crossing in Hopewell Junction. At that time, the ND&C depot in Hopewell Junction was still at its original location near Bridge Street, about two hundred yards west of the crossing point. Early photographs of Hopewell Junction show that the depot was not moved to the crossing until some time after the Borden's creamery was built in 1901. This means that for a period of about nine or ten years, from early in 1892 until after 1901, the ND&C depot was a couple hundred yards from any DC Railroad tracks, which would be inconvenient for transferring passengers and freight. The location of the construction rail connection would have provided access to the depot via ND&C tracks, but there is no record that this route was ever used for passenger service. At least one early photograph shows an open shelter at the crossing. That shelter may have been the only passenger transfer point until the ND&C depot was eventually moved.

Somehow, the DC Railroad had come up with the finances to complete the construction and begin operations. Where did the money come from? Could it be that the DC Railroad had negotiated a deal? The answer to those questions seems to be in the name reference that happened that same month, May 1892. In 1889, several small railroads in Dutchess County had been consolidated into one large line called the CNE&W Railroad with financial backing from the Philadelphia & Reading Railroad. The Dutchess County Railroad had the same officers as the CNE&W Railroad, and so became allied with the Poughkeepsie Bridge Railroad, the Hartford & Connecticut Western Railroad, the Hudson Connecting Railroad, and the Poughkeepsie & Connecticut Railroad. Barely nine days after the opening of the Dutchess County Railroad, Kimball wrote a letter of complaint using the new name, CNE&W Railroad. In later letters he still referred to the line as the DC Railroad, even though it was part of the CNE&W Railroad.

### Volume 33, Page 594, 30 May 1892
*Kimball wrote to Fowler, general superintendent, CNE&W Railroad, complaining that the man assigned to the tower at the Hopewell crossing was frequently drunk.*

In addition to the name change, this was the first mention of a tower at the crossing. Prior to that time, the letters had been about a flagman at the crossing. About April or May 1892, a crossing control tower was constructed at Hopewell Junction. On 8 June 1892, Kimball wrote to the superintendent of the DC Railroad regarding requirements for the crossing tower operator and the agent at Hopewell Junction. There seemed to be a communications gap between the two roads even though their tracks were connected. There was still no arrangement for freight or passenger transfer. Even as late as December 1892, a full six months into the operation, there was still no freight transfer facility between the two roads. Apparently there was no freight house at Hopewell to handle less than carload lots.

View of the former ND&C RR/CNE Rwy crossing at Hopewell Junction, NY. Looking northeast toward Millbrook and Millerton. Building at left is the freight house. The tracks to Millbrook and Millerton were removed in the late 1930s. The Maybrook Line crosses between the depot and the tower. The crossing diamond had already been removed in this photo. From the collection of J. W. Swanberg.

### Volume 34, Page 629, 8 December 1892

We have no arrangement at Hopewell Junction for the interchange of freight between our road and the DC RR except in full car loads.

In early 1892, a man named Archibald McLeod controlled the railroads that were consolidated into the CNE&W Railroad. He renamed it the Philadelphia, Reading & New England Railroad in August 1892. The name Central New England & Western Railroad had lasted only three years when it became the PR&NE Railroad. Even so, the letterbooks kept referring to the Poughkeepsie to Hopewell line as the DC Railroad. Through stock manipulation, McLeod also gained control of the NY&NE Railroad by using PR&NE Railroad stock as collateral. Then the same man controlled both of the railroads that connected to the ND&C at Hopewell, the NY&NE and the PR&NE.

Of course the giant New Haven Railroad saw the growing competition in southern New England and fought back under the leadership of J. P. Morgan. The New Haven began cutting off access to the NY&NE Railroad. Because the NY&NE had close ties with the P&R Railroad, the financial strain, combined with a stock market crash, forced the Philadelphia & Reading into receivership on 20 August 1893. The PR&NE remained in receivership until January 1899 and then was reorganized into the Central New England Railway.

Meanwhile, J. P. Morgan had been buying NY&NE stock at a depressed price and by 1895, had gained control of that road as well. He changed the name from NY&NE Railroad to NE Railroad, the New England Railroad. J. P. Morgan and the New Haven Railroad wanted the bridge route to have access to Pennsylvania coal and connections to the western states, but the CNE Railway owners refused to sell only part of their road. To get the bridge route, the New Haven Railroad was forced to buy the entire CNE Railway in 1904. The line still operated under the name CNE Railway until it was formally merged into the New Haven Railroad in 1927. Once again, in 1904, all the tracks connected to the ND&C Railroad at Hopewell Junction were controlled by one man, but this time it was J. P. Morgan.

During all the name and management changes, the ND&C kept running trains between Dutchess Junction and Millerton. They also kept collecting the monthly trackage rental checks from the NY&NE Railroad, the NE Railroad, and later, the New Haven Railroad. A January 1893 report stated that there were seven inches of snow on the tracks, and the flangers were out clearing the line. The NY&NE was moving about two hundred loads per day and the Erie had about eight hundred cars in Newburgh waiting to cross the ferry. The ND&C had sixty cars of coal caught in the back up. From 7-11 January 1893, the DC Railroad moved 179 loads. The Reading Company had eleven hundred cars waiting at Poughkeepsie.

### Volume 35, Page 257, 3 March 1893

Through our roadmaster I learn that the foreman in charge of the track on the Dutchess County RR at Hopewell Junction has been instructed by his superior office to make no repairs to the automatic interlocking switch and signal apparatus that protects the crossing, which are located on our line.

**Hopewell Junction crossing tower, about 1934. Looking along the Maybrook Line toward Poughkeepsie. Hopewell depot and freight house at left. Former ND&C RR crosses between the depot and freight house.** Photo by John P. Ahrens from the collection of J. W. Swanberg.

**Hopewell Junction freight house, passenger depot and tower.**
Postcard from the Alice Bryden collection. Collection of Heyward Cohen.

This was a direct violation of the Board of Railroad Commissioners' orders. It sounded like a very dangerous way to save a few dollars. A failure there would be disastrous for both railroads. The NY&NE Railroad was handling about a hundred cars each way per day at that time with expectations of doubling that number.

The DC Railroad was handling at least thirty or forty cars a day through Hopewell. With that much traffic, a reliable crossing protection system was an important safety measure. Charles Kimball wrote a letter to Superintendent M. E. Blaine in Hartford pointing out the facts of the commissioners' ruling. There was no indication of any response from Mr. Blaine.

The condition of the Hopewell crossing signal system became an ongoing battle between the ND&C and the PR&NE Railroad. The battle continued for at least eleven years when the owner of the line from Poughkeepsie to Hopewell was the CNE Railway. On 7 February 1898 there was a letter from ND&C vice-president G. Hunter Brown acknowledging a report from the National Switch and Signal Co. Their inspection of the crossing signal system had pointed out safety problems which the ND&C vice-president immediately reported to W. J. Martin, general superintendent of the PR&NE Railroad. Among the problems was the fact that the long distance signal for the ND&C tracks had been disconnected and was not working at all. Since the PR&NE Railroad was responsible for the tower and signal system, Brown asked them to do the repair work and generally overhaul the system.

Mr. Martin's response was a letter to Brown suggesting that the distant signals should be done away with entirely. Brown did not agree, and on 15 March 1898, he sent a letter to John S. Kenyon, secretary, Board of Railroad Commissioners in Albany, explaining the situation. Brown was concerned about running ND&C express trains through Hopewell with an unsafe signal system. The ND&C had been slowing the express trains through Hopewell as a safety measure, which cost time and money. The next letter in the series was on 23 March

1898, and it informed Mr. Martin that the state Board of Railroad Commissioners was sending an inspector to Hopewell Junction this morning. There was no report of inspection results. Since the PR&NE Railroad was operating under control of a court appointed receiver, it is not likely that very much was accomplished. We can only assume that some compromise was reached because both roads continued running trains.

J. P. Morgan already had control of the NE Railroad, and the financial strain was squeezing the PR&NE Railroad, which had been in receivership since 1893.

### Volume 51, Page 457, 3 October 1898

*ND&C vice-president G. Hunter Brown wrote to Everett Garrison (ND&C facilities engineer):*

> The PR&NE RR is to be sold at auction at Poughkeepsie on Thursday October 6th. I should like to be present at the sale for business reasons.

J. P. Morgan and his New Haven Railroad had gained financial control of the NY&NE Railroad in 1895 and changed the name to NE Railroad. In July 1898, the New Haven took over the NE Railroad completely. The section that ran on ND&C rails between Hopewell Junction and Wicopee Junction was then known as part of the Highland Division of the New Haven Railroad. The Central New England Railway bought the Poughkeepsie Bridge from the bankrupt PR&NE Railroad in 1898. J. P. Morgan and his New Haven Railroad then bought a controlling interest in the CNE in order get access to the bridge. J. P. Morgan and the New Haven Railroad either owned or controlled all the tracks that connected with the ND&C at Hopewell Junction and Wicopee.

### Volume 53, Pages 2, 3, 4 and 5, 15 October 1898

> I would also advise it is now contemplated putting on 150 men immediately at Hopewell to grade and prepare the yard there for the New Haven business, in fact 15 men are at work there now and the grade stakes are in position.

The change of ownership did not seem to make much improvement in the condition of the Hopewell crossing signal system. As late as 1904, near the end of the ND&C, there were letters addressed to J. F. Weldon, (actually his name was John F. Hedden) superintendent of the CNE Railway in Hartford, complaining about inoperative signals and incompetent tower operators. It's not likely that John Hedden did anything about the signal system. When the New Haven Railroad bought out the CNE in 1904, he and the previous CNE Railway owners moved to Nevada. The Brock brothers formed the Tonopah & Goldfield Railroad with John Hedden as the general manager.

With the coming of automobiles, the local passenger train business went into a steady decline. The New Haven Railroad wanted the bridge route but not all the other parts of the CNE Railway. They began a program of abandonment. At the end of May 1904 the New Haven Railroad withdrew all passenger service on their Highland Division at Fishkill Landing, which left that market to the ND&C. The Fishkill Landing ferry service was abandoned in August 1904. As of 30 September 1904, the CNE Railway ceased all traffic on the section of the ND&C between Millerton and State Line. The bridge route through Hopewell Junction handled the east-west traffic to and from Connecticut.

Highway trucks began to take most of the short haul freight business. The railroad line from Hopewell Junction to the Poughkeepsie Bridge, however, became the main east-west

Trestle and fill construction to double track the Maybrook line in 1910. This fill was built at Didell in Dutchess County, NY. Original photo taken by James Luyster. Photo owned by Mildred Diddell whose family supplied the timbers for the trestle. Collection of John Helmeyer.

heavy freight traffic artery for the New Haven Railroad, the Maybrook Line. To handle the increasing traffic, the ridge line was double tracked in 1909, but by that time there was no more ND&C Railroad.

In 1905, the New Haven Railroad purchased the ND&C Railroad and merged it into the CNE Railway. The CNE Railway later was merged into the New Haven Railroad in 1927. What had been the ND&C main line east of Hopewell Junction was abandoned in the 1930s, and the crossing signal tower was no longer needed. By 1939, the old ND&C main line from Hopewell Junction to Millerton had been torn up and sold for scrap metal to Japan. It is interesting to speculate on how much of the ND&C Railroad came back to US territory at Pearl Harbor on 7 December 1941.

Early in the twentieth century, passenger trains between Boston and Washington, DC, ran through Hopewell Junction and across the Poughkeepsie Bridge. In the 1960s, long freight trains with two or three GE U25B locomotives would get a running start around Fishkill Plains and thunder through Hopewell Junction to attack the eastbound grade. All this came to a halt when the Poughkeepsie Bridge burned in 1974. With no more through traffic, the local business could not support operations. Conrail made the last local run in 1982 before the tracks were removed.

Dutchess County now owns the roadbed and is planning to use it as a utility corridor and rail trail. Maybe future hikers will pause by Lake Walton on warm summer evenings and listen for the echo of steam whistles from a hundred years in the past. Who knows? Hopewell Junction may even have its own ghost train.

Last Conrail run on the Maybrook between Poughkeepsie and Hopewell Junction in 1982. The tracks were removed in the 1980s. This section of the former Maybrook Line is now owned by Dutchess County, NY. The right-of-way is designated as a utility corridor and rail trail. Collection of Ziegert.

# Meanwhile, Back at the East End

THE NY&NE was not the only railroad to lease trackage rights from the ND&C Railroad. When the ND&C Railroad was formed out of the old D&C Railroad in 1877, The Poughkeepsie and Eastern Railroad was already using a section of ND&C track between Stissing and Pine Plains. The P&E Railroad ran from Poughkeepsie, through Pleasant Valley and Salt Point, to Stissing Junction, then onto ND&C rails to Pine Plains. Beyond Pine Plains, the P&E ran on its own rails again northward through a section of Columbia County to Boston Corners, then back into Dutchess County to Millerton and State Line. The P&E and successor railroads used the short section of track throughout the entire life of the ND&C. There are many references in the ND&C letterbooks over the years. This section of trackage rights became part of the Central New England & Western Railroad (CNE&W).

In 1889, the Central New England & Western Railroad was formed out of several smaller railroads in northern Dutchess County, New York. Included in the CNE&W Railroad were the Poughkeepsie Bridge Railroad, the Hartford & Connecticut Western Railroad, the Hudson Connecting Railroad, the Rhinebeck & Connecticut Railroad, and the Poughkeepsie & Connecticut Railroad. The bridge company built the Poughkeepsie & Connecticut Railroad line parallel with the P&E Railroad through Pleasant Valley and Pine Plains. The CNE&W Railroad used the same set of connecting tracks that the ND&C Railroad owned between Millerton and State Line, to reach Connecticut.

The first mention in the ND&C letterbooks of the CNE&W Railroad is on 30 September 1889, barely two months after it was formed. There is a three page discussion of the CNE&W Railroad operating from Campbell Hall across the Poughkeepsie Railroad Bridge to Silvernails Bridge in Columbia County, a point on the Hartford & Connecticut Western Railroad that they also operated from Rhinebeck to Hartford, Connecticut.

A note on 9 December 1889 further clarifies the operation of the Millerton to State Line connection.

**Volume 28, Page 612, 9 December 1889**

In our State Reports we have given, under the heading of Description of Road and Equipment, the entire length of our main line Dutchess Junction to New York and Connecticut state line, 58.84 miles. However that portion of the road between Millerton Station and State Line, a distance of one mile, is leased to the Hartford and Connecticut Western RR Co., now part of the Central New England and Western RR, at a fixed rental and is operated and maintained by that Co., they paying taxes on same.

By January 1890, it became very evident that the CNE&W Railroad did not want to do any business with the ND&C Railroad. The CNE&W attempted to cut off all business but the ND&C fought back with a legal claim on a contract with the H&CW Railroad, which was part of the CNE&W Railroad. Beyond just ignoring the ND&C, the CNE&W began to actively undercut freight rates.

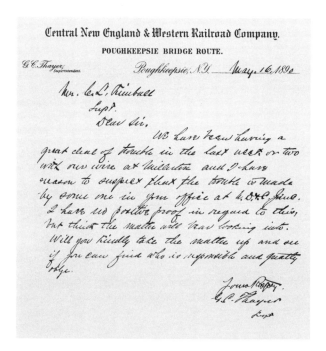

**CNE&W RR letter accusing ND&C RR people of wire tampering.**
Author's collection.

### Volume 30, Page 30, 12 July 1890
*Letter to N. R. Turner, Esq. CNE&W Railroad, Poughkeepsie:*

I understand that you are offering to carry coal from Highland via the bridge route or from Rhinebeck to Pine Plains at $1.40 per ton. This does not agree with our conversation held on the 18th of June at which time you agreed to maintain and adhere to the $1.50 rate to that point. Please explain.
Your Truly   C. L. Kimball

It seems that the CNE&W Railroad was not following the "gentleman's agreement" on price fixing rules.

There are several letters in 1891 dealing with a survey and deed for the sale of land to the CNE&W Railroad. The description says that it is "where the CNE&W crosses at Stissing." Early railroad maps of Dutchess County do not show any such crossing. Tracks are parallel and very close together but there is no crossing. CNE&W tracks do cross the P&E tracks at Stissing but not the ND&C tracks. The question remains. What was this deed for?

### Volume 31, Page 259, 269, 271-272, 13, 16, 17 March 1891
*Letters to Everett Garrison telling him that the general (Schultze) wants*

a survey of the land where the Central New England & Western Railroad crosses at Stissing. The survey is for a description to make a deed to transfer land to the Poughkeepsie and Connecticut Railroad Company.

### Volume 31, Page 643, 27 June 1891
*Kimball wrote to Schultze:*

I enclose herewith map and description made by Mr. Garrison of the land that it is proposed to deed to the CNE&W RR Co. located near Stissing Junction.

Apparently, the ND&C owned land in Stissing that the CNE&W wanted for some reason. There is also mention of an agreement for a freight transfer siding at Stissing with no indication of whether the siding was ever built.

In addition to leasing the State Line connecting track, the CNE&W Railroad also used other ND&C facilities at Millerton, such as the turntable, the engine house, and the depot. On 21 March 1891, Charles Kimball, the ND&C superintendent, wrote to the CNE&W Railroad in Hartford to say that "Our roadmaster complains that your heavy engines are destroying our turntable at Millerton." The CNE&W responded saying that the turntable should be upgraded for heavier locomotives. Kimball wrote back telling the CNE&W that this was not in the lease and if CNE&W locomotives damage the turntable, the ND&C will hold the CNE&W responsible.

**ND&C RR train at Attlebury Farms. Lucius Beebe had Howard Fogg make a painting of this scene.**
Collection of Leroy Beaujon. Courtesy of J. W. Swanberg.

The CNE&W Railroad actually used space in the ND&C depot at Millerton.

### Volume 31, Page 612, 19 June 1891
*Kimball wrote to Agent S. A. Patterson at Millerton*

By the terms of the lease, the CNE&W Railroad was responsible for maintenance of the tracks between Millerton and State Line, but such was not high on their priority list.

### Volume 31, Page 515, 28 May 1891
*Kimball wrote to Mr. Fowler, the general superintendent of the CNE&W Railroad, Hartford:*

The track from the crossing or Y at NY & Harlem crossing to the east end of yard at Millerton needs a general overhauling. In fact it is not a safe track to run over. The ties are rotten, rail is bad, with broken fish plates and many of the bolts are missing. Won't you have it put in order.

In addition to undercutting coal rates, the CNE&W also moved into the milk hauling business. The ND&C shipped milk to New York City via New York Central trains from Dutchess Junction or Millerton, and therefore was dependent on New York Central shipping rates to remain competitive. Charles Kimball appealed to the New York Central Railroad for help.

### Volume 31, Page 560, 6 June 1891

The Central New England & Western RR Co. are moving with all their power to capture the milk from all our stations east of Verbank & will from appearances succeed at Pine Plains, Attlebury, Stissing, Bangall, Millbrook, Bethel & Shekomeko unless your company comes to the rescue.

During the summer of 1891, Kimball wrote to the CNE&W with an interesting inquiry.

### Volume 31, Page 590, 13 June 1891
*Kimball wrote to Milton A. Fowler, attorney for CNE&W Railroad, Poughkeepsie, New York:*

Will you kindly give me the full name of the RR Co. that built the road from Silvernails Bridge to the Poughkeepsie Bridge, and the date when the above Co. transferred their right & interest in said road to the Central New England and Western Railroad Company, and was this transfer made by lease or by absolute sale?

Why was he asking about the name and ownership history of his competitors' railroad? Did he have some sort of scheme in mind? There is no further mention of this subject so we will probably never know what he had in mind.

Early in 1892, the smokestack on the Millerton engine house had to be replaced. Previously, the stacks at Millerton and Dutchess Junction had been made of steel, which did not stand up to the corrosive hot gasses from a coal fire. The ND&C decided to switch over to masonry smokestacks.

**Postcard view of the RR station in Millerton, NY.**
Collection of Heyward Cohen.

### Volume 33, Page 19, 9 January 1892

Have Geo. Crank [?] put the stone smoke stack on the Millerton engine house on the CNE&W side of the house. Holmes has the jack and iron work for same at Dutchess Junction.

With financial backing from the Philadelphia & Reading Railroad, Archibald McLeod bought control of the CNE&W Railroad in January 1892, then in August 1892 he renamed it the Philadelphia, Reading New England (PR&NE). The officers of this road were also the same ones listed for the new Dutchess County Railroad that was being built from Poughkeepsie to Hopewell Junction.

There is an interesting side light to the competition between the railroads. Perhaps it was only wishful thinking or maybe a rumor started to discourage shippers from using the bridge route.

### Volume 34, Pages 5-6, 30 June 1892
*Kimball wrote to Schultze telling about seeing a report on the problems with the piers of the Poughkeepsie Railroad Bridge:*

It is said that the most easterly and most westerly piers are anchored in shelf rock which is giving away.

Watching the Poughkeepsie Railroad Bridge fall into the Hudson River would surely be a spectacular sight. Now, more than one hundred years later we are still waiting.

Beginning in August 1892, the name Philadelphia, Reading & New England Rail-

**Top:** Arrangements for leasing the ND&C RR tracks between Stissing and Pine Plains. Author's collection.

**Right:** School taxes paid by the ND&C RR to the town of Northeast, September 1897. Author's collection.

road was used. There are statements of estimated costs to repair the Millerton passenger depot and also costs to build a new coal shed at Millerton. On 12 October 1892, the ND&C Railroad sent a bill to the PR&NE Railroad for half the cost of repairs to the Millerton depot. The PR&NE Railroad had financial problems and went into receivership in August 1893. It remained in that state until Thursday 6 October 1898, when the PR&NE Railroad was sold at auction in Poughkeepsie. ND&C vice president G. Hunter Brown attended the auction "for business reasons." The Central New England Railway purchased the PR&NE Railroad.

During those years, the ND&C management found it increasingly difficult to extract the payments from the P&E Railroad for the trackage rights between Stissing and Pine Plains. By 1896, the amount owed was $937.50. On 21 February 1896, G. Hunter Brown wrote and threatened to cut their road in half by locking the switches at Stissing and Pine Plains if they did not pay up. A few months later, in May 1896, he gave them permission to use the ND&C turntable in Pine Plains. Again, in July 1896, another letter asked for the back payment of $650. By December 1896, the amount owed was back up to $937.50, and Brown again threatened the P&E Railroad. He quoted the lease wording and threatened to "prevent and debar the trains of the P&E Railway Co. from entering upon or running over our tracks." He served notice that if they did not pay by 1 January 1897, the switches at Stissing and Pine Plains would be locked against the P&E Railroad. While this was happening, the P&E was undercutting the ND&C coal rates for shipments into Dutchess County across the Poughkeepsie Bridge by not living up to the agreed rates. The agreement not to compete was actually written into the lease for the trackage rights.

The P&E trackage lease was due to expire in March 1898, and Brown refused to consider any reduction in the rental. The discussion turned to the possible discontinuance of P&E rights on the ND&C rails. A letter outlines thirteen points to be taken up at a joint meeting in New York of the PR&NE Railroad, the P&E Railroad, and the ND&C Railroad. The meeting was in the office of the receiver of PR&NE Railroad at 192 Broadway on Monday 28 February 1898. Most of the points dealt with agreeing on rates where the lines were in competition. Even amidst the problems of receivership, payments owed, and lockout threats, the main thing on their minds was the rate agreement. By June of that year, the P&E, too, was in receivership under direction of a man named Slocum.

On 1 Aug 1898, Brown wrote to Slocum, receiver of the P&E Railroad, about the track rental price. The rental had been five thousand dollars per year in the past. It was reduced to twenty-four hundred dollars and Brown agreed to reduce it further to two thousand dollars per year with a provision. The P&E agreed to maintain the coal business, which was routed from the Hudson River ferry via the ND&C Railroad to Stissing, then to Poughkeepsie via the P&E through Pleasant Valley. Brown and the ND&C had the upper hand in that round. In 1899, the ND&C Railroad shops at Dutchess Junction were taking in contract repair jobs on P&E Railroad locomotives. The P&E struggled along for several more years and finally merged with the CNE in 1907. By that time, the ND&C was already part of the CNE.

In early 1899, the ND&C letterbooks begin to mention the CNE Railway as the new management of the railroad that was leasing the connection from Millerton to State Line. A CNE Railway engine was housed in the ND&C roundhouse at Millerton each night beginning on 15 Oct 1899. The ND&C night

**Postcard view of ND&C RR #4 at Pine Plains.**
Collection of J. W. Swanberg.

watchman was to take care of the engine for extra compensation. The CNE Railway offered to pay the Millerton night watchman thirty-five dollars per month to take care of their engine. G. Hunter Brown wrote back and said that was not enough and told them to hire their own man for the job. The CNE Railway was billed for half the cost of painting the station buildings at Millerton.

G. Hunter Brown wrote to John W. Brock, president of CNE Railway, Philadelphia, and sent copies of the new lease requesting that the CNE repair and upgrade the track between State Line and the Harlem Railroad. He also agreed to meet their chief engineer, Mr. Ewing, to make arrangements for reconstructing Bridge 71. Brown wrote to Brock again about the CNE engine that was to occupy the second stall in the ND&C engine house at Millerton over the winter nights. He asked the CNE to share in the expense of building a semaphore to protect the movement of this engine after dark.

An unfortunate event happened just before Christmas 1902.

**Volume 74, Page 661, 22 December 1902**
*Letter to Geo. W. Aldridge, secretary Board of Railroad Commissioners, Albany, New York:*

George Thurston, Engineer on Central New England Railway was walking across tracks in our Millerton yard was caught and crushed between two cars and instantly killed today. Regular report by mail.

On 6 April 1903, the turntable at Millerton collapsed. The following day a letter went out to J. F. Hedden, superintendent, CNE, Hartford asking to use the wye at State Line to turn two engines per day until the ND&C turntable at Millerton was repaired. The ND&C actually owned the wye but it was leased to the CNE at that time. Letters went to conductors and agents to couple engines from trains 52 and 50 together when turning at State Line to minimize the number of train movements. Letters also were sent to William Sellers & Company, 1600 Hamilton Street in Philadelphia, requesting immediate shipment of new castings for the Millerton turntable. ND&C management discovered that upgraded parts were available so the turntables could handle heavier engines. They ordered upgraded parts for both the turntable at Millerton and at Dutchess Junction.

In the summer of 1904, the New Haven Railroad withdrew passenger service and ceased operation of the ferry service at Fishkill Landing. Fishkill Landing became a freight only connection with the NYC Hudson line. This cut off much of the ND&C revenue from river crossing freight on the west end of their line. The New Haven Railroad bought the CNE Railway that year. The CNE Railway continued to operate but it was under New Haven control. Was it then really a coincidence that the CNE Railway ceased operation on the connection from Millerton to State Line at the east end of the ND&C line? With no connections to the east or west, the ND&C Railroad would be left with only local business and north-south connections with the NYC Railroad. Of course the ND&C wanted to keep the door open into Connecticut, so they decided to operate the Millerton to State Line section as part of the ND&C Railroad. After all, they owned those tracks.

On 30 September 1904, G. Hunter Brown sent a three-page letter to J. F. Hedden, superintendent of the CNE Railway. After a meeting at State Line, ND&C management had decided to continue operation of the track between State Line and Millerton. The ND&C agreed to a proposition by the CNE. There would be a joint agent and a station at State Line Junction for which the CNE would pay two-thirds and the ND&C would pay one-third. The station would be for passengers and less-than-carload freight. The agent would not be paid more than forty-five dollars per month. The ND&C would allow the CNE to use the turning wye provided that a minimum of three trains per day are turned at a rate of fifty cents each. Telegraph wires would be connected between the State Line agent and the ND&C agent at Millerton. The ND&C proposed a passenger schedule between the two points.

**Volume X, Page 802, 30 September 1904**

We put on a service between Millerton and State Line effective Monday.

Within a week there was a problem. The CNE began to balk at the terms for the agency at State Line even though they were the ones who proposed the deal in the first place. ND&C wanted to stick with the original terms. For two weeks of operation the passenger count between Millerton and State Line had averaged eight. The fare was six cents each so revenue was about forty-eight cents per run. How long could they afford to run trains with revenue at only forty-eight cents per trip?

By 15 Oct 1904, things were looking pretty grim. Due to the business conditions of the company, conductors and crews were asked to perform coach cleaning and other maintenance tasks while waiting for runs. The noose was tightening around the ND&C Railroad.

One of the last surviving entries in the ND&C Railroad letterbooks was on 18 October 1904. There were two cars of freight for the ND&C waiting on the CNE siding at State Line, but the ND&C engines were not allowed on the CNE main to get them. ND&C general freight agent Underhill asked the CNE to deliver them to the ND&C engine on the next trip. We will probably never know for sure, but the cars most likely were transferred.

The New Haven Railroad bought the ND&C Railroad and turned it over to the CNE to operate on 1 August 1905. Because the New Haven really wanted a main east-west freight route across the Poughkeepsie Railroad Bridge, they were not interested in unprofitable local business. The New Haven Railroad (via the CNE Railway) embarked on a program of abandonments to dismantle the ND&C Railroad properties. First to go were the Dutchess Junction shop facilities in 1907, then in 1916, the connection from Dutchess Junction to Wicopee Junction. In 1927, the CNE Railway was absorbed into the parent New Haven Railroad. Later, the line from Millerton to Hopewell Junction was abandoned in sections. By 1939, all that remained was the Maybrook line to the Poughkeepsie Bridge and a section of the old ND&C Railroad between Hopewell Junction and Beacon. Today, the Poughkeepsie Railroad Bridge has not seen any trains since it burned in 1974. Tracks of the Maybrook line have been gone for almost twenty years. Indeed the New Haven Railroad itself is long in the past. But a small part of the ND&C Railroad still survives between Hopewell Junction and Beacon as a section of Metro North Commuter Railroad.

# The Milk Business

A MAJOR SOURCE of revenue for the ND&C came from hauling milk. Milk from area farms was hauled by wagon or by train to processing plants for bottling. The bottled milk was then hauled to the city. Each day, trains made stops along the line to pick up cans of milk and carry them to the processing plants. The ND&C Railroad used two milk cars which ran the length of the line and back each day. In the early years, these milk cars were not much more than wooden boxcars or baggage cars on passenger trains. In the 1880s, the NYC Hudson line did not have milk cars suitable to operate with high speed trains. Hudson line operation required automatic brakes. As a result, much of the milk was shipped to the city by steamboats from the Dutchess Junction dock. The NYC did run the older style milk cars on the Harlem line, so some of the ND&C Railroad milk shipments went by way of Millerton on the NYC Harlem line to 47th Street and Fourth Avenue in New York City.

By the 1890s, milk shippers and dealers were pressuring the railroads to use "refrigerator cars." The NYC Railroad began using updated milk cars capable of running as part of high speed passenger trains. The newer cars did not have mechanical refrigeration as we know it today. They were insulated cars equipped to use ice to keep the milk cold. In 1898, the run from Dutchess Junction to New York City on the NYC Hudson line was increased to four insulated cars.

Dairy farmers who lived close to the plants could bring their milk in by wagon. Quite often, in the ND&C books the processing plants were called *creameries*. Indeed, on today's maps you can still find Creamery Road or Creamery Lane. After bottling, most of the milk was loaded into special train cars then an ND&C train hauled it to Dutchess Junction or Millerton and transferred it to a New York Central train to New York City. In good weather, some of the milk went to the Dutchess Junction dock and was loaded onto river steamboats for the trip to New York City. Steamboats charged a lower rate than the railroad but could not run in winter weather when ice blocked the river.

A standard milk can, used to carry milk from the farm to the processing plant, held forty quarts (ten gallons) of milk. Dairy farmers would fill the cans and put them on a specially built platform next to the tracks. The milk train crew would pick up the cans at each platform. Of course, a full can of milk was quite heavy, so the ND&C railroad posted a notice that they would not accept milk for transportation unless the cans had two secure handles.

An ND&C company report stated the amount of milk carried for the year 1 April 1883 to 31 March 1884. Most of the smaller stations along the line accounted for one thousand to two thousand cans each during the year. Some areas handled a lot more such as Millbrook 10,612, Shekomeko 17,310, and Pine Plains at 24,312 cans. In the case of Pine Plains, that amounted to an average of more than sixty-five cans (or 650 gallons) per day, 365 days a year. Cows did not take weekends or holidays off. The ND&C Railroad total for the year was 97,761, or an average of about 268 cans (2,680 gallons) of milk per day. Because of competition from other railroads, the ND&C shipments from Pine Plains had dwindled from sixty-five cans to about thirty-five cans per day by 1896.

One of Borden's milk processing plants, which was opened in March of 1901, was a large white building in Hopewell Junction. Land under the plant belonged to the ND&C Railroad and was leased to Borden's. ND&C Railroad books mention a Sheffield Farms creamery in Hopewell Junction in 1898, before the Borden's plant was built. Along the ND&C line there were several other milk processing plants in which the railroad had financial interests. Curley & Todd owned the plant at Verbank which Locust Farms later purchased, but the ND&C Railroad held the mortgage. The ND&C Railroad had a contract with Frank Hall of Verbank to build the LaGrange milk plant, but Beakes Dairy Company operated it. The ND&C also owned the ice house at Shekomeko, which was leased to plant operators F. Lahey & Sons. McDermott & Bunger operated the Millbrook plant.

Before mechanical refrigeration, the plants used ice cut from local ponds in the winter and stored in insulated buildings. Some of the ice was hauled in from as far away as Lake Champlain. With proper insulation, the ice would last through the summer months. In February 1892, Charles Kimball ordered 250 bushels of sawdust from William Allen of Hopewell Junction. The stated reason was to cover the ice supply at the ND&C Railroad ice facility at Brinckerhoff. Milk cars were supposed to be cooled with ice starting in May 1892, but the NYC Railroad failed to provide the insulated cars as agreed. Stations along the ND&C had been equipped with ice tongs and hand carts to handle the ice blocks. By July, milk shippers were threatening to use other railroads. Kimball wrote a letter of complaint to the NYC on 26 July 1892. It must have gotten results because ice was actually loaded into "refrigerator" cars starting on 8 August 1892. With luck, it would be enough to keep the milk cold all the way to New York City.

Of course there was the opposite problem in the winter. On many winter occasions, even after insulated cars were in use, the milk arrived in New York City frozen solid. On 17 December 1900, ND&C general freight agent William Underhill wrote a letter to the Hillside Dairy Company, 812 Sixth Avenue in New York City. He explained that the railroad had no way to heat the milk cars. If the milk was arriving frozen he suggested shipping it without the caps to allow for expansion.

In winter, the ND&C Railroad contracted with pond owners for ice, some of which was stored to be used in train cars and some of which was sold to milk plant operators. The ice storage area at the LaGrange milk plant was thirty-nine by seventy-nine by twelve feet for a total of 36,972 cubic feet, which held over 821 tons of ice. The ice delivered to the Borden's milk plant in Hopewell Junction came from a pond in Billings, New York. ND&C record books show that as of 20 March 1901, the new Borden's plant opened with nine hundred tons of ice in storage insulated with sawdust.

On 29 March 1901, the ND&C railroad sent a bill to Borden's for the nine hundred tons of ice in the new Hopewell Junction plant. The total bill was $67.50 for the ice plus $160.61 for shipping charges. That works out to be a little over twenty-five cents per ton. Of course, at that time, a laborer's wages were around $1.35 for a ten hour day or about 13.50 cents per hour. A railroad man earning a good salary might get forty-five dollars per month.

There was competition in the milk hauling business. In the fall of 1885, the New York &

**Postcard view of Millbrook, NY.**
Collection of Heyward Cohen.

New England Railroad proposed a plan to ship milk eastward from Hopewell Junction to make connections into New York City through Putnam County. The ND&C Railroad objected to the plan on the basis that it was a violation of their contract for trackage rights between Hopewell Junction and Wicopee Junction. The contract was for rights to carry through freight and passengers on ND&C rails but not to perform any local business. There was no further mention of the NY&NE shipping milk. The NY&NE was a much larger railroad than the ND&C and was more interested in through freight traffic anyway.

In the northeastern part of Dutchess County, there were other railroads competing with the ND&C in hauling milk to New York City. What had once been the Poughkeepsie & Eastern Railroad had gone bankrupt in 1874 and was reorganized under new management. It was renamed the Poughkeepsie, Hartford & Boston Railroad (PH&B). Their tracks never reached Hartford or Boston but they did reach Boston Corners which is in New York State near the Massachusetts line. This railroad actually leased trackage rights from the ND&C Railroad between Stissing and Pine Plains. For that section of the line, the two railroads ran trains on the same tracks. The PH&B Railroad routed their milk shipments eastward to Boston Corners where they connected with the Harlem line of the NYC Railroad to New York City. On those same tracks between Stissing and Pine Plains, the ND&C trains were hauling milk westward to connect with the Hudson line of the NYC Railroad or a river steamboat at Dutchess Junction to reach the New York City markets.

Dairy farmers in the northeastern part of Dutchess County had a choice of several railroads to haul their milk to market. The decision of which railroad to use was most often made on the basis of shipping charges. Whichever railroad could get the milk to market for the least expense would get the hauling business. There was more at stake than just the number of cans of milk. The railroad that hauled the milk probably also hauled the feed, grain, and supplies. Shipping rate competition was very evident in the ND&C letterbooks. In early February 1884, ND&C Railroad superintendent Charles Kimball wrote a four page let-

**Main St. Crossing, Pine Plains, NY, looking east toward Winchells and Millerton.**
Collection of J. W. Swanberg.

ter to ND&C Railroad president Schultze in New York City discussing the competition from the PH&B Railroad. Here is a quote from the first page.

### Volume 18, Page 59, 4 February 1884

It looks a little as though we should lose our milk shipments from Pine Plains and a part of our shipments from Shekomeko. Milk producers in that vicinity are bound to ship by rail the year round if they can, and I understand that they are soliciting the aid of the PH&B to carry their milk to Boston Corners where connections will be made with the Harlem Road for 47th St. NY City.

The NYC Railroad charged thirty cents per can for their part of the trip to New York City on either the Hudson line or the Harlem line and they refused to reduce the rate. The ND&C Railroad had been averaging about twenty-two cents per can for the Dutchess County part of the trip, but the PH&B Railroad offered to haul the milk for ten cents per can. In the letter, Kimball told Schultze that the ND&C Railroad was faced with either reducing the charge to ten cents or losing the business completely.

Part of the problem was the total quantity of milk to be shipped from Dutchess Junction to New York City. If the ND&C Railroad lost the milk shipments from Pine Plains and Shekomeko, the total at Dutchess Junction dock would not be enough for the steamboats to bother stopping. The ND&C Railroad would then be forced to use the NYC Railroad at a higher rate for all the remaining shipments. A month later, in March 1884, a group of milk producers presented a petition to the ND&C Railroad demanding that all milk shipments go by rail and not by steamboat. Kimball relented and agreed to stop using steamboats to ship milk. Later, business reports

**ND&C Junction, Pine Plains, NY, looking north. Train at right is coming from Pine Plains station and Millerton. Train at left is going toward P&E Junction to Silvernails or Lead Mines. Lower left goes to Poughkeepsie or Dutchess Junction.** Collection of J. W. Swanberg.

show that the ND&C Railroad did indeed change to a ten cents per can rate to meet the competition.

Perhaps the ten cent rate was a bit too steep a cut for the PH&B Railroad (formerly the P&E Railroad). That same year they again declared bankruptcy and began operating under court supervision. Some of the assets were sold off to other lines. Their section of track from Boston Corners to State Line near Millerton was sold to the Hartford & Connecticut Western Railroad. That meant that they no longer had a direct connection into Connecticut. This was a blow to their business prospects.

Apparently, the year 1884 was not very good for railroads in Dutchess County. The ND&C Railroad reported a loss of two thousand dollars for the month of March 1884. The H&CW Railroad, which bought part of the PH&B assets, was losing money at a rate of five thousand dollars per month. The PH&B Railroad declared bankruptcy but managed to recover under a new name. By 1887, the name was New York & Massachusetts Railway (NY&M). In 1893, the name was changed again to P&E Railway. It began as the P&E Railroad and ended as the P&E Railway. After years of struggling, it was merged into the CNE Railway in 1907. By that date, the ND&C Railroad and the H&CW Railroad were already part of the CNE Railway. In 1927, the CNE Railway was absorbed into the New Haven Railroad system. Two companies owned the tracks in Dutchess County. The New York Central owned the Hudson and Harlem lines. All the rest belonged to the New Haven Railroad.

The question of price cutting came up again in 1897 when the P&E Railway cut prices for their milk shipments. ND&C management responded by saying that the price cuts were a violation of the trackage rights contract between Stissing and Pine Plains. Apparently, there was language in the lease agreement that prevented price cutting and business competition between the two railroads. The P&E Railway restored the higher rate for their milk shipments. Laws about price fixing were not as stringent as today. Pricing agreements between competing railroads were common. As long as all parties stuck to the agreement, they could charge as much as they wanted.

In railroading, even a milk run could have its dangers. When the ND&C Railroad milk train #55 pulled into Clove Branch Junction on 8 September 1887, Brakeman Frank Barton was missing from the milk car. The train was immediately reversed for a search back toward Arthursburgh.

Less than a mile back along the line, the crew found his body by the tracks in a cut. His body was badly bruised and his neck was broken. Nobody knew exactly what happened but the theory was that he tried to attract the attention of his sister who lived a short distance away from the tracks. Barton left a pregnant wife and a twenty-one month old child. The ND&C Railroad Company generously agreed to pay for his funeral.

It was not always the train crewmen who were involved in train accidents. In the village of Fishkill on 18 August 1890, a NY&NE Railroad train struck a milk wagon at a local crossing. Both the wagon driver and the horse were killed in that incident.

Weather often played a part in milk hauling. The winter following Barton's demise was an unusually cold and snowy season. On 19 December 1887, the milk train was three and one half hours late due to a snow storm, and that was only the beginning. It took forty men two days to clear the cuts so trains could reach Millerton. The line was blocked again on 27 January 1888. That time they used one hundred men and it still took two days to get a train to Millerton. On 13 February, there was a ten inch covering of snow. The biggest storm of all began on 12 March 1888, the infamous "Blizzard of '88." When the storm hit, there were three trains stranded along the ND&C line. It took more than two hundred men with shovels nine days to get a train through twenty foot deep drifts to Millerton. ND&C trains did not reach Millerton until 21 March, and they were still hauling away snowdrifts in gondolas as late as 29 March. A month later, in April 1888, an ND&C business report outlined the total cost of fighting the great blizzard of 88. The bottom line was a loss of $3771.45. One of the items listed was the loss of revenue from missing shipments for fourteen hundred cans of milk. One wonders wonder what the farmers did with all that milk?

Occasionally, it was traffic problems that delayed the milk. On 26 October 1890, ND&C train #55 was delayed an hour and twenty-six minutes by a NY&NE train blocking the main line east of Hopewell Junction. This caused the ND&C milk train to miss the connection with the NYC train at Dutchess Junction. The NY&NE Railroad had been granted permission to store trains on ND&C tracks east of Hopewell Junction provided they did not interfere with traffic. ND&C superintendent Charles Kimball wrote a strong letter to the NY&NE Railroad saying they could no longer use the ND&C for train storage.

A regular milk train run could also be handy for moving equipment. The ND&C borrowed a derrick from a railroad in New Jersey for a construction job in May 1891. When the derrick arrived at Dutchess Junction, it was coupled onto the milk train and hauled to the work site near Shekomeko.

Building a new creamery or milk processing plant was a sizable project in terms of money and effort. A good illustration is the construction of the milk bottling plant at LaGrange Station on the ND&C Railroad. On 10 December 1896, Mr. Charles E. Brownell, Esq. of LaGrange proposed building the plant. ND&C management responded by saying they would give rights to build on railroad land and would provide $250 as start up money. They would also hire a contractor, then accept payment in time notes for the rest from any "qualified firm." Apparently, it took time to find a qualified firm. The request for construction bids did not go out until almost four years later on 15 November 1900. The ND&C signed a contract with the proposed operator, the Beakes Dairy Company of New York City. A set of specifications was sent out to building contractors the following day. All was not well. On 24 November, the ND&C sent a letter to the Beakes Dairy Company to inform them that the bids were coming back at about double the estimated cost, and one contractor refused to bid on the job. Then a second set of bid requests went out to a different group of contractors.

A few days later, on 30 November 1900, ND&C management sent another letter to Beakes Dairy Company suggesting that they change their specifications to reduce the cost of the LaGrange creamery and meet with the ND&C people to discuss the situation. If Beakes decided to back out, then the ND&C wanted to be paid for work already done on the building foundation and track work for a siding. More than a month later, on 2 January 1901, a letter went out to Beakes Dairy asking what their intentions were for the LaGrange creamery.

Other people in LaGrange were becoming concerned about the slow pace of the creamery project. On 10 January 1901, ND&C general freight agent William Underhill responded to a letter from Charles Burbank of LaGrangeville. He explained that the ND&C was not the hold up in building the creamery. The ND&C Railroad had begun construction of the building and stood ready to complete the project. The problem was that George E. Beakes had been ill and confined to his home for the previous six weeks. Underhill had written to the Beakes company urging them not to abandon the project.

The following day, 11 January, Underhill again wrote to the Beakes company urging them to complete the contract for operation of the creamery. There were prospects for 100 to 150 cans of milk per day, which would be a profitable quantity. Local farmers had increased the number of cows to supply the milk. Eleven days later, on 22 January, Underhill wrote a letter confirming a telephone call from Beakes earlier that day. On that day, the ND&C Railroad signed a contract with Frank T. Hall of Verbank for construction of the creamery building for $3,550. Part of the iron work was to be done at the ND&C Railroad shops at Dutchess Junction. There had been a few minor changes in the specifications. The foreman's room upstairs would not be finished and the ice house walls would be insulated with an air space but not filled with sawdust. The contractor had promised to have the ice house ready for deliveries in about ten days. The first car of material delivered to the LaGrange siding derailed because the curve was too sharp. Negotiations were under way to get ice from a pond in Billings.

The ice was to be purchased for six cents per ton from E. Wright Vail who owned part of the pond. However, to get the ice out, it had to be moved across part of the pond and property that Mr. Ferris owned. Mr. Ferris was to be paid two cents per ton to allow passage over his part of the pond and across his land to the railroad tracks. Since the LaGrange ice house under construction was designed to hold up to one thousand tons of ice, that meant sixty dollars for Mr. Vail and twenty dollars for Mr. Ferris. Ice on the pond was fourteen inches thick, but it was already late in the winter season and the concern was how to get the required one thousand tons of ice before the weather warmed up.

Local farmers were willing to help move the ice as long as it did not interfere with their normal spring farming activities. If a wooden chute was built from the pond to the tracks, the ice could be moved as fast as two hundred tons per day, which would require a special train. At the ice house, a crew of six to ten men plus horses would be needed to move and stack the ice since the ice house was fifty feet from the tracks. The Beakes company decided on a lower cost but slower method. They would haul the ice to the ND&C station siding at Billings. The facilities at Billings station could handle only three cars per day. Instead of a special train, scheduled ND&C trains would move the ice to LaGrange.

ND&C vice president and general manager G. Hunter Brown sent instructions to Conductor Crawford on train 51.

### Volume 66, Page 41, 11 February 1901

We will commence the movement of ice from the Billings pond to the Lagrange creamery almost any day. You must be prepared under the orders of our car accountant to move this ice from Billings to Lagrange in your train and put in place of the loaded cars sufficient number of empties as per his directions.

In early March 1901, there is a notation that the LaGrange ice house contained 821 and three-fifths tons of ice. This was not quite the one thousand tons originally planned, but it was apparently enough for the Beakes company to begin operations. During this same period of time, the new Borden's creamery in Hopewell Junction was also being filled with ice from the pond in Billings. The Borden's plant took nine hundred tons. In the late winter of 1901, Mr. Vail had more than $125 extra money, and Mr. Ferris had over $30 for watching the ice move across his land.

In May 1901, Frank T. Hall, the building contractor, informed the ND&C Railroad that he had completed the construction of the LaGrange creamery and payment was due. By 20 May, the Beakes company had inspected and accepted the new building and begun operation. But all was not well. The Beakes creamery at LaGrange was shipping only fifty-five cans per day and three-quarters of them were not even bottled because the boiler had not arrived yet. They could not wash bottles fast enough. The ND&C was not getting enough revenue from the operation. If all the milk was bottled, the ND&C would make $5.50 per day. Since part of the milk was still in cans, the ND&C got only $3.50 per day. The boiler finally arrived on 18 June 1901, and production settled down, but they still had problems bottling enough cases of milk to fill the New York orders.

In February 1901, while the ND&C Railroad was busy getting the LaGrange creamery operational, the Borden's Condensed Milk Company decided to locate an even larger plant in Hopewell Junction. It was to be located on ND&C Railroad land next to the depot and leased for ninety-nine years. This plant was planned to handle three hundred or more cans of milk per day. This quantity of milk would be about one thousand cases of bottled milk per day shipped from Hopewell Junction to Dutchess Junction, and then to New York City on the NYC Railroad.

When word about the new Borden's operation got around, the ND&C Railroad was "besieged with inquiries from farmers located at

*The Milk Business*

**Above:** Postcard view of Hopewell Junction, about 1905. Large white building at right is the Borden's creamery. White building at left is the Hopewell Inn, still in operation in 2002. The ND&C RR depot is at the right in its original location. Collection of the author.

**Below: Borden's Creamery, Hopewell Junction, c. 1910.** Collection of the Hudson Northern Model RR Club.

**ND&C RR milk train at the Bordens plant in Hopewell Junction, NY.**
Postcard from the Alice Bryden collection. Collection of Heyward Cohen.

Brinckerhoff and Johnsville." William Underhill wrote a letter to Isaac Milbank, vice president of Borden's Condensed Milk Company in New York asking exactly when the new plant would be ready to accept milk from the farmers. Other milk processing plants in the area would try to get the farmers to commit milk shipments for six months or more. A firm opening date before 1 April would assure a supply of milk over the summer months.

It was getting late in the winter season, so Borden's elected to use a special ND&C train dedicated to hauling ice before the weather changed. ND&C conductor J. A. Frost was assigned to get the job done with box cars and drop side gondolas from LaGrange and Hopewell Junction. The ice house at LaGrange was already full, so the equipment was free to use on the Borden's job. The "ice train" returned to Dutchess Junction for minor servicing each night. By 20 March 1901, the Borden's plant in Hopewell Junction had nine hundred tons of Billings Pond ice in insulated storage. In addition to $67.50 for the ice, the ND&C Railroad billed Borden's $160.61 for the special shipping.

To handle the bottled milk from the Borden's plant, the ND&C wanted to build a siding next to the building. This presented a small problem. The CNE Railway controlled the signal tower for the crossing at Hopewell Junction. Wiring for the western semaphore was buried under where the siding should be. Two weeks later, there was a letter to Judge Samuel Phillips inquiring about the legal responsibility for the buried wiring. There is no record of how it was resolved, but the siding was built and served Borden's milk for many years.

About a year and a half later, in October 1902, the Borden's milk output consigned to 33rd Street in New York City had increased to the maximum capacity of the forty thousand pound NYC train cars assigned to the run. G. Hunter Brown wrote to D. B. McCoy superintendent of the NYC Hudson Division, requesting that sixty thousand pound cars be assigned because the shipments were going to be even higher in the future. At times, the milk cars were loaded with six hundred cases when the maximum was supposed to be five hundred. Three cars a day left from Hopewell Junction, and occasionally the overflow had to be loaded into the car from Millbrook. There were actually six insulated cars in rotation to serve just the Borden's plant at Hopewell Junction. Total milk shipments on the ND&C were running as high as eight hundred cans (eight thousand gallons) per day which would translate into about two thousand, four hundred cases of bottled milk every day.

ND&C Railroad record books have letters concerning meetings that the milk-shipping railroads held. These meetings were really price setting sessions. Representatives from railroads around New York State would meet in New York City to decide how much they were going to charge. As long as all the parties charged the agreed amounts, they could set their own rates because the milk producers had no reasonable alternatives for getting milk to market. Along with hauling the milk, railroads also carried the supply of empty bottles and coal for fuel.

The railroad grip on the milk shipping business lasted for many years until the advent of highways and trucks. By the 1920s, trucks were hauling milk point to point without a heavy investment in tracks and locomotives. Highways were built with taxpayers money. Milk producers did not have to build platforms along the tracks and wait for a scheduled train. A dairy farmer with a Ford Model T truck could haul his milk to the processing plant or a collection point. Tanker trucks meant that the processing plants did not have to be located near a railroad line. Trucks cut the travel time of bottled milk shipments significantly. Within a few more years, the trucks had mechanical refrigeration units to keep the milk cold.

Then it was the railroads who were out in the cold.

# The Coal Business

ONE of the main incentives for building an east-west railroad across Dutchess County was to haul coal. Coal from the mines in Pennsylvania was used to power much of the industry in New England. Of course, the finished products could then be hauled back to Pennsylvania and the western states. Coal also heated many of the homes and businesses in the northeast. Another big customer was the railroads themselves. Most of their engines burned coal, and coal heated their stations. The Erie Railroad at Newburgh and the Delaware & Hudson Canal at Rondout near Kingston both brought large quantities of coal to the Hudson River. Situated between the Hudson River and the Connecticut state line, Dutchess County was in an ideal position to take advantage of the coal hauling business.

At that time, there was no bridge across the river. To take advantage of this coal traffic, the D&C railroad had built ferry dock facilities at Dutchess Junction, which was directly across the river from the Erie Railroad docks in Newburgh. By the time the ND&C Railroad was formed out of the bankrupt D&C Railroad in 1877, the coal was already flowing across the river. Coal barges came down the river from Rondout and train cars carried on barges, called car floats, came across the river from Newburgh. Railroad tracks on the dock bridge connected directly with tracks on the barge deck so that train cars could be rolled on and off. The Pennsylvania Coal Company actually owned the car floats that the ND&C used. The car floats were a bit slow and there was also the problem of the river freezing over in the winter, just when coal was needed the most. The ferry was not exactly ideal, but it was the best available at the time.

As early as 1872, the D&C Railroad dock at Dutchess Junction ran more than seven hundred feet along the Hudson River east bank. Part of the dock had railroad tracks and a ferry bridge to handle train cars on car floats. This section could move as much as four hundred tons of coal per day. Another part of the dock was equipped with two steam-driven hoists to move coal and other heavy freight from river barges. The dock hoists could move about three hundred tons of coal per day from river barges to train cars. The dock also handled up to one hundred tons of merchandise freight plus passengers that the steamboat *Fanny Garner* and other river boats carried. As much as three hundred tons of freight was handled per day on the north end of the dock, which had a three hundred-foot-long piling trestle extension with train tracks. Two of the ND&C's smaller steam locomotives were assigned to switching duties in the dock and yard areas. On a good day, the Dutchess dock facilities could move one thousand tons of coal and freight plus passengers. Dutchess Junction dock was a busy place.

Trainloads of coal would leave Dutchess Junction and then struggle up the hill and across the Tioronda Bridge high over Fishkill Creek. Beyond Wicopee and Matteawan they would pass through Glenham and Fishkill on the trip eastward. Near Millerton in the northeast corner of Dutchess County the coal trains could make connections with railroads in Connecticut. Of course some of the coal was delivered to retail dealers and industries in towns

**Coal storage facilities still standing in Beacon.**
Photo by author, March 2002.

along the line in Dutchess County. Just about every town had at least one retail dealer who, in turn, sold coal to local customers. A listing of coal dealers and industries in 1892 contained more than thirty-five locations scattered along fifty-eight miles of track.

The ND&C Railroad enjoyed the benefits of this arrangement for the first few years of operation. The picture changed when the NY&NE Railroad built competing ferry facilities at Fishkill Landing in 1881 and contracted for trackage rights on eleven miles of ND&C rails. Fishkill Landing was only about two miles north of Dutchess Junction, and the NY&NE rails joined the ND&C at Wicopee Junction near Matteawan. NY&NE trains were then hauling loads of coal on ND&C tracks through Glenham and Fishkill and on through Hopewell Junction, where the NY&NE branched off eastward to reach Connecticut.

The NY&NE ferry operation at Fishkill Landing had advantages over the ND&C ferry service. Being much newer, the NY&NE ferry had a bigger, more efficient steamboat called the *William T. Hart*, which could move train cars across the river at a much faster rate than the ND&C car floats.

At Fishkill Landing, the trains crossed over the NYC Railroad Hudson line on an overpass, so there was no traffic conflict. At Dutchess Junction, ND&C trains had to cross the double track Hudson main line at grade which required careful timing and backup moves. ND&C Railroad management understood the situation and soon contracted with the NY&NE to carry train cars and freight across the river. Beginning on 11 January 1883, the NY&NE ferry service at Fishkill Landing handled all ND&C carload freight. Cars were transferred to and from the ND&C Railroad at Wicopee Junction. The pace of ND&C Railroad operations at Dutchess Junction dock slowed considerably without the car floats, but barge, freight, and passenger operations continued. On ND&C Railroad timetables, Newburgh was treated as the last stop even though it required a ferry ride to get there from Dutchess Junction.

With both railroads running on one set of tracks between Wicopee Junction and Hopewell Junction, the friction and competition grew. The NY&NE needed ND&C rails for access to the Fishkill Landing ferry and the ND&C needed the monthly check for the trackage rights. They had to live together, but it was an uneasy relationship. In addition to taking part of the Connecticut coal business, the NY&NE also began encroaching on local ND&C business. In December 1882, the NY&NE announced plans to build a coal yard at Wicopee Junction and charge thirty cents per ton for hauling coal across the river. This was not good news for the ND&C. Their rate for the same service was seventy cents per ton.

Of course, not all the coal was of highest quality. A letter in April 1884 outlines the results of testing Towanda coal as locomotive fuel. An ND&C locomotive used seventy pounds of coal per mile on Towanda coal. This compared with forty-eight and a half pounds per mile for the "regular fuel." ND&C Railroad superintendent Charles Kimball wrote to the coal company saying that their price of three dollars per ton for the Towanda coal was too high, and the ND&C would "continue with the present supplier."

As with most other railroad activities, there were potential dangers in hauling coal. Something as simple as the grade on a customer's siding could be a problem.

**Volume 34, Page 51, 11 July 1892**

Notice to all engineers;
Do not under any circumstances enter the Howard Haight and Co. coal track at Millbrook except with the engine headed east.
The grade of this track is equal to 4 inch rise in 11 feet of track, and should you back your engine onto this siding you would bare the crown sheet and damage it.

The notice did not have to mention the explosive possibilities of a damaged crown sheet in a locomotive boiler.

In the fall of 1887, there was a major bottleneck in the flow of coal across the river. The NY&NE ferry slip in the Erie Railroad yard in Newburgh had to be rebuilt. On the east side of the river, coal was in short supply with winter weather coming. Dock facilities at Dutchess Junction were straining to hoist as much coal as possible out of barges into train cars while crews of men with shovels were recruited to assist in moving the coal. The ND&C Railroad had a total of 225 coal cars and 103 of them were trapped on the west side of the river. Some of them were empties on the way to the coal mines, and twenty-three cars were loaded with iron ore consigned to Glendon, Pennsylvania. On the east side of the river, coal supplies were getting low, and twenty cars were assigned to haul coal from the Pennsylvania Coal Company and D&H coal barges docking at Dutchess Junction. Only about one hundred tons per day were available from the dock and it was being rationed out to the retail dealers and industries. The remainder of the ND&C cars were being unloaded on other railroads in New England.

The Newburgh ferry slip was repaired and train cars once again began moving across the river on the steamship *William T. Hart*. Coal supplies were still low on the east side of the river. In November, the ND&C Railroad management discovered that the NY&NE were unloading some of the carloads of coal consigned to the ND&C at Fishkill Landing instead of transferring it at Wicopee Junction. This amounted to hijacking, and the ND&C lodged a protest. Over the winter, coal supplies were replenished until 15 February 1888. That was when the steamship *William T. Hart* broke down, and train cars once again began to clog the Erie yard in Newburgh. None of the people involved could know at that point, but the coal supply was still low three weeks later when the infamous blizzard of 1888 buried the Hudson Valley in several feet of snow.

An ND&C Railroad report in May 1889 stated the amount of coal delivered in Dutchess County for the year 1888 broken down by locations. This did not include coal that was routed through the ND&C to other railroads. In addition to local dealer sales, stations along the line used coal for heat and also locomotive fuel. Coal burning stoves heated passenger cars. Water towers had to be kept from freezing in the winter. By far the largest amount was for Matteawan, which used 10,915 tons. The hoist engines on Dutchess dock used 444 tons. Hopewell Junction, for example, used 344 tons while Millbrook used 2,456 tons. The smallest usage was for the Shunpike station at 32 tons. The ND&C Railroad delivered a total of 25,231 tons for the year 1888. That amounts to about 435 tons of coal delivered per mile of track.

The pattern of coal shipments across the Hudson River changed again when the Poughkeepsie Railroad Bridge opened in December 1888. Trains using the bridge route could cross the river in a matter of minutes without resorting to labor intensive steamboats or car floats. And the bridge crossed high over the winter ice, so it could be used all year round. This was stiff competition for the barge and ferry services.

Just as they had done in the milk business and other ventures, the ferry service railroads fought back with the "gentlemen's agreement" on hauling rates. A letter to the general freight agent of the Central New England & Western Railroad, who owned the bridge, illustrates that point.

**Volume 30, Page 30, 12 July 1890**
*Letter to N. R. Turner, Esq.*
*CNE&W. Railroad, Poughkeepsie:*

I understand that you are offering to carry coal from Highland via the bridge route or from Rhinebeck to Pine Plains at $1.40 per ton. This does not agree with our conversation held on the 18th of June at which time you agreed to maintain and adhere to the $1.50 rate to that point. Please explain.

Yours Truly   C. L. Kimball

Another letter two years later, in 1892, complained about the same situation. In July 1896, a competitor was selling coal at Millerton for a lower price than the ND&C agent could because his coal came via the bridge route. This was in violation of their previous agreement about maintaining rates. Other lines were not following the price fixing rules.

Coal hauling competition became even more intense when the Dutchess County Railroad opened a line in 1892 from the Poughkeepsie Bridge directly to Hopewell Junction to connect with the NY&NE Railroad. Trains crossing the bridge could then more easily handle coal and other freight for the southern part of Connecticut via the NY&NE Railroad line to Danbury. This also meant that coal crossing the bridge could be easily hauled to Hopewell Junction in competition with the ND&C, which hauled coal via the Fishkill Landing ferry. Occasionally, the winter temperature would drop to ten or twenty degrees below zero and the ice blocked ferry traffic just when coal was needed. Meanwhile DC Railroad coal trains rolled across the Poughkeepsie Bridge. The Dutchess County Railroad line from the Poughkeepsie Bridge to Hopewell Junction later became one section of the New Haven Railroad Maybrook line, which carried coal to New England until the Poughkeepsie Bridge burned in 1974.

Coal hauled across the Poughkeepsie Bridge could be delivered faster, more reliably, and at a lower cost than coal moved by ferry. The competition began to show in the ND&C tonnage reports. A report dated July 1896 used Hopewell Junction as an example. In the year 1891, there were 611 tons of coal delivered to Hopewell Junction. By 1895, the number had dropped to 267 tons. In the first six months of 1896, there were only two carloads of coal totaling thirty-nine tons delivered to Hopewell Junction. The ND&C was almost out of the local coal hauling business in Hopewell.

In an effort to compete with the coal traffic

over the Poughkeepsie Bridge, in 1898, the ND&C worked out an agreement with the P&E for a new coal yard in Poughkeepsie. The arrangement was that the ND&C would haul coal northeast from the Dutchess Junction dock to connect with the P&E at Stissing. The P&E would then haul the coal southwest through Pleasant Valley to Poughkeepsie. This route was many miles longer than the bridge route, which ran directly into Poughkeepsie off the bridge. It was longer, more expensive, and involved a transfer at Stissing. This route also had the problem of winter ice at the Dutchess Junction dock, but ND&C coal could be delivered to Poughkeepsie. Major customers would be the State Hospital and Vassar College. Of course, this route would be viable only if the bridge road honored the "gentlemen's agreement" to maintain rates at a higher level.

In December 1898, trains began hauling coal via Dutchess Junction, Stissing, and Pleasant Valley to Poughkeepsie. The D&H Canal Company sent barges down the river from Rondout to Dutchess Junction dock. Meanwhile, the ND&C was looking for more customers such as the Poughkeepsie Electric Railway. All did not go as smoothly as planned. In April 1899, the Hudson River State Hospital refused the only railroad bid for coal delivery. They wanted to get coal by boats and teams of horses and wagons at the Poughkeepsie waterfront. After all, the D&H coal barges passed within sight of the State Hospital on the way down the river to Dutchess Junction. William Underhill, who was the ND&C Railroad general freight agent, went to Poughkeepsie to meet with the State Hospital managers. He came back with a signed contract to haul the coal by rail all the way from Dutchess Junction to Stissing and back to Poughkeepsie. I would certainly be interested in knowing how he convinced them.

Coal was being delivered via Stissing and Pleasant Valley, but it was only a matter of time before the arrangement began to unravel. In early 1901, there were letters of complaint stating that the "Bridge Road" was not respecting the agreements to maintain rates on coal shipments. Despite the competition, the ND&C obtained fifteen used flat bottom 7,000 series metal coal cars that the New Haven Railroad delivered in April 1901 via the B&O Railroad from the Monongahela River Railroad. ND&C coal deliveries to other locations continued. In May 1901, the ND&C signed a contract to deliver several thousand tons of bituminous coal to Millerton. Coal shipments were halted for a time in 1902 due to a strike at the mines.

Even as late as 1904, just before the end of the ND&C Railroad, they were still talking about pricing agreements. The descriptive language in a 1904 letter sounds more like a formal contract. The ND&C had entered into an agreement with the CNE Railway to maintain "reasonable and standard" rates on shipping anthracite coal to points "common and competitive and thus removing the vicious competition through cutting of rates."

Basically, the railroads agreed not to compete with rate cuts and the customers had no real alternative for obtaining coal. Surely, the railroads kept their profits high with these agreements, but it was certainly not very good for the customers. It would not be very many years in their future when trucks would change the picture.

In the summer of 1904, the New Haven Railroad abandoned the Fishkill Landing ferry service. The Poughkeepsie Bridge had won the competitive battle. This meant that the ND&C no longer had any way to transfer train cars across the river. At the other end of the line, the CNE Railway had further isolated the ND&C by cutting train service from Millerton into

**Postcard view of ND&C RR second #8 built by Baldwin Locomotive Works, 1895.**
Collection of J. W. Swanberg.

Connecticut. All the New Haven really wanted was the bridge route, which became the Maybrook line. With the loss of east-west freight traffic and revenue, the ND&C was in serious trouble. The Dutchess Junction dock was still in operation for dwindling barge traffic. The ND&C still had connections with the NYC Hudson line at Dutchess Junction and the NYC Harlem line at Millerton. There was also the line from Poughkeepsie to Hopewell Junction and Danbury, which was the New Haven Railroad Maybrook line. All of this was still not enough to keep the ND&C Railroad alive. In 1905, the CNE Railway, backed by the New Haven Railroad, took over the assets of the ND&C. Then all the east west lines across Dutchess County belonged to the CNE Railway/New Haven Railroad organization. There was no longer any need for a "gentleman's agreement" on rates. The New Haven and CNE could set their own rates without any competition—that is, until trucks came along.

# Coping with Weather

FROM THE VERY BEGINNING, one of mankind's major concerns has been coping with weather extremes. This was just as true of the early railroads as it is today. Nature can conjure up challenges seemingly at a moment's notice. A summer storm can wash away a bridge or winter snow can block tracks. Keeping a steam engine running when the temperature is below zero can be tricky. Railroaders had to learn to deal with every situation to keep the trains rolling.

Winter cold, snow, and ice were probably the biggest challenges facing the railroads. Steam engines depended on a lot of water, which tended to freeze in the winter unless the tanks and pumps were kept warm. If a pump house fire went out during the winter, the steam driven pumps and pipes would soon freeze solid, and most likely they would be ruined. On 15 January 1881, there was an entry in the ND&C letterbooks with detailed instructions on draining all the water out of the Fishkill water pump engine to prevent damage. Keeping watch over the tank house fires was a vital part of winter railroading.

**Volume 16, Page 136, 23 March 1883**
*Instructions to local agents to discontinue the fires in the tank houses:*

In case the weather turns cold so as to endanger freezing again, you can start a fire but at present there is no need of it and probably will not be.

Thick ice on the Hudson River also posed problems for the ferry operations. When ice clogged the river, no steamboats could operate. During icy winters, the car floats could not transfer freight cars across the river to or from Newburgh. Boat passenger and local freight service also stopped. Before the Poughkeepsie railroad bridge was built, traffic across the river came to a halt until the river thawed enough for boats to move. Winter weather could be tough for railroaders. The physical work increased and the revenue decreased. Fog could also be a problem.

**Volume 34, Page 640, 9 December 1892**

In a heavy fog yesterday at about 4:30 near Tioronda trestle engine #7 struck our hand car which two section men were trying to get off the track. Both men were injured and the hand car is a wreck.

**Station Agent G. S. Wells at Moores Mills coping with the snow. Note the white shirt, tie, bowler hat, and snowshoes.** Collection of Heyward Cohen.

Even the wind can be a problem. On Christmas Eve, 24 December 1881, there was an empty box car parked on a siding by the Hopewell Junction water tank. A strong wind moved the car through a switch and onto the main line. A Grant engine on train #8 hit it head on. Damage to the engine required ordering new parts from Grant Locomotive Works.

Trying to keep the tracks clear in winter snow was a big problem. It often resulted in exhausted crews and broken equipment. In early February 1881, crews were trying to free up stuck trains and open the line. About a mile north of Moores Mill, engine #1 broke a parallel rod, which then whipped around and destroyed the running board on that side. It also bent the rod on the other side and bent the crank pin. A bolt pulled out of the boiler and let out all the steam. In addition to snow drifts, the crew now had a dead, mangled engine blocking the line. One can imagine the blue language on that occasion.

The winter of 1887-88 turned out to have some of the worst weather on record. The first mention of weather problems came on 19 December 1887 with a note that the milk train was three and a half hours late due to the snow storm. On the following day, 20 December, a note stated that trains could not get through to Millbrook. An engineer and forty men were clearing snow from the cuts. That was only the beginning.

### Volume 25, Page 270, 27 January 1888

Line is blocked with snow east of Shekomeko. Cannot get to Millerton.

### Volume 25, Page 278, 28 January 1888

Train leaving at 6:00 AM with all available men to clear the snow.

### Volume 25, Page 279, 30 January 1888

Finally got a train to Millerton at 4:22 on Jan 29. Worked 100 men and paid $2.00 a day. Cuts on the mountain were all full, hard packed and the cold intense.

### Volume 25, Page 284, 30 January 1888

Six broken rails since last Thursday.

Cold winters caused more rail breakage. Early rails were made of iron, which tended to break more easily in colder weather. For example, the Clove Branch had eight miles of track and experienced eight broken rails during the winter of 1883-84. This was considered to be a great improvement over the previous season. The Clove Branch had a particularly high rate of iron rail breakage, mainly because of heavy ore cars coming out of the mine at Sylvan Lake. On 27 February 1888, the letterbooks have a cost estimate for replacing twenty-five miles of iron rails with new steel rails. Eventually, over a period of several years, the iron rails were replaced by more durable steel rails. By the fall of 1889, the ND&C Railroad had almost forty-four miles of steel rails with thirteen miles of iron rail remaining.

Now, back to the winter of 1887-88.

### Volume 25, Page 328, 13 February 1888

We had 10 inches of snow on Saturday.

Perhaps the best known weather battle was the great blizzard of March 1888. Volume 25 of the ND&C letterbooks contains the saga of dealing with the infamous Blizzard of '88. On 10 March 1888 the conditions were so dry that sparks from the stack of NY&NE engine #98 set a half dozen grass fires that threatened the Van Wyck buildings in Fishkill Village. Two days later the snow reports began coming in.

### Volume 25, Page 440, 12 March 1888

Worst storm we ever had and growing

worse. Road completely blocked. Cannot move a train. Have got to wait until storm abates.

### Volume 25, Page 440, 12 March 1888

Road completely buried. Heavy drifts all the way. Weather cold and blowing. Have three engines out but all alive. Am trying to open road to Hopewell today. Kisselbrack at Millbrook, Hemingway at Moores, Stowell stuck in a drift at Verbank.

Three trains with crews and passengers were stuck.

### Volume 25, Page 441, 13 March 1888

We are blocked with snow. Please discontinue sale of tickets to points on ND&C RR until further notice.

### Volume 25, Page 441, 14 March 1888

Storm has apparently stopped. Have got road open to Brinkerhoff. Stowell is also working between Moores and Millbrook. Will take several days to open the road I fear.

### Volume 25, Page 444, 16 March 1888

Snow is much heavier than I supposed it was. We may get to Pine Plains tomorrow night. We hope to have 150 men today. We shall open to Hopewell by noon today.

To this point it had taken four days to get from Beacon to Hopewell Junction, a distance of eleven miles.

### Volume 25, Page 446, 17 March 1888

We expect to get road open as far as Pine Plains tonight. But shall not reach Millerton before Tuesday.

### Volume 25, Page 447, 17 March 1888

Work train to leave Dutchess Junction before 6:30 AM tomorrow to the snow drift beyond Millbrook.

### Volume 25, Page 455, 19 March 1888

All mail from Millerton for our line up to noon today has been sent around by Boston Corners. Am working all the men I can hire to open the road through Millerton and hope to tonight or tomorrow. The drifts have been enormous the whole length of road.

### Volume 25, Page 459, 21 March 1888

20 ft. snow in Husted cut which is partly cleared.

Nine days after the storm started there, was still twenty feet of snow in the cuts.

### Volume 25, Page 460, 21 March 1888

I hoped to get through to Millerton today as we now have but those 20 ft. cuts to dig out but the rain prevents work. We have worked all the men we could get, some 200, ever since the blizzard let up but our road seemed to catch it even worse than our neighbors.

### Volume 25, Page 479, 29 March 1888

We must take an engine and some gondolas and take out some of the worst banks of snow from the worst cuts east of Husteds.

More than two weeks after the storm and with two hundred men working, they were still moving snowdrifts. A month later, on 25 April, Superintendent Charles Kimball wrote a summary letter to President John Schultze describing the battle. He included a statement of expenses and business losses due to the storm. Here are his words:

> This is the first time that we have been prevented from getting a train through the entire length of the road some time in the course of 24 hours since I took charge of the road, Nov. 1st 1871.
>
> The storm or blizzard of March 12th 1888 blocked our road so that we did not get it

**Main Street Matteawan in the blizzard of March 1888. Building with the tower at left was a hat factory. Note the horse drawn car behind the snow bank.**
Collection of the Beacon Historical Society.

open through to Millerton until Sunday March 25th. We opened the road from Dutchess Junction to Millbrook so as to run regular trains west of the latter point commencing March 17th, and the following day we opened the road to Shekomeko so that all regular trains were run west of that point commencing March 19th.

Sunday the 18th, we ran the milk train from Pine Plains.

We were a whole week clearing the road east of Shekomeko where we found the cuts nearly all full of heavy snow, some of which we had to remove by cars, a very slow process, and much of it was handled six times in casting it out of the cuts.

The road was cleared however without damage to property or injury to person which might have resulted if we had adopted the course of neighboring roads. The storm of March 12th continued until the morning of the 14th, and was the most severe snow and wind storm that the oldest inhabitant ever experienced in this or any other section of this country.

The wind during this time blew at the rate of 60 to 80 miles per hour, as reported by the signal stations through this section of the country. It is estimated that three to four feet of snow fell during the storm which was driven into solid banks wherever it found a place to lodge.  Yours Truly  C. L. Kimball

The major portion of Kimball's expense listing was for hiring and feeding the extra men fighting the snow. Typical wages for shoveling snow was one dollar per day. Shovels and snow goggles were included on the expense list, as well as expenses for the acting mail clerk to reroute delayed mail.

Business losses included $100 lost revenue from passenger service and $125 revenue lost from mail service. The largest business loss was $140 for 1,400 cans of milk at ten cents each. It seems that a lot of milk went to waste during the storm. The bottom line showed a total loss of $3,771.45 from the great blizzard of 1888. This was a substantial sum of money in the economy of that time.

One would imagine that both management and workers were glad to see spring that year, but spring weather brought its own problems. Cold winter weather would freeze the ground solid under the roadbed to a depth of several feet. When weather warmed up in the spring, the thaw was not always even. Expansion and contraction of the frozen earth shifted the tracks. Engineers reported frost heaves in the track so bad that the tender frame would jump up and catch on the foot board of the engine and slip off again. One can imagine fast stepping fireman trying to keep the fire hot on that run.

In the fall of 1889, the ND&C Railroad installed Baker heaters in their passenger coaches. The following winter, there was a letter to the Baker Heater Company saying that the weather had not been cold enough to really test the car heaters but they seemed to work.

**Snow problems on Winchell Mountain, 1916. Note the derailed cars and a crane in the rear.**
Collection of J. W. Swanberg.

### Volume 29, Page 173, 4 February 1890

The waste pipe is defective. It will freeze up when the mercury stands at 20 degrees above. We have had great trouble with your fittings. Nearly all the joints proved to be leaky after a week or so in service.

It was not long before the coach heaters were put to the test. Winter temperatures on the ND&C Railroad could reach twenty degrees below zero. On more than one occasion milk shipments to New York City arrived frozen solid.

### Volume 29, Page 281, 6 March 1890

A fearful snow and wind storm set in about 1:00 o'clock this AM which comes from the N. E. and is still raging with unabated force. The thermometer at 6:00 AM stood at 10 degrees above 0. About five inches of snow have fallen but it is drifted and is still drifting.

Even when there was little snow, ice would build up on the rocky sides of the narrow cuts. On 9 February 1899, a note stated that the ice build up in Oak Summit cut had grown to the point where it scraped the sides of the coaches and damaged the battens. That same month there was more snow.

### Volume 55, Page 397, 15 February 1899

Our Hopewell division was opened for all traffic by noon on Feb. 14th, balance of road opened today as far east as Shekomeko. Three engines & plow working west from Millerton; have only made 3 miles since Monday. We will resume all train service tomorrow except through train from Millerton. Expect to clear road by Thursday night. We were ready to handle New Haven business before it could be delivered to us. Worst storm since the blizzard.

An occasional rain and wind storm could knock down the telegraph lines or the telephone lines. Storms sometimes would wash out a bridge or flood a section of track. Hot weather in the summer posed an additional set of problems. If the weather was dry, there could be grass fires along the line from the engine smokestack sparks. Sparks from the stacks were the reason that most of the stations along the lines had slate roofs.

Hot weather also threatened to spoil any perishable freight. This was particularly true of milk shipments to New York City. Before mechanical refrigeration, the best way to keep milk cool in the summer was with ice in insulated cars. The ice was harvested from ponds in the winter and stored in large, well insulated buildings. The ND&C Railroad owned several ice storage buildings. Milk processing plants along the line usually had their own ice house. The Borden's plant in Hopewell Junction had an ice storage area that held over nine hundred tons of ice, which they purchased from the ND&C Railroad. The railroad contracted with local pond owners and hauled the ice to each using plant. In this industry, the cold winter weather helped to cool milk in the summer. All you had to do was figure out a way to save the ice with good insulation.

With the widespread use of the telegraph, railroads took the lead in opening communications in rural areas. In addition to telegraph messages, the ND&C Railroad had been providing standard time signals from the Cambridge Massachusetts Observatory starting in November 1885. By November 1898, all the stations of the ND&C were posting daily weather reports from the US Weather Bureau at Cornell University in Ithaca, New York. I wonder if those reports were any more or less accurate than today's television forecasts?

# The Lighter Side of Railroading

AS WITH ANY OCCUPATION, there were events in railroading life that can only be classified as "the lighter side of life." At the time, many of these events were serious and even traumatic for the participants, but when viewed from a safe distance, they tickled a good sense of humor. For example:

**Volume 29, Pages 516 and 518, 10 May 1890**

Vulgar and offensive writing on the walls of the Millbrook water closet.

It seems that times have not changed all that much since 1890. Another good example is the problem with straw hats, which were popular in the "Gay Nineties."

**Volume 30, Page 25, 10 July 1890**
*Letter to C. N. Chevalier, superintendent, NY&NE Railroad, Fishkill on Hudson:*

Enclosed please find copy of a letter from Wm. Carroll of Mattewan, NY & hat manufacturer, who complains of the damage done to straw hats and stock by sparks and coals from your engines and especially engine 40. Will you please give the matter your attention and have the matter remedied as soon as possible.

*Yours Truly   C. L. Kimball*

A flaming straw hat could be a great laugh for everybody except the wearer. A potentially more dangerous situation was uncovered in 1881. The Shenandoah Mining Company was shipping consignments of dynamite in plain wooden boxes marked *merchandise*. On one occasion, Superintendent Charles Kimball chewed out a conductor for his placement of a shipment of wool. The wool was shipped in an open gondola just behind the engine. I wonder what color the wool was when it arrived and how many burn holes there were from smokestack sparks?

Charles Kimball, who signed the above straw hat letter, was a veteran railroader. Over a period of forty years or more he had been employed by several railroads and had worked his way up from track laborer to superintendent. Because of this background, he often was directly involved in the daily work along the line. He knew every job as well or better than the men who were doing the work. Here is an example:

**Volume 31, Page 317, 28 March 1891**
*Kimball wrote to Robert. G. Weeks, New York, complaining about poor quality wooden maul handles:*

I commenced as a track laborer in 1852 and have been connected with track building and in charge of track ever since, as foreman, roadmaster, contractor and superintendent. During this period of almost 40 years I have handled, used, bought and inspected a good many maul handles and I ought to be a tolerable judge of such goods.

I wonder if any of today's "superintendents" are that concerned with the quality control of track crew maul handles? Speaking of quality control, a batch of tickets was sent back to be reprinted because a station name was spelled wrong. Tickets for Shunpike were printed as Stunpike.

In a business as spread out as railroading, it

**ND&C RR employee's trip pass.**
Author's collection.

is difficult to keep an eye on just what employees are doing at any point in time. To add to the problem, some of the people hired as laborers are not always of the highest educational level or moral standing. In one case, a farmer complained that train crews were stopping and stealing apples from his orchard. A shipment of lager beer for Hopewell arrived with half empty bottles and the corks put back. Charles Kimball signed a letter with authority for the local agents to allow installation of wall pockets at depots to hold temperance literature. By 1882, the railroad required that all shipments of boots and shoes be strapped shut to prevent loss.

Losses were not always confined to freight. Sometimes there were problems with checked baggage. In the fall of 1897, the ND&C finally agreed to go along with the NYC&HR Railroad in the rules for checking baggage through. The NYC&HR required that any checked bicycles must have attachments such as bells and lights removed before checking, or else the passenger must sign a release form. The ND&C did not have such a rule but they did agree to inform the passengers that the rule would be applied when they changed trains at Dutchess Junction.

Ordinary horseplay could be a problem too. One hot July day, a gentleman arrived at Dutchess Junction on a train from New York. While waiting for the train to Millbrook, he was reading while seated on a bench in front of the ND&C depot. Without warning he received a plaster of soft blue clay. A fireman of engine #4 had thrown the clay, while "skylarking with other employees." Charles Kimball made an example out of the errant fireman and discharged him the following day, but there is no indication of whether the railroad paid to have the gentleman's clothes cleaned.

One of the more interesting tales of the ND&C Railroad happened in the hot summer weather of July 1896. A shipment of a large bag of smoked meat arrived at the ND&C depot in Fishkill, New York. It was consigned to a butcher shop on Main Street in Fishkill Landing. Recall that this was in the days before mechanical refrigeration, so the bag had been in very warm conditions. By the time it reached the Fishkill depot the bag was beginning to be a bit "fragrant."

The Fishkill agent decided he did not want the bag in his depot very long, so he put it on the next train to Matteawan. Of course the agent at Matteawan was just as interested in moving the bag out of his depot as well. A local delivery wagon was summoned to carry the load to the butcher shop at the other end of Main Street. A little imagination brings up the image of a horse drawn delivery wagon clopping along in the hot July sun past the Howland Library with the driver perhaps having a clothespin on his nose.

When the deliveryman arrived at the shop, the butcher absolutely would not allow the bag onto his premises, saying that the Board of Health would likely close down his shop. In desperation, the deliveryman took the bag to a local lard rendering plant and beat a hasty retreat.

In a series of letters, the questions began. The shipper wanted to know who was going to pay for the meat. The railroad wanted to know who was going to pay the shipping charges. The butcher was still looking for his supply of meat. There was no word on where the deliveryman went. After the initial flurry of letters and telegrams, there was no indication of how the matter was resolved. We will probably never know how the case of the rotten meat was settled.

In that same year, 1896, the ND&C vice president Mr. G. Hunter Brown showed his sense of humor. Brown and his wife had been invited to the Poughkeepsie Bridge to see the Intercollegiate Rowing Races on June 26th. Since his wife was not particularly interested, Brown wanted to substitute William Underhill, general freight agent, to conduct some business while there. Brown's response was:

### Volume 43, Page 8, 22 June 1896

Will the pass which I hold to the Bridge Watchman be sufficient to cover Mr. Under-

**ND&C RR E. Main St. crossing, Matteawan, NY.**
Collection of the Beacon Historical Society.

hill, or shall I be obliged to put him in skirts in order to get through the lines?

There is no indication of whether Underhill had to wear a skirt. Vice president Brown was a fairly young college graduate and, incidentally, the nephew of ND&C president, J. Crosby Brown. He was also a sports fan. In November 1896, he received tickets to a Yale-Princeton football game. He responded with a telegram.

### Volume 43, Page 447, 9 November 1896

Look out for Princeton. She is playing a very strong and offensive game. Their full back, Baird, is certainly the best I have seen this year in the field.

G. Hunter Brown also made arrangements for the ND&C Railroad to donate an engraved silver loving cup to be presented to the winner at the Millbrook Golf Club. It seems that he understood where the influential people lived. Not all the influential people lived in Millbrook, however. On the first of March 1899, he wrote a letter to Honorable John Henry Ketcham, House of Representatives, Washington, DC:

> Dear sir, Kindly accept my thanks for the package of seeds received from you yesterday. I have turned them over to Mrs. Brown who has charge of our garden. Your Truly G. Hunter Brown

There is an old saying about rank having privileges. Our vice president and general manager G. Hunter Brown took advantage of that idea for some of his household purchases. He had arranged with a Mrs. Skidmore of Clove Valley to send a package of fresh butter by train to his home in Garrison every Friday. This plan worked for a while, but then some shipments went astray. He traced the problem to improperly made out waybills and sent out a letter to agents and assistants to correct the situation. Brown also used train services to his advantage. In one instance, he sent his wife's chinchilla muff and hat to a store on Fifth Avenue in New York City to be placed in special storage for the summer months "to prevent the fur being attacked by moths and other insects."

G. Hunter Brown extended some of those privileges to a few of the railroad's more affluent and influential customers such as Mrs. John D. Wing of Millbrook. He wrote a letter to all conductors stating:

> This will be your authority to allow Mrs. John D. Wing or a member of her family to carry one fox terrier dog in the passenger coaches of this company.

G. Hunter Brown was also interested in keeping up with some of his affluent social friends. He and William Underhill wrote to John Van Benschoten in Poughkeepsie to arrange for a test drive in a 1902 Oldsmobile. Van Benschoten drove to Matteawan from Poughkeepsie to demonstrate his horseless carriage to Underhill, Brown, and another man named Peavy.

In reading the ND&C letterbook entries signed by G. Hunter Brown, it becomes apparent that he was not really very interested in the every day work of railroading. His letters talked about obtaining wall murals for the company offices or meeting friends at *the* club in New York. There were times when he did have to deal with the job at hand. Here are some examples.

### Volume 43, Page 551, 11 December 1896
*Letter to S. A Colwell, Matteawan:*

> Our overflow pipe to our wash bowl has been stopped up for a week. Your son came here one day this week and tinkered around here for an hour or two and left the building with our cupboard door open and a slop pail half full of water on the floor, and the whole outfit in an upset and disorderly condition, and we have not seen him since. Such foolish and unbusinesslike attempts as this to remedy a defect in this overflow pipe is very annoying to say nothing of the seriousness of this condition of affairs.
>
> I shall call the attention of the Health Officer to this matter today and leave it with you to take such action as you deem best after receiving this letter.

### Volume 43, Page 582, 22 December 1896

> It will be necessary to make some arrangement at Arthursburgh station for installing a stove at that point. Complaints from the public have been so numerous of late to the effect that tramps are occupying

**THE TRANSPORTATION CLUB**
MADISON AVENUE AND 42D STREET

NEW YORK, Oct. 1st, 1901

Mr G H Brown
Matteawan Dutchess Co.
N.Y.

DEAR SIR:

Your non-resident membership dues for the three months ending Jan. 1st, 1902, and amounting to $5.00 are now payable. Check should be drawn to the order of The Transportation Club, and sent to the undersigned.

Respectfully
MARSHAL L. BACON
*Treasurer*

Transportation Club dues reminder to ND&C Vice President G. Hunter Brown
Collection of the Beacon Historical Society, Beacon, NY.

**Transportation Club dues reminder to ND&C vice president G. Hunter Brown.** Collection of the Beacon Historical Society.

Arthursburgh station night and day, and that it is unsafe for a patron of the road to approach the spot unprotected that we must make some move to give better service at that place.

### Volume 43, Page 587, 23 December 1896

The ND&C will pay Mrs. Theodore Horton of Arthursburgh $5 per month to unlock the station one half hour before each train and lock it again after the train has gone.

### Volume 48, Page 69-70 and 77-78, 7 and 8 October 1897

*Brown wrote a two-page letter to S. A. Coldwell (landlord?) complaining about water from the building cesspool leaking through the retaining wall and onto the tracks. This was weakening the wall and washing away ballast, so he was afraid it would cause the wall to collapse and wreck a train. Also, there was a sewage odor where trains stopped at the station.*

He sent a similar letter to Dr. J. G. Dawson, president of the Health Board. Apparently, plumbing was a big problem at the ND&C offices. It must have been quite a leak to wash away part of the ballast.

Some of the more interesting tales come under the heading of unusual cargo. For example, Conductor Hemingway got a note from Superintendent Kimball saying that on Saturday morning his train was to carry one cow from Hopewell Junction to Pine Plains. Just where the cow was supposed to ride was not specified. In the ND&C letterbooks, there are at least two letters explaining that the fare is double the standard adult rate for carrying corpses to the cemetery. The ND&C Railroad charged a rate of six dollars per car for hauling the Barnum and Bailey Circus from Millerton to Shekomeko, while they hauled stock for free if the animals had been exhibited at the state fair in Syracuse.

General Freight agent Underhill wrote special instructions to agent G. H. Bontecou at Dutchess Junction regarding the handling of five carloads of willow blocks. The blocks were to be loaded on a Hudson River schooner and shipped to A. A. Marks, 701 Broadway in New York City. Mr. Marks, it seems, was a manufacturer of artificial limbs, and the blocks of willow wood were destined to become wooden legs and arms.

The Empire State Sugar Beet Company of Lyons, New York, marketed the leftover beet pulp as cattle food. However, on one occasion there was a problem with the paperwork. A gondola loaded with soggy beet pulp sat in the NYC&HR Railroad Fishkill Landing yard for a number of days in warm weather before being delivered to the ND&C and consigned to Fishkill Village. After one sniff, the consignee refused the shipment. ND&C general freight agent, William Underhill wrote to the NYC&HR Railroad saying that they were to blame for the delay and should therefore pay the shipping and disposal charges.

> The car of beet pulp on hand at our Fishkill station is a total loss. It is absolutely unsaleable and there will be some further expense entailed to dispose of it if we can get any one to touch it at all.

Two days later, Underhill wrote to the Empire State Sugar Beet Company:

> This beet pulp arrived in a worthless condition. This car is standing on our side tracks untouched, refused by consignee who advises us that no disposition whatever can be made of it. The accrued freight charges on this car under special low rates made to cover the case are $40.50. To this will be added the expense for unloading this car to some dump or we will gladly return it free to New York Central at Dutchess Junction, if they will accept the same, upon receipt of your check for the $40.50.

Nine days later, another carload of beet pulp was refused because the consignee served notice that he would not accept it. Apparently, the Empire State Sugar Beet Company had found a sneaky way to dispose of unwanted byproducts.

Another perhaps even more odorous cargo was manure. In the days before automobiles, horses were the main mode of local transportation. In some urban areas, there were almost as many horses as there were people. This could add up to a rather large problem. The ND&C arranged with the Jersey City Horse Manure Transportation Company to haul horse manure in twenty ton carload lots to the Dieterich estate in Millbrook. This is the same estate that later became the home of Timothy Leary and his LSD drug cult. Each day, Train #51 would pick up the empty manure cars and return them for the next load. I am sure that the well-heeled train riders from Millbrook did not relish the idea of carloads of manure in the ND&C mixed trains, especially during station stops in the hot summer months.

In many of the small towns along the line, the railroad depot was the center of social activity. In addition to things like daily weather reports and standard time signals by telegraph, the depot was a center for local news, Western Union telegrams, and even town meetings. In the 1880s, the train depot often had the only telephone in town. Items ordered by mail often came to the depot by way of Railway Express. The very idea that the tracks by the depot could carry you thousands of miles to the other side of the continent was a heady thought to people who had never been farther than a few miles from the farm where they were born.

The ND&C letterbooks have many examples that illustrate the influence of the railroads on rural life. For example on 8 January 1897, a supply of posters was distributed to each ND&C depot. The posters advertised Hi Henry's minstrel show, which was scheduled for Peatties Academy of Music at Fishkill on Hudson. The day after the minstrel, a report stated that the railroad had carried 175 passengers to the show. On various occasions, there were posters for John Philip Sousa's marching band or dramas. In many cases, the railroad would provide extra passenger cars or extra trains to handle the load for these events. There were special trains scheduled to carry passengers to the Chrysanthemum Festival in Millbrook or to connect at Hopewell Junction

Okay! What do we do about this mess? August 1899 photo of a wreck on the ND&C RR. A story with the photo says there were two stock cars of sheep in the train accompanied by two Englishmen who were asleep. What a rude awakening. The location of this accident was not specified on the photo.
Collection of the Beacon Historical Society, Beacon, NY.

with the NY&NE trains to the Connecticut State Fair at Danbury. Excursions to lakes and parks were popular. These extra trains were a welcome addition to the rural social scene. They boosted the attendance at local events and at the same time added to the railroad revenue. Of course, most of that business dried up when Henry Ford's Model T arrived.

In December 1897, the ND&C Railroad agreed to have the Automatic Vending Machine Company install candy and gum vending machines in twelve stations along the line. These machines proved to be a double-edged sword. On one hand, they provided a service for the passengers and revenue for the railroad. On the other hand, they were a constant source of customer complaints and also a target for burglars. Over the next few years, there were several instances of depot burglaries and vending machines broken open.

Of course, all that activity around a depot was bound to attract a bit of the other side of life. There was a good example of this in March 1899 at the Clove Branch Junction station. A homeless tramp named Barney was drunk one Saturday morning and standing on the platform as an express train was passing by. The breeze of the train blew his hat off, and while attempting to catch it, he staggered into the side of a passing train coach. He was thrown to the ground and sustained a compound fracture of his right arm. The train stopped and they took the man to LaGrange where the coroner happened to be at the station. On the advice of the coroner, they then took the injured man to the General Hospital

A wreck on the ND&C could always draw a crowd. This photo shows engines #4 and #6 nose to nose in August 1899. The location of this accident was not specified on the photo.
Collection of the Beacon Historical Society, Beacon.

at Matteawan where the railroad surgeon set his broken arm.

This was not the end of the story, however. Because the man was homeless, he remained in the hospital. The railroad did not feel obligated to pay for his keep after a few days of recovery. ND&C vice president G. Hunter Brown wrote a letter to Isaac Carman, the county superintendent of the Poor at Oak Summit, to get the injured homeless man moved to the county poor house. The hospital was willing to keep the man for five dollars per week, but Brown asked the county to take over the case because the railroad was in no way responsible. How times have changed! In the hands of today's lawyers, a case like that would be worth millions.

One of the most important measures of a railroad's performance was running trains on time. Late trains got a lot of attention. On 7 February 1901, ND&C vice president G. Hunter Brown wrote a scathing two-page letter to Engineer Cronkrite chewing him out for running out of coal and making his train twenty minutes late. In today's railroad world, would a vice president be writing letters and threatening actions against an engineer for being twenty minutes late?

Well before the coming of computers, the ND&C Railroad had its own version of a millennium bug. The problem was in the ticket date stampers that agents used at each depot. It seems that the number wheels did not have all the required digits to change the century date. The errant date stampers were sent to E. J. Brecks and Company in New York to have the wheels updated when the year 1900 rolled by.

*The Lighter Side of Railroading*

They did'nt wait for the "Yankee" robin's to fly North back in those days. Spring was here the day the Cannonball made it's first stop for the crew to take a dip in Fishkill Creek.

The cartoons on these pages and the next of life on the CNE were drawn by Ed Ross of Hopewell Junction as a birthday gift for William Turner. They were presented to the Beacon Historical Society by Mr. and Mrs. Andrew Fedorchak of Beacon. Note that the locomotive lettering shows the CNE Rwy, however, the locomotive numbers are from the NH RR. The Hopewell Junction depot is in the background of the top drawing on the next page.

"Well the round house leaks, maybe the rain warped it!"

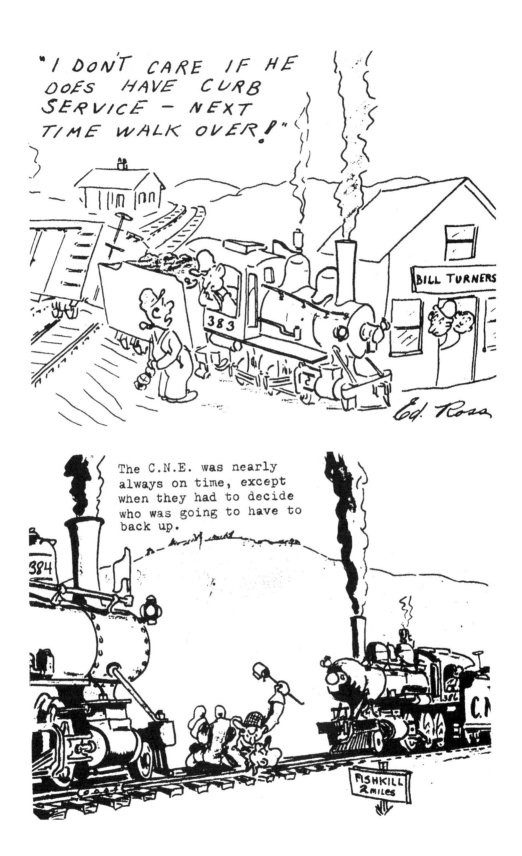

# After the ND&C Railroad

IN THE EARLY YEARS, before the ND&C Railroad, the rails across southern Dutchess County had several different owners. After the ND&C passed from the scene, those same rails saw several more owners. At the end of the ND&C, the next owner was the Central New England Railway, which was actually part of the New Haven Railroad organization. New Haven money bought the ND&C assets in 1905, but the CNE Railway was given the task of operating the new acquisition.

The New Haven bosses did not really want the ND&C Railroad. They were mainly interested in east-west freight service across the Poughkeepsie Bridge and access to the NYC Hudson River line. The only part of the ND&C that they had any use for was the section from Hopewell Junction to Wicopee Junction for access to the Fishkill Landing connections with the NYC Hudson line. With this in mind, they embarked on a program of abandonments. New Haven Railroad Fishkill Landing ferry service had been discontinued in 1904. New Haven Railroad passenger service from Fishkill Landing also had been abandoned in 1904, leaving that market to the ND&C and CNE. The first ND&C facility to go was Dutchess Junction. The CNE sold most of the shops and buildings for salvage in 1907.

Passenger and freight service continued on the old ND&C from Dutchess Junction to Millerton, but it was not profitable. Meanwhile, the NH/CNE Maybrook line, which crossed at Hopewell Junction, was being upgraded for more Poughkeepsie Bridge traffic. The Maybrook line curves were straightened a bit and a second track was added in 1910. CNE train service at Dutchess Junction ceased operation in June 1916. The rails up to Wicopee Junction were removed and the great Tioronda Bridge over Fishkill Creek was sold for scrap. All that remains today are the high stone abutments standing guard over the creek. The NYC Hudson line served Dutchess Junction for a time, but even that service would not last. Today, there are only trees and a few scattered bricks to show where Dutchess Junction was. Amtrak and Metro-North trains thunder by every day, and nature has reclaimed Plum Point.

Other parts of the ND&C managed to last a while longer. What had once been the ND&C main line still connected towns in Dutchess County from Beacon all the way to Millerton. The CNE Railway operated the line until 1927. On 10 May 1927, the CNE was formally absorbed into the New Haven Railroad. The old ND&C Railroad line became part of the New Haven Railroad.

With Dutchess Junction gone, the major activity on what had been the ND&C Railroad shifted to Hopewell Junction. The yard at Hopewell Junction was the base for pusher engines used to help heavy freight trains going eastward over the mountain to Connecticut. Over the years, several types of steam engines were assigned to pusher service at Hopewell Junction. The largest of these engines was the Santa Fe L-1 class with a wheel arrangement of 2-10-2. They were very large and powerful engines but not very fast. From the ground up they were designed to move heavy trains over mountains. First delivered to the New Haven Railroad in 1918, they were not suited for high

**Railbus on the former Rhinebeck & Connecticut/Central New England Rwy, at Copake station, November 1932. At that time, this was part of the NH RR. Railbuses like this were used on the NH RR and other lines to cut costs in the last few years of passenger service.** Collection of Heyward Cohen.

speed main line service. That same year they were assigned to pusher service in Hopewell Junction. The service facilities at Hopewell included coal, water, and minor repairs. As many as thirty engines a day were serviced at the Hopewell roundhouse. Hopewell was a very smoky and sooty town in those days.

The New Haven continued its program of abandonments. The former ND&C line from Hopewell Junction to Millerton was next in line in 1938. By 1939, the tracks had been removed and the scrap sold to Japan. It is tempting to speculate about how much of the old ND&C came back to American soil at Pearl Harbor on December 7th 1941. All that remained of the old ND&C line was the eleven-mile section from Hopewell Junction to Wicopee Junction in Beacon.

Most of the Santa Fe steam engines were gone by 1947, when diesel engines took over.

There was no longer a need for the roundhouse, the coal tower, and the water tower. Most of the railroad activity in Hopewell Junction had changed drastically by 1950. The use of coal was declining rapidly on the railroads as well as in the town. Early diesels still required pushers on the mountain on rainy days. Wet rails could cause the diesel engines to slip on the grade. An occasional steam pusher could be seen at Hopewell as late as 1950, but the coal and water facilities were no longer needed when even the pushers were diesels.

With declining traffic on the Maybrook line, one set of rails was torn up, and the line reverted to single track operation in 1961. As diesels were built with higher and higher horsepower and weight, even the pushers were no longer needed. The engine service roundhouse building was rented out to a plastics company, and in 1955, the roundhouse burned. Eventually, only the old ND&C depot building remained as a lonely reminder of the glory days of steam trains in Hopewell Junction.

The New Haven Railroad survived and operated the Maybrook line until the ill-fated Penn Central Railroad (PC) was formed in February 1968, and PC took over the New Haven Railroad on 1 January 1969. The PC Railroad was an attempt to salvage the railroads of the northeast by combining the New York Central Railroad, the Pennsylvania Railroad, and the New Haven Railroad into one giant railroad. It did not work, and the federal government stepped in and created CONRAIL in 1976 to prevent total collapse of the railroads. CONRAIL then became custodian of what had once been part of the ND&C Rail-

**Right: Charles Miller worked for the NH RR in Hopewell Junction. He was the father of Harry Miller and grandfather of Dennis Miller. Dennis Miller is the current superintendent of highways in East Fishkill.** Collection of Harry and Mary Louise Miller.

**Below: Removing the rails of the former ND&C RR mainline, 1938. Heisler locomotive pulls a scrap train at Main St. in Pine Plains.** Photo by L. Haight. Collection of J. W. Swanberg.

road between Beacon and Hopewell Junction. CONRAIL also operated the Maybrook line and the Poughkeepsie Bridge.

The final blow was the 1974 fire on the Poughkeepsie Bridge. With no traffic across the Hudson River, the local rail customers could not support the cost of train operations. The last CONRAIL local run on the Dutchess County portion of the Maybrook line was in 1982. Shortly after that, the tracks were removed from Poughkeepsie to Hopewell Junction. Now weeds grow in what used to be one of the busiest places in Dutchess County. The county purchased the right of way and plans are underway to bury water lines under it and pave the surface to create a recreational rail trail connecting Poughkeepsie and Hopewell Junction.

The Housatonic Railroad acquired the line from Beacon to Hopewell Junction and into Connecticut. They later sold the line to the MTA Metro-North Railroad but retained the rights to run freight on the line. Today, there is no rail service on the line either freight or passenger. Occasionally a hi-rail inspection truck travels the line, and sometimes you can see a train of equipment being moved between the Hudson line and Connecticut. The Danbury Railroad Museum occasionally runs a fan trip to view the fall foliage, but there is no regular train service. Metro-North uses the Hopewell Junction yard as a track equipment training facility. Metro-North or the Housatonic Railroad may someday find a use for these tracks, but for now the rails look pretty rusty.

If you look closely enough, you may still find parts of the ND&C Railroad. The rails, bridges, and crossing signs are still in place from Hopewell Junction to Beacon, but there is little train traffic to bother the motorists. Some

**Danbury RR Museum fan trip at Hopewell Junction.**
Photo by the author, November 2000.

**Hopewell Junction Depot, November 1980.**
Author's Collection

ND&C buildings have been put to new uses in Millerton, Millbrook, and Verbank. The headquarters building in Matteawan is now part of the city of Beacon and includes businesses and apartments. In Hopewell Junction, the tracks are gone from the depot, but the building still stands awaiting restoration into a museum at the end of the planned Dutchess County rail trail.

There is a much more intangible legacy from the ND&C Railroad and its peers. Railroads opened up communications between formerly isolated places. Along with the railroads came the telegraph, the telephone, and daily newspapers deliveries. Railroads carried rural farm products to the cities but they also brought city culture and life to the farms. A farmer and his wife could enjoy a concert in town and be home for the next day's chores. Mail-order catalog shopping thrived with the goods delivered by rail.

In a matter of a generation it became possible for the average person to travel three thousand miles across the continent in less time than it took a colonist to ride a horse from Boston to Philadelphia. Consumer goods and food could be moved long distances at reasonable cost. Winter time city dwellers in the northeast could buy oranges from Florida and fresh lettuce from California. City dwellers could spend a weekend in the mountains or at the beach, and vacation resort areas flourished with rail service providing the customers. Entire industries and towns grew up along the rail lines, and for some people, commuting to work in the city became a way of life. Railroads influenced daily life in countless ways. Our modern lifestyle owes much to men like George Brown, Charles Kimball, G. Hunter Brown, and William Underhill. They probably did not realize it in their own time, but they changed the world simply by doing what they did best-running a railroad.

# Appendices

### Appendix A: Rosters

This appendix contains locomotive rosters for the following railroads:
- Dutchess & Columbia Railroad
- Clove Branch Railroad
- Boston, Hartford & Erie Railroad
- New York, Boston & Northern Railway
- New York, Boston & Montreal Railway
- Newburgh, Dutchess & Connecticut Railroad

These rosters have been compiled by Leroy Beaujon, who is a retired New Haven Railroad towerman now living in Roseville, California. Lee has been very active in the New Haven Railroad Historical and Technical Society and has contributed much to the New Haven RR archives at the Thomas J. Dodd Research Center of the University of Connecticut campus at Storrs, Connecticut. Lee is also a charter member of the Ontario & Western Railway Historical Society.

### Appendix B: ND&C Railroad Maps

This appendix contains segments of old USGS maps dating from the 1890s to the early 1900s. The route of the ND&C Railroad can be traced from Dutchess Junction to Millerton with a branch to Sylvan Lake and Clove Valley.

These maps are available via the Internet from the University of New Hampshire: http://docs.unh.edu/nhtopos/nhtopos.htm

### Appendix C: Adams's Photographs

This appendix contains a collection of ND&C Railroad station photographs from the collection of the late Robert B. Adams. He was a retired executive of *Trains* and *Model Railroader* magazines. Adams was interested in the history of the Central New England Railway, which of course included the ND&C Railroad.

The photographs in this section were intended for a book that Adams was writing about the CNE and ND&C. Unfortunately he passed away before the manuscript was completed and the book was never published. Some of these pictures have been published previously in other books but never together as far as I know.

The sequence follows the line of the ND&C Railroad from the Matteawan station to Shekomeko. You may note a very jaunty car that seems to be in most of the pictures. My guess is that it may have been his car or the car of someone who took the photos for him.

The copies of the pictures in this group were obtained from Heyward Cohen who lives in Amenia, New York, and has an extensive collection of railroad photographs and postcards for sale.

### Appendix D: Adams/Westman Drawings

This appendix contains a collection of ND&C Railroad station drawings also from the collection of the late Robert B. Adams. The drawings were done by Victor Westman, a retired railroader living in Danbury, Connecticut, and were intended for the Adams book that was never published. They are presently in the collection of Heyward Cohen.

Some of these pictures have been used previously as Christmas card illustrations but never together. The sequence follows the line of the ND&C RR from Hopewell Junction station to Millerton.

## DUTCHESS & COLUMBIA RAILROAD
## (9/4/66 - 11/5/68)
## BOSTON, HARTFORD & ERIE RAILROAD (D&C DIV.)
## (11/6/68 - 3/19/71)
## CLOVE BRANCH RAILROAD
## (11/21/68 - 12/17/72)

### Locomotive Roster

| NBR. | NAME | BUILDER | CONST.# | DATE | CYL. | DRIV. | WHEELS | NOTE |
|------|------|---------|---------|------|------|-------|--------|------|
| 100 | DUTCHESS | Schenectady | 526 | 12/68 | 16"x24" | 60" | 4-4-0 | 01 |
| 101 | FISHKILL | Schenectady | 528 | 12/68 | 17"x24" | 54" | 4-4-0 | 02 |
|  | TIORONDA | M.W.Baldwin | 707 | 6/30/56 | 14"x24" | 60" | 4-4-0 | 03 |
|  | WASHINGTON | Breese, Kneeland & Company | ? | 1856 | 16"x20" | 70" | 4-4-0 | 04 |
|  | PINE PLAINS | Breese, Kneeland & Co. | ? | 1856 | 16"x24" | 70" | 4-4-0 | 05 |
| 1 | MILLBROOK | Grant L.Wks. | 699 | 4/70 | 17"x24" | 60" | 4-4-0 | 06 |
| 2 | BANGALL | Grant L.Wks. | 700 | 4/70 | 17"x24" | 60" | 4-4-0 | 07 |
| 3 | VERBANK | Schenectady | 627 | 4/70 | 16"x24" | 60" | 4-4-0 | 08 |
| 4 | LAGRANGE | Schenectady | 616 | 3/70 | 18"x24" | 60" | 4-4-0 | 09 |
| 5 | - | Danforth L&M | 804 | 3/30/72 | 18"x24" | 56" | 2-6-0 | 10 |
| 6 | - | Danforth L&M | 805 | 4/05/72 | 18"x24" | 56" | 2-6-0 | 11 |

The Dutchess & Columbia Railroad turned out to be more of a "Paper" railroad company than an "Active" railroad company. From it's inception in 1866 until it's demise sometime in 1884, the D&C's actual operation of it's line was only for a little over two years total. No portion of it was open for business until after being leased to the BH&E RR in late 1869. For most of the intervening years, it's locomotives and rolling stock were leased out to other carriers. It is thought that the D&C's locomotives stayed lettered "D&C RR" plus stayed numbered and/or named as originally assigned until the New York, Boston & Montreal Rwy came in to existence in early 1873. At that time new equipment was ordered and all existing locomotives were renumbered and probably the names were dropped by that time. A roster of the NYB&M's locomotives follows this roster.

NOTE 01 - Diverted by the D&C RR from the Schenectady Loco. Works to the BH&E RR becoming their #10 but kept the name "DUTCHESS"; Cost new $11,787.50; Operated on the BH&E's D&C Division, a newly opened line between Dutchess Jct. and Millbrook, NY; Went to the NY&NE RR after the BH&E's demise and renamed the "ONWARD" but kept the same number; Was scrapped in 1895.

(To NY&NE #10 "ONWARD")

NOTE 02 - Diverted to the D&C RR from the Schenectady Loco. Works to the BH&E RR becoming their #7 but kept the name "FISHKILL"; Cost new $12,812.50; Operated on the BH&E's D&C Div., a newly opened line between Dutchess Jct. and Millbrook, NY; Went to the NY&NE RR after the BH&E's demise keeping the same name and number; Sold by the NY&NE in 1870 to an unknown party.

(To NY&NE #7 "FISHKILL")

D&C RR Pg. 2 -

NOTE 03 - Bought from the North Pennsylvania RR (their #5 "Neshaminy" and delivered by boat to Dutchess Jct. area on Feb. 8, 1869; Was a woodburner and used mostly on the **Clove Branch** RR; Owned by the Estate of James Brown, former D&C Pres.; Taken out of service in 1877 and sold for scrap in Sep., 1881 for $350.00.
(To NYB&M #16; D&C/CB "TIORONDA")

NOTE 04 - Ordered from Breese,Kneeland & Co. by the East Tenn. & Va. RR that defaulted on payment and was in turn sold to the Hampshire & Hamden RR in Mass. becoming their #1; The H&H later became the New Haven & Northampton RR (Canal Line) The drivers were rebuilt from 60" to 70" by the builder prior to the sale to the H&H RR; Sold to the D&C RR for $4000.00 and delivered by boat to the Dutchess Jct. area on Feb. 15, 1869; Was a woodburner and used mostly on the **Clove Branch** RR; Said to have been sold to a construction company in Delaware in Apr.,1884 for $500.00 with payment going to the **Clove Branch** RR; Final dispostion unknown.
(To NYB&M #17; D&C/CB "WASHINGTON)

NOTE 05 - Origin similar to locomotive described in "Note 04" except was H&H/NH&N #2; Apparently used mostly on the **Clove Branch** RR during time that the D&C RR was operated by the NYB&M Rwy; Supposedly sold in Jun.,1876 by the Estate of James Brown, former D&C Pres., to an unknown railroad in Quebec, Can.; Final dispostion unknown.
(To D&C/CB "PINE PLAINS")

NOTE 06 - Bought by the D&C RR but leased to the NYB&M Rwy in 1873; Reverted back to the Trustees of the D&C RR after the NYB&M Rwy's demise in late 1876 and leased to the new ND&C RR in Feb.,1877; Finally sold to the ND&C RR on Feb.16,1884 for $4750.00.
(To NYB&M #13; D&C/CB (1st) #1)

NOTE 07 - Bought by the D&C RR but leased to the NYB&M Rwy in 1873; Reverted back to the Trustees of the D&C RR after the NYB&M Rwy's demise in late 1876 and leased to the new ND&C RR in Feb.,1877; Finally sold to the ND&C RR on Feb.16,1884 for $4750.00.
(To NYB&M #14; D&C/ND&C #2; CNE #212)

NOTE 08 - Bought by the D&C RR but leased to the NYB&M Rwy in 1873; Reverted back to the Trustees of the D&C RR after the NYB&M Rwy's demise in late 1876 and leased to the new ND&C RR in Feb.,1877; Finally sold to the ND&C RR on Feb.16,1884 for $2750.00.
(To NYB&M #12; D&C/CB (1st) #3)

NOTE 09 - Bought by the D&C RR but leased to the NYB&M Rwy in 1873; Reverted back to the Trustees of the D&C RR after the NYB&M Rwy's demise in late 1876 and leased to the new ND&C RR in Feb.,1877; Finally sold to the ND&C RR on Feb.16,1884 for $4750.00.
(To NYB&M #11; D&C/ND&C #4; CNE #213)

NOTE 10 - Bought new by the D&C RR but apparently almost immediately sold in early 1873 to the NYB&M Rwy; Did not revert back to the D&C RR on the demise of the NYB&M Rwy in late 1876 but was sold to the ND&C RR by the Trustees of the NYB&M Rwy in early 1877.
(To NYB&M #15; ND&C (1st) #8, (2nd) #3; CNE (1st) #3)

D&C RR Pg. 3 -

NOTE 11 - Bought by the D&C RR but was sold almost immediately to the Poughkeepsie & Eastern Railroad in Oct.,1872 for $12,000.00 becoming their (1st) #4; Was traded in to the Rogers Loco. Works on Apr.25, 1895 as part payment (value unknown) on new P&E Rwy (2nd) #2 "OLIVIA".
(To P&E RR #4; PH&B RR #4; NY&M Rwy #4; P&E Rwy (1st)

## NEW YORK, BOSTON & NORTHERN RAILROAD
(12/18/72 - 1/20/73)
## NEW YORK, BOSTON & MONTREAL RAILWAY (D&C DIV.)
(1/21/73 - 8/10/76)
## CLOVE BRANCH RAILROAD
(12/18/72 - 8/10/76)

### Locomotive Roster

| NBR. | NAME | BUILDER | CONST.# | DATE | CYL. | DRIV. | WHEELS |
|---|---|---|---|---|---|---|---|
| * | PINE PLAINS | Breese, Kneeland & Co. | ? | 1856 | 16"x24" | 70" | 4-4-0 |
| 1 | - | Brooks | 185 | 5/31/73 | 16"x24" | 60½" | 4-4-0 |
| 2* | - | Brooks | 188 | 6/14/73 | 16"x24" | 60½" | 4-4-0 |
| 3 | - | Brooks | 189 | 6/19/73 | 16"x24" | 60½" | 4-4-0 |
| 4* | - | Brooks | 190 | 6/24/73 | 16"x24" | 60½" | 4-4-0 |
| 5* | - | Brooks | 191 | 6/30/73 | 16"x24" | 60½" | 4-4-0 |
| 6* | - | Brooks | 193 | 7/17/73 | 16"x24" | 60½" | 4-4-0 |
| 7* | - | Brooks | 194 | 7/22/73 | 16"x24" | 60½" | 4-4-0 |
| 8 | - | Brooks | 195 | 7/26/73 | 16"x24" | 60½" | 4-4-0 |
| 9 | - | Brooks | 196 | 7/30/73 | 16"x24" | 60½" | 4-4-0 |
| 10 | - | Brooks | 197 | 8/05/73 | 16"x24" | 60½" | 4-4-0 |
| 11* | LAGRANGE | Schenectady | 616 | 3/70 | 16"x24" | 60" | 4-4-0 |
| 12* | VERBANK | Schenectady | 627 | 4/70 | 16"x24" | 60" | 4-4-0 |
| 13* | MILLBROOK | Grant L.Wks. | 699 | 4/70 | 17"x24" | 60" | 4-4-0 |
| 14* | BANGALL | Grant L.Wks. | 700 | 4/70 | 17"x24" | 60" | 4-4-0 |
| 15* | - | Danforth L&M | 804 | 3/30/72 | 18"x24" | 56" | 2-6-0 |
| 16* | TIORONDA | M.W.Baldwin | 707 | 6/30/56 | 14"x24" | 60" | 4-4-0 |
| 17* | WASHINGTON | Breese,Kneeland | ? | 1856 | 16"x20" | 70" | 4-4-0 |
| 18 | HILAND HALL | Mason L.W. | 241 | 10/10/66 | 15"x22" | 66" | 4-4-0 |
| 19 | LUTHER PARK | Baldwin L.W. | 1520 | 9/28/66 | 14"x24" | 60" | 4-4-0 |
| 20 | A.L.MINER | Baldwin L.W. | 1527 | 10/16/66 | 14"x24" | 60" | 4-4-0 |
| 21 | C.G.LINCOLN | Baldwin L.W. | 1529 | 10/20/66 | 14"x24" | 60" | 4-4-0 |
| 22 | LEBANON | Nthn.RR of NH Concord Shops | | 1862 | 14"x20" | 60" | 4-4-0 |
| 23 | PACIFIC | Rogers L.W. | 773 | 5/23/57 | 14"x20" | 66" | 4-4-0 |
| 24 | G.F.CARMAN | Rogers L.W. | 166 | 3/30/49 | 14"x20" | 66" | 4-4-0 |
| 25 | MTN. BOY | Schenectady | 563 | 6/??/69 | 16"x24" | 66" | 4-4-0 |
| 26 | MTN.GIRL | Schenectady | 564 | 6/??/69 | 16"x24" | 66" | 4-4-0 |

Only locomotives shown with "*" believed to have been assigned to and/or used on D&C Div.of NYB&M Rwy; Balance of locomotives assigned to other divisions and may never have operated over the D&C RR's lines in Dutchess Co., NY.

NOTE 01 - Was a woodburner and used mostly on the **Clove Branch RR**; Supposedly sold by the Estate of James Brown (former D&C Pres.) about Jun.,1876 to an unknown railroad in Quebec, Can.; Probably never carried a NYB&M Rwy number and sister locomotives "WASHINGTON" or "TIORONDA" may have filled in on the **Clove Branch RR** after the sale; Final disposition unknown.      (See D&C RR Note 05)
                                                     (Was D&C/CB "PINE PLAINS'

NOTE 02 - Was assigned to the Harlem Extension Div. of the NYB&M Rwy; Became Bennington & Rutland RR #10 "C.E.HOUGHTON"in late 1876.

NYB&M Rwy Pg. 2 -

NOTE 03 - Purchased new by the NYB&M Rwy; Remained on the D&C Div. after the demise of the NYB&M Rwy in late 1876 and was leased to the ND&C RR in Feb.,1877; Sold by the NYB&M Rwy's Trustees to the ND&C RR on Sep.30,1888 for $500.00; Was rebuilt at Dutchess Jct. in late 1888; Was condemned by the CNE Rwy on Sep.9,1909.      (To ND&C #5; CNE #2

NOTE 04 - Was assigned to the Harlem Extension Div. of the NYB&M Rwy; Became Bennington & Rutland RR #11 "M.S.COLBURN" in late 1876; Was rebuilt at the Taunton Loco. Works in May,1882 and renumbered to (2nd) #7 with new name "H.W. STAFFORD".

NOTE 05 - Purchased new by the NYB&M Rwy; Remained on the D&C Div. after the demise of the NYB&M Rwy in late 1876 and was leased to the ND&C RR in Feb.,1877; Was reboilered at the Schenectady Loco. Works in Jan.,1884; Sold by the NYB&M Rwy's Trustees to the ND&C RR on Sep.30,1888 for $1500.00; Was rebuilt at Dutchess Jct. at the end of 1888 costing $4540.00; Was damaged in the Dutchess Jct. roundhouse fire of Nov.23,1893 in the amount of $1700.00; Was rebuilt at the Schenectady Loco. Works in early 1895 costing $3443.00; Was condemned by the CNE Rwy on Sep.9, 1909.      (To ND&C #7; CNE #2

NOTE 06 - Was assigned to the Harlem Extension Div. of the NYB&M Rwy but was moved to High Bridge, NY on Sep.25,1875 from storage at Dutchess Jct. for use on the NYC&N RR; Leased to the Freehold & New York RR (N.J.) in late Dec.,1879 by the NYB&M Rwy's Trustees.

NOTE 07 - Purchased new by the NYB&M Rwy; Remained on the D&C Div. after the demise of the NYB&M Rwy in late 1876 and was leased to the ND&C RR in Feb.,1877; Sold by the NYB&M Rwy's Trustees to the ND&C RR on Sep.30,1888 for the amount of $1000.00; Was rebuilt in Nov.,1888 at Dutchess Jct.; Was condemned by the CNE Rwy on Dec 31,1912 for value of $500.00 and sold for scrap soon after.
      (To ND&C #6; CNE #2

NOTE 08 - Leased to the Freehold & New York RR (N.J.) by the NYB&M Rwy's Trustees and was shipped to them on Aug.13,1877 from storage at Dutchess Junction.

NOTE 09 - Became Erie RR #496 after the demise of the NYB&M Rwy in late 1876; Was renumbered to Erie #199 in 1889; Renumbered again to Erie #40 in 1895; Was rebuilt by the Baldwin L.W. in Apr.,1897 to a Vauclain Compound becoming BLW #15295 and reclassified to a Class D-6 by the Erie and once more renumbered to Erie #373; Sold to the NYS&W RR in Oct.,1911 becoming their #18

NOTE 10 - Became Erie RR #497 after the demise of the NYB&M RR in late 1876; Was scrapped by Jun.,1889.

NOTE 11 - Became Erie RR #498 after the demise of the NYB&M RR in late 1876; Was scrapped by Jun.,1889.

NYB&M Rwy Pg. 3 -

NOTE 12 - Purchased new by the D&C RR and was leased to the NYB&M Rwy in early 1873; Reverted back to the Estate of James Brown (former D&C Pres.) after the demise of the NYB&M Rwy in late 1876; Leased to the ND&C RR in Feb.,1877; Was rebuilt at Dutchess Jct. in Mar.,1883; Was sold to the ND&C RR on Feb.16,1884 for $4750.00; Was damaged in a fire at the Dutchess Jct. roundhouse on Nov.23,1893 in the amount of $1700.00; Was sold by CNE Rwy on Aug.9,1906 to Sinsman & Fisher Co.(scrap dealer) for $525.00.          (See D&C RR Note 09)
(Was D&C #4 "LAGRANGE";To D&C/ND&C #4; CNE #2:

NOTE 13 - Purchased new by the D&C RR and was leased to the NYB&M Rwy in early 1873; Reverted back to the Estate of James Brown (former D&C RR Pres.) after the demise of the NYB&M Rwy in late 1876; Was leased to the ND&C RR in Feb.,1877 and sold to them on Feb.16,1884 for $2750.00; Was rebuilt at Dutchess Jct. in Jun.,1888; Was taken out of service in early 1891 to allow ND&C RR (1st) #8 to be renumbered as (2nd) #3 to fill in the gap; Final disposition unknown but thought to have been used as a stationary boiler at Dutchess Jct. at least until 1902 when mention made of it again as still being on the property but unused.          (See D&C RR Note 08)
(Was D&C (1st) #3 "VERBANK"; To D&C/ND&C (1st) ;

NOTE 14 - Purchased new by the D&C RR and was leased to the NYB&M Rwy in early 1873; Reverted back to the Estate of James Brown (former D&C RR Pres.) after the demise of the NYB&M Rwy in late 1876; Was leased to the ND&C RR in Feb.,1877 and finally sold to them on Feb.16,1884 for $4750.00; Cylinders were rebuilt to 17"x 24" at the Schenectady Loco. Works in 1885; Loco. was rebuilt again in 1888; Was rolled out to safety at the Dutchess Jct. roundhouse fire on Nov.23,1893; Sold to loco. broker Benjamin Watson of N.Y. City on Mar.26,1902 for $2000.00 who in turn sold it to the Chestnut Ridge Rwy. in Penna.; Final disposition unknown.(See D&C RR Note 06)
(Was D&C #1 "MILLBROOK"; To D&C/ND&C (1st) ;

NOTE 15 - Purchased new by the D&C RR and was leased to the NYB&M Rwy in early 1873; Reverted back to the Estate of James Brown (former D&C RR Pres.) after the demise of the NYB&M Rwy in late 1876; Was leased to the ND&C RR in Feb.,1877 and sold to them on Feb.16,1884 for $4750.00; Cylinders were rebuilt to 17"x 24" in Apr.,1888; Loco. was rebuilt again in early 1891 at a cost of $2671.25; Was condemned by the CNE Rwy in Jun.,1907 for value of $562.50 and was scrapped soon after.          (See D&C RR Note 07)
(Was D&C #2 "BANGALL"; To D&C/ND&C #2; CNE #2]

NYB&M Rwy Pg. 4 -

NOTE 16 - Purchased new by the D&C RR but was sold in early 1873 to the NYB&M Rwy; Became their #15 when new Brooks built 4-4-0 #5 was delivered in Jun.,1873; Was leased by the NYB&M Rwy's Trustees to the N.J.Midland RR from May 8, 1876 until Apr.14,1880 and was leased to the ND&C RR from Apr.,1880 until purchased by them on Sep.30,1888 for $1200.00; Was rebuilt during June/July,1882 and again at the Cooke Loco. Works in Sep.,1891 for $4707.00; Was damaged in the Dutchess Jct. roundhouse fire on Nov. 23,1893 in the amount of $1565.00; Was condemned by the CNE Rwy in March,1907 and sold to W.B.Seymour Co.(scrap dealer) for $626.25.          (See D&C RR Note 10)
                (Was D&C #5; To ND&C (1st) #8 - (2nd) #3; CNE (1st)

NOTE 17 - Was a woodburner and assigned to the **Clove Branch RR**; Was taken out of service in 1877 and sold for scrap in Sep.,1881 for the amount of $350.00; Proceeds went to the Estate of James Brown who was the former D&C RR President.              (See D&C RR Note 03)
                (Was D&C "TIORONDA"; to D&C/CB "TIORON

NOTE 18 - Was a woodburner and first used on the **Clove Branch RR**; Said to have been assigned to NY & Boston RR Division service by the NYB&M Rwy for a short period of time; Sold by the Estate of James Brown (former D&C RR Pres.) in Apr.,1884 to a construction company in Delaware for $500.00; Payment went to the account of the **Clove Branch RR**; Final disposition unknown.   (See D&C RR Note 04)
                (Was D&C/CB "WASHINGTON"; to D&C/CB "WASHINGT

NOTE 19 - Originally assigned to the Harlem Extension Div. of the NYB&M Rwy; Became Bennington & Rutland RR #1 after the NYB&M Rwy's demise in late 1876; Was sold or scrapped by 1900.

NOTE 20 - Originally built for the Bennington & Rutland RR (#2) and was assigned to the Harlem Extension Div. of the NYB&M Rwy; Reverted back to B&R RR #2 again after the NYB&M Rwy's demise in late 1876; Was scrapped in 1894.

NOTE 21 - Originally built for the Bennington & Rutland RR (1st) #3 and assigned to the Harlem Extension Div. of the NYB&M Rwy; Reverted back to B&R RR #3 again after the NYB&M Rwy's demise in late 1876; Was sold or scrapped by 1889 when new B&R (2nd) #3 received.

NOTE 22 - Originally built for the Bennington & Rutland RR (#4) and was assigned to the Harlem Extension Div. of the NYB&M Rwy; Reverted back to B&R #4 again after the NYB&M Rwy's demise in late 1876; Was sold or scrapped by 1900.

NOTE 23 - Originally the Northern RR of New Hampshire RR's "JAMES SEDGELY"; Was sold to the Long Island RR and subsequently to the Bennington & Rutland RR in Aug., 1869 becoming their (1st) #5; Was assigned to the Harlem Extension Div. of the NYB&M Rwy; Reverted back to the B&R RR after the NYB&M Rwy's demise in late 1876 but was sold or scrapped by 1891 when new (2nd) #5 was received.

NYB&M Rwy Pg. 5 -

NOTE 24 - Originally built for the Long Island RR and was named "PACIFIC"; Was acquired by the NYB&M Rwy and assigned to their Harlem Extension Div.; Became the Bennington & Rutland RR's #6 "MANCHESTER" after the NYB&M Rwy's demise in late 1876; Was sold or scrapped by 1891 when new (2nd) #6 was received.

NOTE 25 - Originally built for the NY & New Haven RR but was diverted to the NY & Harlem RR becoming their "ALBANY"; Was assigned to the Harlem Extension Div. of the NYB&M Rwy; Became Bennington & Rutland RR (1st) #7 "G.F.CARMAN" after the NYB&M Rwy's demise in late 1876; Was sold or scrapped by May,1882 when new (2nd) #7 was received.

NOTE 26 - Built for the Lebanon Springs RR and was assigned to the Harlem Extension Div. of the NYB&M Rwy; Became Bennington & Rutland RR #8 after the NYB&M Rwy's demise in late 1876 and named the "FRANK C. WHITE"; Was renamed to the "E.D. BENNETT"; Became Rutland RR #60 in 1901 and NYC RR #1060 in 1905; Was scrapped in Jul.,1914.

NOTE 27 - Built for the Lebanon Springs RR and was assigned to the Harlem Extension Div. of the NYB&M Rwy; Became the Bennington & Rutland RR's #9 after the NYB&M Rwy's demise in late 1876 and was named the "C.J.McMASTER"; Became Rutland RR #61 in 1901 and NYC RR #1061 in 1905; Was scrapped in Aug., 1906.

## DUTCHESS & COLUMBIA RAILROAD (3rd)
### (8/11/76 - 1/31/77)
## NEWBURGH, DUTCHESS & CONNECTICUT RAILROAD
### (2/1/77 - 7/31/05)
## CLOVE BRANCH RAILROAD
### (8/11/76 - 12/31/97)

### Locomotive Roster

| NBR. | NAME | BUILDER | CONST.# | DATE | CYL. | DRIV. | WHEELS |
|---|---|---|---|---|---|---|---|
|  | TIORONDA | M.W.Baldwin | 707 | 6/30/56 | 14"x24" | 60" | 4-4-0 |
|  | WASHINGTON | Breese, Kneeland & Company | ? | 1856 | 16"x20" | 70" | 4-4-0 |
| (1st) #1 |  | Grant | 699 | 4/70 | 17"x24" | 60" | 4-4-0 |
| (2nd) #1 |  | Rogers | 3339 | 8/31/83 | 15"x22" | 46" | 2-4-4T |
| #2 |  | Grant | 700 | 4/70 | 17"x24" | 60" | 4-4-0 |
| (1st) #3 |  | Schenectady | 627 | 4/70 | 16"x24" | 60" | 4-4-0 |
| (2nd) #3 |  | Danforth | 804 | 3/30/72 | 18"x24" | 56" | 2-6-0 |
| #4 |  | Schenectady | 616 | 3/70 | 16"x24" | 60" | 4-4-0 |
| #5 |  | Brooks | 188 | 6/14/73 | 16"x24" | 62" | 4-4-0 |
| #6 |  | Brooks | 193 | 7/17/73 | 16"x24" | 62" | 4-4-0 |
| #7 |  | Brooks | 190 | 6/24/73 | 16"x24" | 62" | 4-4-0 |
| (1st) #8 |  | Danforth | 804 | 3/30/72 | 18"x24" | 56" | 2-6-0 |
| (2nd) #8 |  | Baldwin | 14276 | 4/95 | 18"x24" | 69" | 4-4-0 |
| (1st) #9 |  | Rogers | 3339 | 8/31/83 | 15"x22" | 46" | 2-4-4T |
| (2nd) #9 |  | Baldwin | 21016 | 9/02 | 19"x24" | 69" | 4-4-0 |
| #10 |  | Baldwin | 19461 | 8/01 | 18"x24" | 69" | 4-4-2 |

The Dutchess & Columbia RR (under Trusteeship) began operations for a third time in Aug.,1876 on the demise of the NYB&M Rwy; The property (excluding the locomotives which were leased to the ND&C RR) was apparently sold to the ND&C RR just prior to it's first date of operation which was on Feb.1,1877.

Although the CNE Rwy began operating the ND&C RR on Aug.1,1905, it's locomotives probably were not immediately relettered and renumbered until after the Poughkeepsie & Eastern Rwy was taken over by the CNE Rwy in 1907.

NOTE 01 - Was used on the **Clove Branch RR** but may have been taken out of service in early 1877; Owned by the Estate of James Brown (former D&C RR Pres.) and was sold for scrap in late Sep., 1881 for the amount of $350.00.      (See D&C RR Noter 03
(Was D&C/CB "TIORONDA"; NYB&M

NOTE 02 - Was the property of the **Clove Branch RR**; Wrecked at Sylvan Lake on Mar.15,1883 and removed from service until sold to John J. Hurley (probably a loco. broker) of New York City i early Apr.,1884 for $500.00 with proceeds going to the **Clov Branch RR**; Said to have been resold to a construction compa in Delaware; Final dispostion unknown. (See D&C RR Note 04)
(Was D&C/CB "WASHINGTON"; NYB&M

ND&C RR Pg. 2 -

NOTE 03 - Leased by the Estate of James Brown (former D&C RR President) to the ND&C RR in Feb.,1877 and finally sold to them on Feb. 16, 1884 for $4750.00; Cylinders rebuilt from 16"x24" at the Schenectady Loco. Works in Jul.,1885; Rebuilt again in 1888; Was rolled out and saved from the roundhouse fire at Dutchess Jct. on Nov.23,1893; Sold to loco. broker Benj. Watson of New York City on Mar.26,1902 for $2000.00 who in turn sold it to the Chestnut Ridge Rwy in Penna. becoming their (2nd) #1; Final disposition unknown.  (See D&C RR Note 06)
(Was D&C #1 "MILLBROOK"; NYB&M #13)

NOTE 04 - See "Note 14" below; Renumbered from (1st) #9 to (2nd) #1 in Sep.,1902 on delivery of new (2nd) #9 from Badlwin Loco. Wks.
(Was **CB RR** "GENL.SCHULTZE")

NOTE 05 - Leased by the Estate of James Brown (former D&C RR Pres.) to the ND&C RR in Feb.,1877 after the NYB&M Rwy demise in late 1876 and finally sold to them on Feb.16,1884 for $4750.00; Cylinders were rebuilt from 16"x24" to 17"x24" in Apr.,1888; New boiler was installed at the Schenectady Loco. Works in Jun.,1891 costing $2239.00 plus additional work was done at Dutchess Jct. in Jul.,1891; Was condemned by the CNE Rwy in May, 1907 for value of $562.50 and scrapped in June,1907.
(See D&C RR Note 07)
(Was D&C #2 "BANGALL"; NYB&M #14; CNE #212)

NOTE 06 - Leased by the Estate of James Brown (former D&C RR Pres.) to the ND&C RR in Feb.,1877 after the NYB&M Rwy's demise in late 1876 and finally sold to them on Feb.16,1884 for $2750.00; Was rebuilt in Jun.,1888 at Dutchess Jct.; Replaced by (1st) #8 in Jan.,1892 and was probably used as a stationery boiler at the Dutchess Jct. roundhouse until scrapped some time in or after late 1902.  (See D&C RR Note 08)
(Was D&C (1st) #3 "VERBANK"; NYB&M #12)

NOTE 07 - See "Note 12" below; Became (2nd) #3 in Jan.,1892; New boiler installed in Sep.,1891 at the Cooke Loco. Works at a cost of $4707.41; Damaged in the Dutchess Jct. roundhouse fire of Nov.23,1893 to the amount of $1565.00; Condemned by the CNE Rwy in Mar.,1907 and sold to a W.B.Seymour Co. (scrap dealer) for $626.25.  (See D&C RR Note 10)
(Was D&C (1st) #5; NYB&M #15; To CNE (1st) # 3)

NOTE 08 - Leased by the Estate of James Brown (former D&C RR Pres.) to the ND&C RR in Feb.,1877 after the NYB&M Rwy's demise in late 1876 and was finally sold to them on Feb.16,1884 for the amount of $4750.00; Rebuilt in Mar.,1883 at Dutchess Jct.; Received a major rebuilding at the Grant Loco. Works in Aug., 1887 (cylinders changed to 17"x24"); Was damaged in the Dutchess Jct. roundhouse fire of Nov.23,1893 to the amount of $1700.00; Sold to a Sinsman & Fisher Co. (a scrap dealer) by the CNE Rwy on Aug.9,1906 for $525.00.
(See D&C RR Note 09)
(Was D&C #4 "LAGRANGE"; NYB&M #11; To CNE #213)

NOTE 09 - Leased to the ND&C RR in Feb.,1877 by the Trustees of the NYB&M Rwy and finally sold to them on Sep.30,1888 for $500.00; Rebuilt in Oct.,1888 at Dutchess Jct.; No indication has been found that this locomotive was used on the ND&C RR from late 1890 until early 1892 and it may have been either leased or loaned to Genl. Schultze's (ND&C RR Pres.) other railroad which was the Freehold & N.Y. RR in N.J.; Was condemned by the CNE Rwy on Sep.9,1909.
(See NYB&M Rwy Note 03)   (Was NYB&M #2; To CNE #214)

ND&C RR Pg. 3 -

NOTE 10 - Leased to the ND&C RR in Feb.,1877 by the Trustees of the NYB&M Rwy; Used mostly on the docks at Dutchess Jct.; Received a major overhaul at the Schenectady Loco. Works in May,1883; Sold to the ND&C RR by the Trustees of the NYB&M Rwy on Sep.30,1888 for $1000.00; Rebuilt in Nov.,1888 at Dutchess Jct.; Condemned by the CNE Rwy on Dec.31,1912 for value of $500.00 and scrapped soon after.
(See NYB&M Rwy Note 07)          (Was NYB&M #6; To CNE #2)

NOTE 11 - Leased to the ND&C RR in Feb.,1877 by the Trustees of the NYB&M Rwy; Used mostly on the docks at Dutchess Jct.; Reboilered at the Schenectady Loco. Works in Jan.,1884; Sold to the ND&C RR by the Trustees of the NYB&M Rwy on Sep.30, 1888 for $1500.00; Rebuilt at Dutchess Jct. in late 1888 costing $4540.00; Damaged in the Dutchess Jct. roundhouse fire of Nov.23,1893 to the amount of $1700.00; Received a major rebuilding in early 1895 at the Schenectady Loco. Works costing $3443.00; Condemned by the CNE Rwy on Sep.9, 1909. (See NYB&M Rwy Note 05)          (Was NYB&M #4; To CNE #2)

NOTE 12 - Leased to the ND&C RR on Apr.15,1880 by the Trustees of the NYB&M Rwy and finally sold to them on Sep.30,1888 for $1200.00; Rebuilt at Dutchess Jct. in Jun./Jul.,1882 and at the Schenectady Loco. Works in 1883; Received a new boiler at the Cooke Loco. Works in Sep.,1891 at a cost of $4707.41; Additional work done at Dutchess Jct. in Oct. and Nov.,1891; Became (2nd) #3 in Jan.,1892; Damaged at the Dutchess Jct. roundhouse fire on Nov.23,1893 in the amount of $1565.00; Condemned by the CNE Rwy in Mar.,1907
(See D&C RR Note 10 and NYB&M Rwy Note 16)
(Was D&C (1st) #5; NYB&M #15; To CNE (1st) #

NOTE 13 - Ordered new on Mar.16,1895 at a cost of $8744.04 that was payable in installments of $242.89 per month for 36 months; Delivered on May 10,1895; An attempt was made in Apr.,1898 to sell the locomotive back to Baldwin due to several problems encountered; but, apparently nothing came of it; Condemned in Mar.,1925 by the CNE Rwy.
(To CNE #226 - (2nd) #3

NOTE 14 - Built and lettered for the **Clove Branch RR**; Cost new was $8030.00 and was paid for on Sep.29,1883; Went to the ND&C RR on Jul.1,1896 when the **Clove Branch RR** was shut down; Cylinders rebuilt to 15"x24" and drivers reduced to 40"; Used on the work train removing rails from the Clove Branch RR in Nov.,1898; Became ND&C RR (2nd) #1 after delivery of new Baldwin (2nd) #9 in Sep.,1902; Remained out of service at Dutchess Jct. for about three years until sold by the CNE Rwy to a W. B. Seymour (loco. broker) on Feb.28,1906 for $500.00; Supposedly resold to a lumber company railroad in Georgia; Final disposition unknown.
(Was CB #9 "GEN.SCHULTZE

NOTE 15 - Purchased new by the ND&C RR for $10,365.00 which was paid with 50% down and 18 monthly installments of $301.59 per month, including interest, for the balance; Condemned by the CNE Rwy in Jul, 1926.          (To CNE #227 - (2nd) #3

ND&C RR Pg. 4 -

NOTE 16 - Purchased new by the ND&C RR for $11,053.00 which was paid with 50% down plus installments of $321.61 per month, including interest, for 18 months; Shipped from Baldwin in Philadelphia, Pa. on Sep.16,1901 and delivered to the ND&C on Sep.23,1901; Letter of complaint was sent to Baldwin on Apr.26,1902 regarding driver and trailing truck spring problems but unknown whether or not resolved; Condemned by the CNE Rwy in Jul.,1926.                    (To CNE #228 - (2nd)

**Facing page, top:** Dutchess Junction and Dennings Point south of Beacon, NY. Wicopee Junction was the point where ND&C and NY&NE tracks came together.

**Bottom:** Beacon, Glenham, and Fishkill. ND&C RR tracks crossed Fishkill Creek twice in Glenham (center).

*Twenty-Five Years on the ND&C - Appendix B: ND&C Railroad Maps*

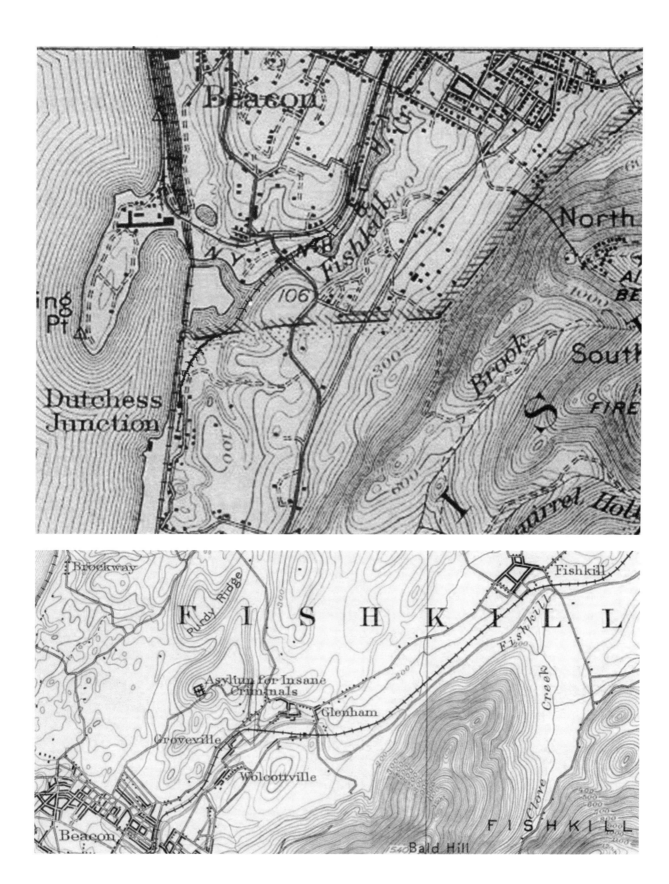

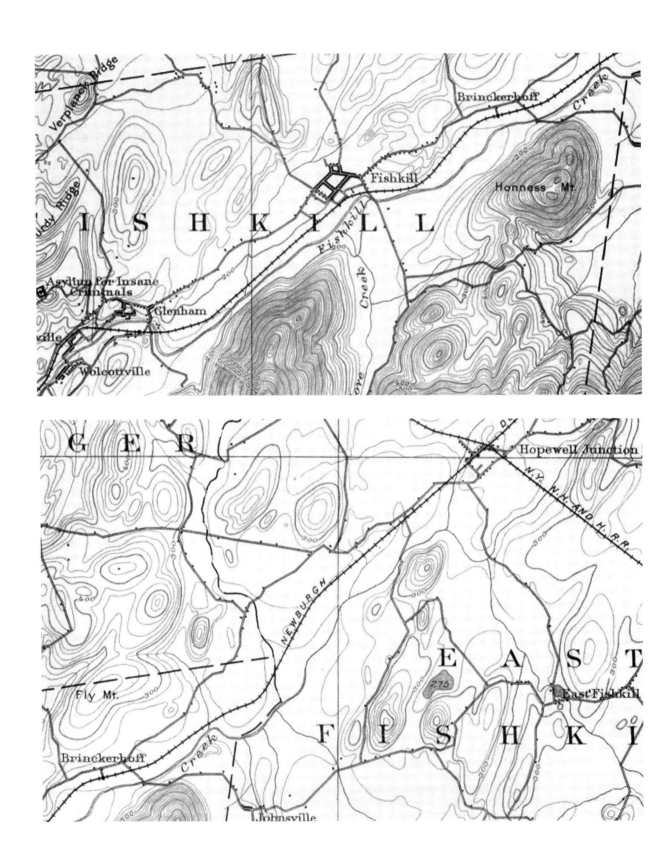

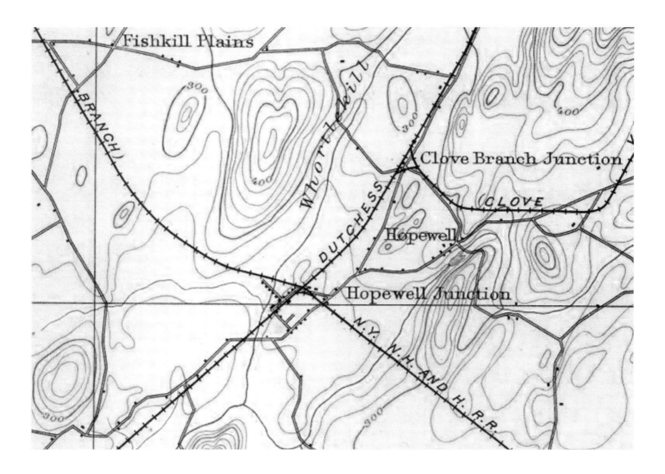

Above: Hopewell Junction and Clove Branch Junction. The ND&C RR ran parallel to Rte. 82 at the top. The Clove Branch RR ran off to the right where it crossed Beekman Road. Tracks at upper left from Poughkeepsie later became the Maybrook Line.

Facing page, top: Glenham, Fishkill, and Brinckerhoff.

Bottom: Brinkerhoff, Sprout Creek, and Hopewell Junction. ND&C RR tracks crossed Sprout Creek just left of center.

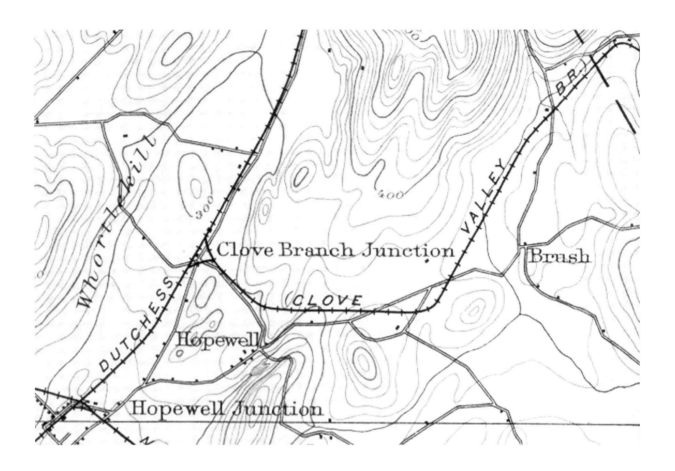

The Clove Branch RR ran toward Sylvan Lake at top right. Map label shows "Clove Valley BR" but actual name was Clove Branch RR. The ND&C ran north to Arthursburg at top center.

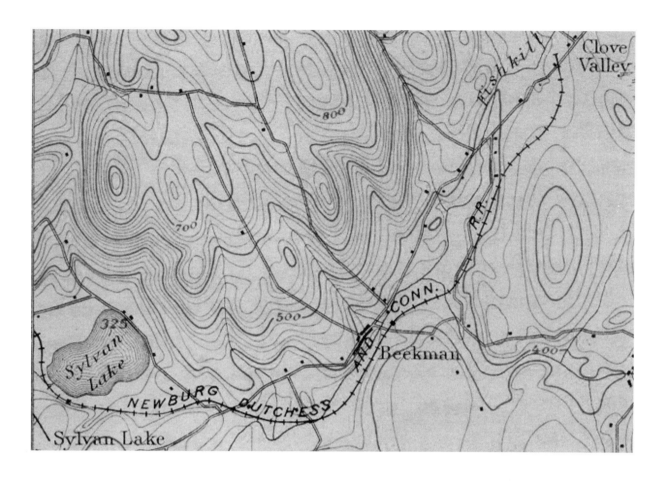

Clove Branch RR to Sylvan Lake, Beekman, and Clove Valley. Before it was abandoned, the Clove Branch RR became part of the ND&C RR.

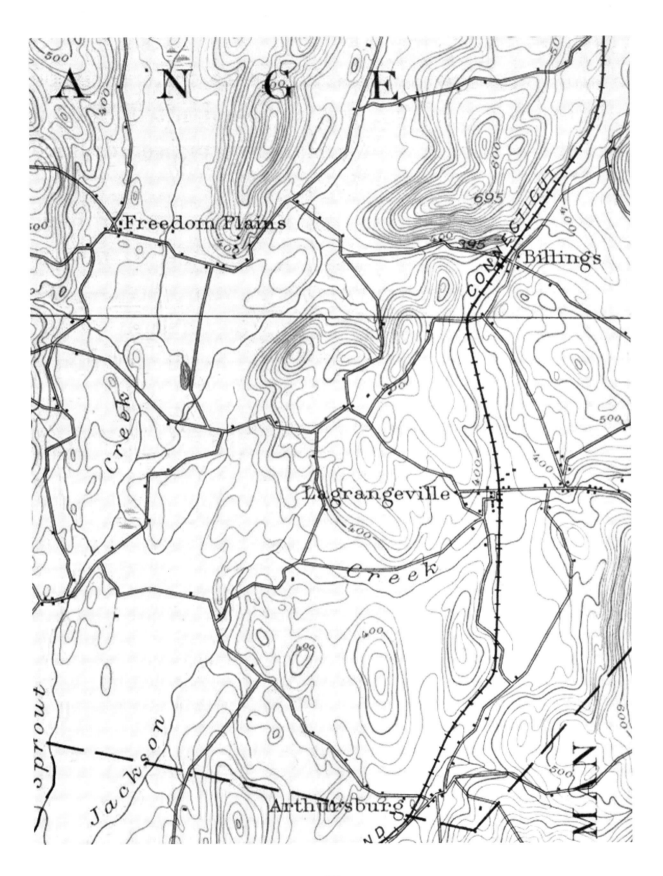

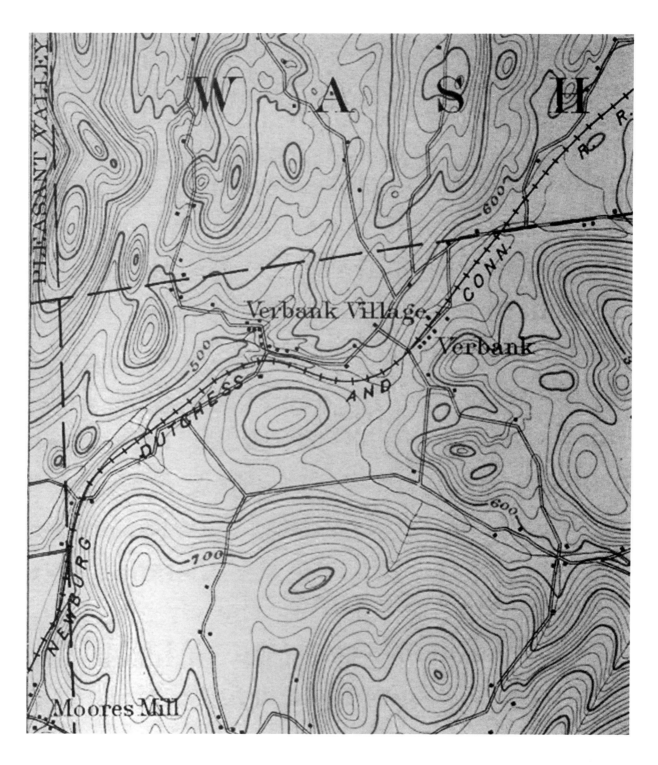

Above: Moores Mills and Verbank.
Facing page: The ND&C ran north through Arthursburg, Lagrangeville, and Billings.

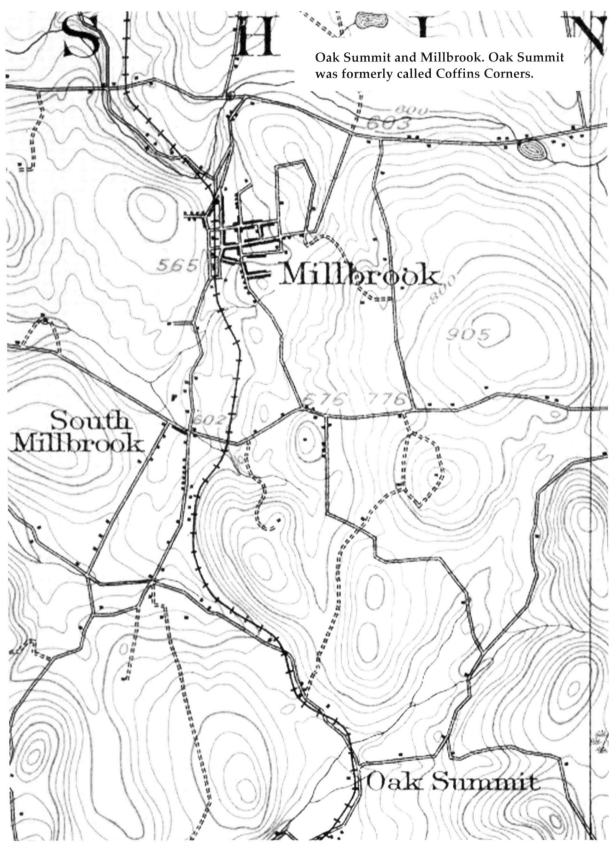

Oak Summit and Millbrook. Oak Summit was formerly called Coffins Corners.

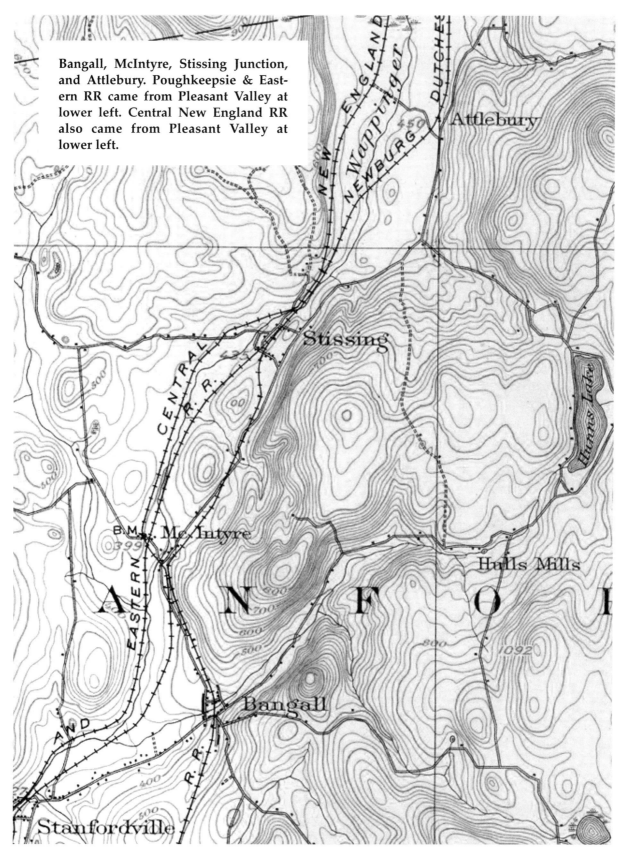

Bangall, McIntyre, Stissing Junction, and Attlebury. Poughkeepsie & Eastern RR came from Pleasant Valley at lower left. Central New England RR also came from Pleasant Valley at lower left.

Attlebury, Pine Plains, and Bethel. The ND&C RR turned east and ran to Bethel and shekomeko (lower right).

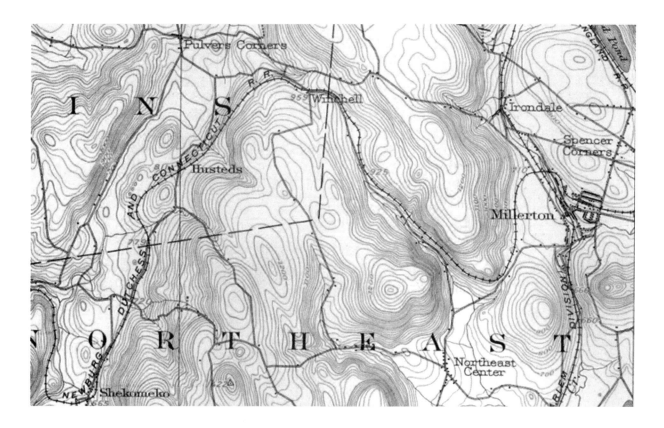

The ND&C RR ran from Shekomeko at lower left to Husteds, Winchell, and Millerton. At Millerton, the ND&C connected with the Harlem Line north and south. East of Millerton, the ND&C had a connection into Connecticut to Waterbury and Hartford.

Above: Former ND&C RR station at Fishkill, NY, November 1932. Below: Former ND&C RR station at Brinckerhoff, NY, November 1932.

Facing page, top: Former ND&C RR station and headquarters, Main Street, Beacon, NY, 1932. This station was called Mattewan before the city of Beacon was formed in 1913. Middle: Former ND&C RR station at Glenham, NY, November 1932. Bottom: New Haven RR 2-6-0 #393 at Glenham.

All of the photos in Appendix C were made for a Robert Adams book that was never completed and are from the collection of Heyward Cohen.

Above: Former ND&C station at Hopewell Junction, NY, November 1932. Former NH RR double track Maybrook Line crosses in the foreground.

Below: Former ND&C station at LaGrange, NY, November 1932. The original station burned and this one was built with insurance money in 1904. It is still in use as a private home.

Above: Former ND&C RR station at Billings, NY, November 1932. The overpass in the background is now the location of Rte. 55.

Below: Former ND&C station at Moores Mills, NY, November 1932.

Above: Former ND&C RR station at Verbank, NY, November 1932. Below: Former ND&C RR freight house, Verbank, NY, November 1932.

Facing page, top: Former ND&C RR station at Oak Summit, NY, November 1932. Middle: Former ND&C RR station at Millbrook, NY, November 1932. Bottom: ND&C RR and P&E RR station at Stissing Junction, NY, November 1932. P&E RR to salt Point, Pleasant Valley, and Poughkeepsie to the right.

Above: Former ND&C RR at Pine Plains, NY, November 1932.

Below: Former ND&C RR station at Shekomeko, NY, November 1932.

Signal station 196 on the Central New England Railway was located at Hopewell Junction, New York, on the double track Maybrook Line between Danbury, Connecticut, on the east and Maybrook-Campbell Hall on the west. The former ND&C single track from the Connecticut state line, via Millerton and Pine Plains to Beacon on the Hudson River crossed at Hopewell Junction. A light, late winter snow is dusting the crossing frogs in this springtime 1921 view as a long westbound freight train gathers speed following its stop for coal and water in the yards behind. The massive 3200-series New Haven Class L-1, 2-10-2, assigned to the CNE, is pouring all 72,000 pounds of its tractive effort rating against those ten, 63-inch drivers to get a roll on the train for its 40 mile run via the Poughkeepsie Bridge to Highland and on to Maybrook, leaving behind a haunting trail of coal smoke and soot to mark its passing.

Prowling the rails of the former Newburgh, Dutchess & Connecticut line, a rail bus is seen approaching Oak Summit station, just south of Millbrook, New York, on its run from Pine Plains to Beacon. The site originally was named Coffin's Summit for a businessman of prestige in the area; but the honor did not survive his passing, and the name was changed around the year 1890.

In similar manner, the rail bus signified the passing of steam trains in passenger service on rural lines for reasons of economy. The ND&C had been purchased in 1904 by the New York, New Haven & Hartford and was given to the Central New England Railway to operate. In June 1927, the CNE was merged into the NYNH&H, the same year that all passenger service on the CNE east of Copake and Pine Plains, New York, ended. The lonely rail bus depicted was one of two such units operating in suffrage of a decree of the Public Service Commission of New York that passenger service must be continued. July 9, 1933, was the date of the last timetable issue covering the rail bus operations, and the cars stopped running shortly thereafter, following PSCs belated granting of permission for abandonment. There wasn't any public left to be served.

The Vanishing Series

The last of the mixed trains operating between Hopewell Junction and Pine Plains via Millbrook ceased to burnish the rail in 1929 when a trestle north of Millbrook and another near Bangall were deemed too weak to support the weight of a moving train. Freight then was rerouted from Hopewell Junction to Poughkeepsie and then northeast to Stissing Junction and Pine Plains, although light gasoline rail cars for passengers continued to use the restricted route until 1933.

Depicted in this scene is one of the last of the mixed trains to use the route, No. 916 northbound out of Hopewell Junction at 7:00 a.m., on its outbound trip to Pine Plains. It has successfully traversed both of the slow order, weak trestles at Millbrook and Bangall and is beginning to pick up speed on the tangents north of Bangall toward Stissing Junction and Pine Plains, whistling loudly for the acute-angled highway crossing of Route 82 (earlier Route 82A). Speed was essential here to make up time from the delaying slow orders over the bridges and make its appointed arrival time of 9:55 a.m. in Pine Plains.

Stissing Junction, New York, revisited December 1912.

The New York, New Haven & Hartford has completed its take-over and consolidation as Central New England Railway of the former Newburgh, Dutchess & Connecticut (left). An eastbound train from Fishkill Landing to Pine Plains waits on its main in deference to a through freight from Campbell Hall to Hartford via the former Poughkeepsie & Eastern (right). The P&E roadbed has just been upgraded for heavy-duty trains and renamed "Main Line Division." Joint trackage from here east to Pine Plains Junction, 4.8 miles, required close coordination in use of facilities. The station building was a joint venture of the former ND&C and P&E roads and was the second erected at this location. The original was destroyed by fire in the fall of 1881.

Pine Plains Peddler

During the years of World War I and after, the Central New England Railway considered its main line between Pine Plains and State Line, New York, to be that of the former Poughkeepsie & Eastern via Ancram Lead Mines and Boston Corners due to its lower grades. Next best was the former Rhinebeck & Connecticut route via Silvernails, Copake, and Boston Corners. The heavy grades over Winchell Mountain via the former Newburgh, Dutchess & Connecticut route from Millerton via Shekomeko became the least desirable.

In the 1921 setting depicted here, a wreck or other blockage of the usual routes has caused the detour of a westbound freight via Millerton and over the rugged Winchell summit into the safe haven of the valley floor at pine Plains. The little Class F-4 Brooks-built (2-6-0) Mogul was the heaviest freight engine allowed to use the line. It was one of six such engines built in 1910 numbered 400-405, then renumbered in 1913 as 125-130, and rebuilt with Walschaert valve gear in 1919. Indicative of the era is the high-riding Model A Ford parked behind the station, designed to straddle the rutted, muddy dirt roads of rural America in the early 1920s.

A light snow has dusted the ground and roof tops of Shekomeko, New York, on a crisp December morning in the 1920s. A drab, grey overcast presages more to come. The CNEs morning mixed train from Pine Plains has just arrived and, after slaking its thirst at the bluff-mounted water tank, will proceed to switch the creamery siding before returning on its appointed rounds.

*Facing page:*
Down Brakes—Trouble Ahead

Following a long, steep, four-mile climb westward from Millerton, New York, via the former Newburgh, Dutchess & Connecticut Railroad, the summit of the mountain range was crested with a long and very narrow cut, originally named Russells Summit and later changed to Winchells. The clearance for passing trains was virtually negligible, and crews were warned never to attempt to stand on or near the tracks while a train was passing through.

The picture denotes that a broken brake beam on a passing freight probably has caused a derailment thereby choking the cut. A lookout is stationed high on a narrow ledge near the top of the bank to watch for smoke signals of approaching trains; while the rear brakeman of the disabled freight dashes to flag the engine as he scampers for the safety of the wider mouth of the cut.

Engine No. 204 was one of twenty-eight locomotives inherited by the Central New England Railway from acquired connecting lines. All of them were renumbered into the 200 series. Formerly 204 had been the Poughkeepsie & Eastern No.2, "Olivia", a 4-4-0 product of the Rogers Locomotive Works In Paterson, New Jersey, construction No. 4848, year 1893. It Was renumbered 204 and ran in this distinctive livery from 1907 to 1912. Thus, here is depicted the anomaly of an ex-Poughkeepsie & Eastern locomotive on ex-Newburgh, Dutchess & Connecticut trackage, pulling a Central New England train over the highest point on its system west of the Harlem Railroad.

The Millerton engine terminal of the former Newburgh, Dutchess & Connecticut Railroad was unobtrusively tucked away on undeveloped land just northwest of the crossing of the Harlem Division of the New York Central and the highway crossing of present Route 22, at the foot of the 1.5% grade over Winchell Mountain. Facilities included water, coal (hand shoveled from open gondolas into tenders), a cinder pit, a fifty-four-foot turntable, and a two-stall engine house.

Depicted is the arrival of the morning CNE local from Hartford to Millerton, having dropped its passengers at the Dutchess Avenue CNE station and proceeded on west to turn, service the engine, and have the cars cleaned. Some passengers undoubtedly have transferred from the ND&C station to the Harlem Division station and boarded the northbound Harlem Division train (right) just getting under way between the crossing gates protecting the CNE track.

# Sources

Beacon Historical Society, PO Box 89, Beacon, NY, 12508. Bound volumes of Newburgh, Dutchess & Connecticut Railroad office records. Also historical local photos.

Leroy Beaujon, Roseville, CA. Retired New Haven RR towerman, compiled locomotive rosters, letters, and photos.

J. W. Swanberg, Branford CT. Retired from the New Haven and Metro-North RR, supplied photos and letters.

Heyward Cohen, Amenia, NY. Postcard and photo dealer who supplied copies of the photos and drawings from the Adams/Westman manuscript.

Baker Library, Harvard Business School, Boston, MA. Letters and records of the ND&C RR and the NY&NE RR.

New Haven Railroad Historical and Technical Association. Publishers of *Shoreliner* magazine.

Kenneth Shuker, Cornwall, NY. Postcards and photos.

Dudley J. Stickels (deceased). Collection of photos obtained by Leroy Beaujon and now at the Dodd Research Center, University of Connecticut at Storrs.

Thomas Dodd Research Center, University of Connecticut at Storrs. Extensive collection of New Haven RR archives.

Robert B. Adams (deceased). ND&C RR photo and drawing collection originally intended for a book that was never completed.

Robert W. Nimke, Westmoreland, NH. Author of a three-volume set of the history of the Central New England Railway.

East Fishkill Historical Society, Hopewell Junction, NY. Photo of Hopewell depot in 1905.

William McDermott, Clinton Corners, NY. Author of *Dutchess County Railroads*.

Lyndon A. Haight, Pine Plains, NY. Author of *Pine Plains and the Railroads*, Volume IV.

Dutchess Northern Model Railroad Club, Hopewell Junction NY. Local history photos.

George B. Greenwood, Pleasant Valley, NY. Author of *Til There Was One*. (The story of two railroads and one remaining station in Pleasant Valley, New York.)

Harry and MaryLou Miller, Hopewell Junction, NY. Photo of Charles Miller.

Inglis Stuart (deceased). Author of *The Dutchess & Columbia R. R. and Its Associates*.

Frank Ziegert, Formerly from Poughkeepsie, now in Florida. Photo of Conrail last run.

Victor Westman, Danbury, CT. Retired railroader and artist who drew the illustrations for the Robert Adams book that was never completed.

John Helmeyer, Wappingers Falls, NY. John obtained photos of the 1910 Maybrook line construction. James Luyster took the original photos which are now in the collection of Mildred Diddell.

# Index

Abandonment, 118, 55, 47, 108, 153, 54, 93
Abutment Stones, 86, 89, 97
Adams, Robert B., 158
Aerial Photos, 49, 98, 99
Air Brakes, 42, 82
Air Signals, 68
Albany & W. Stockbridge RR, 10
Albany, 9, 10, 11, 41, 100
Aldridge, Geo. W., 116
Allen, William, 120
Amenia, 10
American Wheel Engine, 66
Amtrak, 35, 48
Angle Bars, 101
Arch Bars, 42
Arthursburgh, 19, 49, 92, 124, 145, 176
Atlantic Type Loco., 67, 89
Attlebury Farms, 112, 179
Auction, 108, 115
Austin, H. D., 52
Automatic Vending Mach. Co., 148
Automobiles, 48, 93, 108
Axles, 41, 42
Baggage, Mail and Smoke Car, 44
Baker Heater Co., 42, 140
Baldwin Loco. Works, 32, 61
Baldwin, Peter, 56
Ballast Cars, 44
Bangall, 12, 28, 88, 91, 113, 179, 191
Bankrupt, 50, 51, 123
Baptist Church, 55
Barges, 36, 38, 39, 48, 130
Barges, D&H, 20
Barnes, Oliver Weldon, 11

Barnum & Bailey Circus, 146
Barton, Frank, 124
Battleship Maine, 65
Bay Trestle, 43
Beacon Historical Society, 7, 24
Beacon NY, 7, 10, 11, 25, 38, 65, 71, 85, 131, 171
Beakes Dairy Co., 120
Beakes, George E., 125
Bearings, Journal, 42
Beaver Falls & Fort Pitt Bridge Co., 91
Beebe, Lucius, 112
Beekman, 49, 52, 55, 59, 175
Beet Pulp, 146
Belt, Main, 44
Bethel, 113, 180
BH&E RR, 12, 14, 27, 36, 71
Bicycles, 143
Bids, Construction, 41, 47
Bidwell, L. B., 71, 78
Bill of Sale, 56
Billings, 68, 120, 128, 176, 184
Bituminous Coal, 134
Blacksmith Shop, 42
Blaine, M. E., 107
Blank Bolts and Nuts, 42
Blizzard, 9, 39, 124, 132, 137
Bloomer, Frank, 39
Blueprint, CNE, 49, 96
Board of Directors, 56, 66, 70
Board of RR Commissioners, 53, 54, 89, 99, 107, 116
Boiler, 56
Boiler, Steel, 42
Bontecou, G. H., 146
Bordens Condensed Milk Co., 120, 127, 128, 141

Bordens Creamery, 104
Bored Wheels, 41
Boston Corners, 53, 110, 121
Boston, 73
Boston, Hartford & Erie RR, 11
Bottling, 119
Bowen, George S., 94
Brace Rods, 86
Brakeman Frank Barton, 124
Brakeman H.D. Austin, 52
Brakeman, 39, 88
Brakes, 82
Brass Foundry, 35, 42
Brass Lamps, 42
Brass Scrap, 42
Brass Vacuum Gauges, 46
Breakneck Quarry, 90
Breakneck Ridge, 10
Brewster NY, 17, 30, 72
Brick Chimney, 46
Brick Factory, 35, 46
Bridge Company, 94, 110
Bridge Piers, 114
Bridge Route, 38, 84, 133, 134
Bridge Seats, 90
Bridge St. Hopewell, 100
Bridge Stringers, 67
Bridge Upgrade, 78
Bridge, BH&E RR, 36
Bridge, Pedestrian, 36
Bridge, Poughkeepsie, 38, 48, 79, 83, 94, 108, 110, 114, 133, 153
Bridge, Steel, 53
Bridges, 85
Briggs, H. C., 32, 60
Brigham, Conductor, 78
Brinckerhoff, 11, 84, 120, 172, 183
Bristol, 83

Brittle Iron Rails, 64
Brock Brothers, 108
Brock, John W., 116
Broken Rails, 64
Brown Family, 46, 53
Brown, G. Hunter Jr., 40, 46, 53, 56, 144, 157
Brown, George H., 11, 12, 15, 16, 17, 22, 25, 30, 46, 49, 53, 71, 157
Brown, J. Crosby, 20, 46, 53, 144
Brown, James, 32, 33, 60
Brown, Melville, 41, 43
Brownell, Charles E., 125
Brussels Aisle Carpet, 70
Bryant, C. W., 54
Bryant, J., 53
Budd Brick Works, 46
Budd, D., 46
Buffalo Wheels, 69
Bulletin Boards, 47
Bullinger, E. W., 93
Burbank, Charles, 125
Burglars, 148
Burnham, Parry & Williams, 63, 65, 89
Burrows Fixtures, 70
Business Cards, 47
Business Manager, 46
Buying Equipment, 60
Campbell Hall, 84, 94, 110
Campbell, Mr., 102
Camping Excursion, 55
Canal Boats, 26
Candle Power Lamps, 45
Cans, Milk, 119
Car Ferry, see Ferry
Car Fixtures, 44
Car Floats, 26, 37, 39, 82, 130
Car Repair Shop, 35, 41
Cards, Business, 47
Carload Freight, 38
Carman, Isaac, 149
Carpenter Shop, 35, 42
Carpenters, 93

Carpet, 68, 70
Carroll Straw Hat Works, 88
Cartoons, 150, 151, 152
Catastrophes, 83
Cayuta Wheel and Foundry Co., 41
CB RR Extension, 31
CB RR, 31, 50, 54, 56, 59, 60, 86, 88, 137
Cease Operation, 117
Cemetery, 146
Central New England Railway, see CNE Rwy
Cesspool Leak, 146
Channel, 39
Charcoal Cars, 52
Charter, 55
Chatham, 10, 17
Chevalier, C. N., 142
Chief Eng. Everett Garrison, 43
Chimney, Brick, 46
Chimney, Iron, 46
Chinchilla, 145
Chocolate Brown, 34
Chrysanthemum Festival, 147
Chute, Loading, 59
City of Beacon, 65
Cleaning, Coach, 48
Clogged Sidings, 80, 96
Clove Branch Extension, 54
Clove Branch Junction, 18, 49, 53, 54, 56, 57, 124, 173, 174
Clove Branch RR, 11, 17, 18, 21, 30, 49, 59
Clove Valley Extension, 51
Clove Valley, 11, 18, 51, 52, 55, 56, 59, 95, 175
Club, Railroad, 46, 146
CNE Blueprint, 49, 96
CNE Rwy, 22, 47, 48, 59, 66, 68, 93, 105, 108, 123, 134, 153
CNE&W RR, 101, 104, 110, 133
Coach #7, 53
Coach #16, 68
Coach #427, 41

Coach Cleaning, 48, 117
Coaches #5 and #7, 68
Coaches, 39, 42
Coachman, 45
Coal and Water Facilities, 35
Coal Bin Hatch, 47
Coal Business, 115, 130, 131
Coal Furnace, 47
Coal, 58, 79, 82, 111
Coat Hooks, 70
Cofferdam, 90
Coil Syphons, 46
Cold Spring NY, 31, 90
Colored Man, 45
Columbia Bridge Co., 91
Columbia County, 10, 15, 110
Columbia PA, 57
Colwell, S. A., 145
Combination Car, 44
Commissioners, 41, 53, 54, 56, 57, 89, 99, 100, 107, 116
Commuting, 157
Competition, 79, 94, 115, 122, 134
Complaints, 56
Condemnation, 57
Conductor Brigham, 78
Conductor Crawford, 126
Conductor Fairchild, 53
Conductor Frost, 128
Conductors, 48, 117
Conflict, 77
Connecticut Western RR, 15
Connecticut, 9, 93
Conrail, 9, 109, 155
Consolidated Car Heaters, 68
Consolidation Engines, 77, 78
Construction Bids, 41, 47, 125
Construction Connection, 96
Contractors, 125
Cook, James, 33
Copake, 52, 54
Copper, Lake Ingot, 42
Cornwall NY, 92
Corpses, 146
Correspondence Course, 47

County Poor House, 149
Coupling Pins and Links, 80
Court Case, 39, 83
Cracks, Firebox, 68
Crane, Wrecking, 39
Crank, Geo., 114
Crawford, Conductor, 126
Creameries, 119, 104, 124
Crocker Bros., 18
Cronkrite, Engineer, 149
Crosby Steam Gauges, 46
Crossing Frog, 101
Crossing Signals, 100, 107
Crossing, Hopewell, 99, 128
Crown Sheet, 132
CT State Fair, 148
Cuba, 65
Curley & Todd, 120
Curtains, Pantasote, 70
Cuspidors, 68
CW RR, 15, 20
D&C RR, 11, 13, 16, 20, 25, 33, 36, 49, 51, 85, 110, 130
D&H barges, 20
D&H Canal, 36, 130, 134
Dairy Farmers, 119
Danbury RR Museum, 156
Danbury, 133
Danforth Loco. Works, 32, 33, 61
Date Stampers, 149
Davis, J. C., 31
Dawson, J. G., 146
DC RR, 9, 10, 16, 84, 95, 102, 133
Dealers, Coal, 131
Deans, John Sterling, 89
Debar, 115
Deck Bridge, 86, 88
Deeds, 56
Defects, 41
Defer Maintenance, 40, 45
Delaware & Hudson Canal, 15
Delinquent Rent, 39
Dennings Point, 12, 27, 36, 71
Depot, 52, 66, 111
Depot, Hopewell, 103

Depot, Millerton, 113
Derail Points, 102
Derailment, 52, 125
Derailment, Washington, 62
Derrick, 36, 92, 124
Didell NY, 109
Diesel Engines, 154
Dieterich Estate, 92, 147
Directors, 56, 73
Disaster, 45
Discontinued Service, 47
Dismantle, 118
Disposal of Property, 55
Dock Engines, 40
Dock, 35, 36, 37, 39
Double Ended Engine, 61
Double Tracked, 97, 98, 109
Dover Plains, 10
Drawings, 189
Dredge, 39
Drug Cult, 92, 147
Druggist Greene, 79
Drunk, Tower Man, 104
Dutchess & Columbia RR, see D&C RR
Dutchess Cnty RR, see DC RR
Dutchess Cnty Soil & Water Conservation District, 50, 99
Dutchess Junction Brick Co., 46
Dutchess Junction, 9, 11, 12, 15, 18, 22, 26, 27, 35, 37, 39, 47, 48, 49, 56, 57, 62, 70, 82, 96, 117, 118, 130, 153, 171
Dwyer, E. L., 94
Dynamite, 142
Dynamo, 45
E. H. Wilson & Co., 57, 62
E. J. Brecks & Co., 149
East Fishkill, 71, 94
East Glenham, 86
Election, 57
Electric Lights, 45
Ellis Bumper Posts, 47
Ellis, Charles G., 33
Elm Trees, 54, 56, 57

Emancipation, 45
Empire State Sugar Beet Co., 146
Engine #1, 33, 45, 46, 55
Engine #2, 33
Engine #3, 33, 39, 87
Engine #4 Millbrook, 33, 42, 43, 148, 149
Engine #5, 31
Engine #6, 28, 66, 148, 149
Engine #7, 31, 136
Engine #8, 34, 65, 87, 135
Engine #9 Gen. Schultze, 52, 54, 57, 59, 63
Engine #10, 67
Engine #15, 31
Engine #42, 81
Engine #100, 77
Engine #119, 74
Engine #125, 83
Engine House, 41, 42, 44, 52, 111
Engine Inventory, 69
Engine Rosters, 159
Engine Second #1, 66
Engine Second #8, 135
Engine Second #9, 66, 68
Engine Tioronda, 60
Engine Washington, 30, 52, 60
Engineer Miller, 78
Engineers, 47
Engines #3, #4 and #7, 46
Engines #4, #8, #3, and #9, 42
Engines #5, #6, #7, and #8, 33
Engines #6 and #7, 34, 40, 42
Engines, Dock, 40
Engines, GE U25B, 109
Engines, Mogul, 34
Eno, Lawyer, 41, 100
Erection Crew, 90
Erie Canal, 10
Erie RR coach #427, 41
Erie RR, 10, 15, 36, 37, 41, 80, 96, 130
Erlandson, O., 101
Estate of James Brown, 32
Ewing, Mr., 116

Excursion, 53, 55, 102
Extension, CB RR, 17, 51
F. Lahey & Sons, 120
Fairchild, Conductor, 53
Fall Brook Hoppers, 58
Fan Trip, 156
Fanny Garner, Steamboat, 15, 26, 36, 130
Fedorchak, Mr. & Mrs., 151
Felton, G. M., 81
Fence, 38, 42
Fenders. Dock, 39
Fernstrom, H., 47
Ferris, Mr., 125
Ferry William T. Hart, 37
Ferry, 26, 35, 38, 47, 71, 73, 78, 83, 93, 94, 108, 117, 130, 131
Financial Losses, 56
Financial Panic, 50
Fire, 18, 19, 36, 45, 81
Firebox Repairs, 40, 68
Firemen, 47
Fireproof Paint, 86
Fishkill Creek, 11, 36, 48, 85, 130
Fishkill Landing, 10, 11, 12, 37, 47, 65, 71, 73, 74, 75, 93, 96, 117
Fishkill Methodist Sunday School, 53
Fishkill Plains, 109
Fishkill, 11, 124, 130, 171, 172, 183
Fisk, Delafield & Chapman, 61
Fixtures, Car, 44
Flag Stop, 57
Flagman, 99, 102
Flaming Hats, 142
Flat Wheels, 80
Floats, Car, 26, 36
Flues, 40
Fog, 136
Fogg, Howard, 112
Football, 46, 144
Force or Injunction, 100
Ford, 93
Foreman Joseph Rico, 57

Foundation, Scale, 44
Fowler, Milton A., 95, 101, 113
Freehold & NY RR, 19, 30, 31, 60
Freeze, 136
Freight Bills, 50
Freight Cars, 42
Freight Dock, 35
Freight House, 47, 78, 107
French Plate Glass, 69
Frog, Crossing, 101
Frost Heaves, 140
Frost, J. A., 128
Fuel Economy Class, 47
Furnace, 59
Furniture, 46
Fusible Plug, 68
Gardiner Hollow, 56
Garrison, Everett, 43, 51, 67, 86, 100, 111
GE U25B Locos, 109
Gen. Schultze, Loco. #9, 30, 52, 57
General Schultze, see Schultze, John
Gentleman's Agreement, 79, 111, 133
Gilbert Car Mfg. Co., 44
Giness, 19
Glass, Plate, 69
Glenham, 11, 58, 71, 77, 85, 130, 171, 182
Golf, 46, 59, 145
Goodman, Mr., 100
GPS Satellite Rec., 98
Grade Crossing, Hopewell, 100
Grade Curve, 62
Grant Loco. Works, 32, 61, 64
Graphite Paint, 89
Grass Fires, 81
Gravel Train, 73
Great Lakes Region, 53
Green, Tweed & Co., 44
Greene, Druggist, 79
Greenwich Village, 10
Greenwood Lake Ice Co., 31
Gauges, Steam, 46

Guard Rails, 89, 90, 91
H&CW RR, 104, 110, 123
Haight, Howard, 132
Haight, L., 155
Hall, B. T., 41
Hall, Frank T., 120, 125
Hams Bridge, 93
Hand Brakes, 20, 82
Hand Car, 136
Handwriting, 24
Harlem RR, 10, 11, 30, 112, 116, 121
Harlem NY, 10
Harpel, Landowner, 57
Hart, William T., Ferry, 37
Hartford & Connecticut Western RR, 20
Hartford, 83, 94
Hartford, Providence & Fishkill RR, 10
Hartshorn Rollers, 70
Hatch, Coal Bin, 47
Havana Harbor, 65
Hawleyville, 83
Haystacks, 81
Headlights, 63
Headquarters, 24, 157
Health Board, 146
Hedden, John F., 108, 117
Heisler Loco., 155
Hemingway Conductor, 138, 146
Hicks, Allison, 92
High Bridge, 31, 40
Highland Division of NH RR, 84, 108
Highland, 111, 133
Highways, 129
Hillsdale, 15
Hillside Dairy Co., 120
Hi-Rail Truck, 156
Hiring an Engine, 63
Hoist Engines, 36, 130, 132
Holbrook, E., 81
Holmes, G. B. Master Mechanic, 19, 40, 41, 42, 56

Hopewell Junction, 9, 11, 12, 15, 34, 37, 49, 57, 71, 72, 94, 103, 104, 107, 108, 120, 126, 127, 153, 157, 173, 184, 189
Hopper Cars, Fall Brook, 58
Hopper, 70
Horses, Teams of, 57
Horton, Mrs Theodore, 146
Housatonic Railroad, 9, 156
Howard Haight & Co., 132
Howe Scale Co., 44
Hoyts, J. Q., 19
Hudson Connecting RR, 104, 110
Hudson NY, 32, 60
Hudson River Line, 10, 11, 12, 15, 27, 36, 121
Hudson River, 10, 11
Hurley, John J., 65
Husted Cut, 138, 181
Ice House, 48, 125
Ice Train, 128
Ice, 83, 119, 133, 136, 141
Illinois Central RR, 63
Improvements, Dutchess Junction, 47
Indebtedness, 56
Injunction, 100
Inspection Train, 70, 86
Inspector of Railroads, 56
Insulated Cars, 119
Insurance, 41, 44, 52
Interchange, Hopewell, 105
Interlocking, Hopewell, 106
Inventory of Locos, 69
Invitation, 102
Iron Chimney, 46
Iron Furnace, 57
Iron Mine, 59
Iron Ore, 52, 54, 58, 82
Iron Rails, 78, 137
Iron Works, Tower Bros., 59
Italians, 57
Jackson & Sharp Co., 69
James Brown Rolling Stock, 33
Japan, 109, 154

Jersey City Manure Co., 147
Jno. Crosby Trustee, 20
Johnsville, 128
Journal Bearings, 42
Judge Samuel Phillips, 129
Judson & Hancock, 45
Judson, Roswell S., 15
Keenan, W. T., 81
Kenyon, John S., 107
Kernahan & Patterson, 40
Ketcham, John Henry, 145
Keyport NJ, 19, 31, 61
Kimball, Charles, 9, 18, 19, 25, 31, 36, 38, 40, 46, 49, 52, 53, 71, 95, 100, 157
Kingston NY, 15, 36, 130
Kisselbrack, 138
Ladne, Stephen E., 93
Lager Beer, 143
Lagrange, 94, 120, 184
Lagrangeville, 125, 176
Lake Champlain, 120
Lake Ingot Copper, 42
Lake Trucks, 42
Lake Walton, 96, 109
Lamps, Brass, 42
Lamps, Candle Power, 45
Land Sale, 78
Landmarks, 56
Landowner Harpel, 57
Lapi, G., 51
Lasher, H., 32, 62
Lathe, Wheel, 41
Lattice Span Bridge, 57
Lawry, James, 30
Lawyer Eno, 41, 100
Lead Mines, 123
Leaky Fittings, 42
Leary, Timothy, 92, 147
Legacy, 157
Letterbooks, 18, 23, 30, 38, 46, 47, 48, 77
Link and Pin Couplers, 20
Links and Coupling Pins, 80
Loading Chute, 59

Lobdell Wheels, 69
Lockout Threats, 115
Loco. #1, Washington, 30, 33, 45, 46, 52, 55, 60, 137
Loco. #2, 33
Loco. #3, 33, 39, 87
Loco. #4 Millbrook, 28, 33, 42, 43, 143, 148, 149
Loco. #5, 31
Loco. #6, 30, 66, 148, 149
Loco. #7, 31, 136
Loco. #8, Mogul, 33, 34, 65, 87
Loco. #9 Gen Schultze, 30, 52, 54, 57, 59, 63
Loco. #10, 67
Loco. #15, 31
Loco. #42, 81
Loco. #100, 77
Loco. #119, 74
Loco. #125, 83
Loco. Inventory, 69
Loco. Overhaul, 40
Loco. Repair Shop, 35
Loco. Second #1, 66
Loco. Second #8, 135
Loco. Second #9, 66, 68
Loco. Tioronda, 32, 60
Locos. #4, #8, #3, and #9, 42
Locomotive Rosters, 159
Locos #3, #4 and #7, 46
Locos #5, #6, #7, and #8, 33
Locos #6 and #7, 34, 40, 42
Locos, GE U25B, 109
Locust Farms, 120
Lois, Gorham P., 72
Losses, 53
Low Tide, 39
LSD Drug Cult, 92, 147
Lumber Shed, 45
Lumber, 46
Lunch Table, 70
Luxury, 70
Machine Shop, 41, 42, 44, 48
Mahogany, 69
Mail Handling Fixtures, 44

Mail Service, 53
Main Belt, 44
Main Street Matteawan, 38
Main Valves, 61
Maintenance, 40, 45
Malleable Castings Co., 70
Management Reports, 39
Manhattan, 10
Manure, 147
Maps, USGS, 171
Marine Nat. Bank, 32, 60
Marks, A. A., 146
Martin, J. W., 107
Mary Ann's Bridge, 93
Mason Gang, 90
Masonry Smokestack, 113
Masons, 93
Massachusetts, 10
Master Mechanic Holmes, 19, 40, 41, 42, 56
Master Mechanic, 33
Mateer, Robert, 47
Matteawan, 7, 11, 25, 36, 38, 57, 65, 73, 79, 88, 130, 139, 182
Maul Handles, 142
Maybrook Line, 93, 109, 118, 135, 153, 156
Maybrook, 97
McCoy, D. B.NYC RR, 129
McDermott & Bunger, 120
McKinley, President, 65
McIntyre, 179
McLeod, Archibald, 105, 114
Mead & Taft, 92
Meat, Smoked, 143
Merchandise, 36
Metro North Railroad, 9, 35, 48, 118, 156
Midnight Run, 71
Miles, W. A., 54
Military Forces, 65
Milk Business, 22, 82, 112, 119
Milk Wagon, 124
Millbank, Isaac, 128
Millbrook, 9, 11, 25, 49, 92, 113, 119, 138, 178, 187

Millbrook, Engine #4, 28, 42, 43
Millennium Bug, 149
Miller, Charles, 155
Miller, Dennis, 155
Miller, E. I., 54
Miller, Engineer, 78
Miller, Harry, 155
Millerton, 9, 10, 11, 15, 18, 20, 30, 39, 70, 93, 108, 110, 113, 115, 137, 138, 181, 196
Mine, 49
Mining, 58
Minstrel Shows, 147
Mogul #3, 87
Mogul #8, 33
Mogul Engines, 34, 72
Monmouth County NJ, 31
Monongahela River RR, 134
Montreal, 9, 16, 50, 55
Moore, W., 65
Moores Mills, 136, 177, 185
Morgan, J. P., 84, 105
MTA Metro-North RR, 156
Muldoon, Jno. P., 32, 60
Murals, 46
National Paint Works, 89
National Switch & Signal Co., 107
ND&C Junction, 123
ND&C RR, 20, 24, 25, 35, 36, 50, 51
NE RR, 84, 106
Nelson, Homer A., 94
Nevada, 108
New Depot, 41, 47
New England, 10
New Hamburgh NY, 45
New Haven RR, see NH RR
New York & Harlem RR, 10
New York & New England RR, see NY&NE RR
New York City, 9, 10, 16, 36, 50, 55, 57, 120
New York, Boston & Montreal Rwy., see NYB&M Rwy

New York, Boston & Northern RR, see NYB&N RR
Newburgh, 9, 10, 15, 26, 36, 75, 94
Newburgh, Dutchess & Connecticut RR, see ND&C RR
Newspaper, 44
NH RR, 9, 22, 47, 84, 93, 105, 117, 123, 134, 153
Niagara Stamping & Tool Co., 46
Nickel Plating, 42
Night Dispatching, 82
Night Shift, 77
NJ Midland RR, 31, 34
NJ Southern RR, 31
Note Payment, 64
NY&M RR, 52, 94, 123
NY&NE RR, 34, 37, 47, 71, 94, 110, 121, 131
NYB&M Rwy, 16, 17, 20, 34, 40, 50, 51
NYB&M Rwy, Trustees, 33
NYB&N RR, 16, 50, 51
NYB&W RR, 34
NYC RR, 58, 93, 112, 123, 131, 135
NYC&HR RR, 26, 35, 37, 39, 40, 47, 48, 73
NYNH&H RR, see NH RR
O&W RR, 100
Oak Summit, 178, 187, 190
Oak Pilings, 39
Ochre Yellow, 34
Office Car, 73
Officers and Directors, 73
Ohio & North Western RR, 19
Old Hopewell, 11
Oldsmobile, 93, 145
Onion Skin Paper, 23
Opening, DC RR, 102
Ordering Parts, 64
Ore Business, 95
Ore Trestle, 52, 62
Ore, 52, 54, 58, 82
Overflow Pipe, 145
Overhaul, 40
Overpass, 73, 131
P&C RR, 94, 104, 110

P&E Junction, 123
P&E RR, 20, 34, 58, 94, 110, 121, 134
P&R RR, 114
PA RR, 91
Page Harris & Co., 44
Paint Shop, 35, 44
Paint, 34, 46, 66
Paint, Graphite, 89
Painting Crew, Bridge, 85, 93
Painting Engine General Schultze, 63
Palace Car, 70
Panic, Financial, 50
Pantasote Curtains, 70
Parallel Rod, 137
Parkway, Taconic, 49
Partitions, 70
Pass, 143
Passenger Cars, 68
Passenger Shelter, 48, 103, 104
Paterson NJ, 33, 64
Patterson, Mr., 96
Patterson, S. A., 112
Pay, Track Crew, 79
Pearl Harbor, 109, 154
Peat, 73
Peattie, William, 59
Peatties Academy of Music, 147
Pedestrian Bridge, 36
Penn Bridge Co., 91
Penn Central RR, 9, 155
Penn Steel, 91
Penn. Coal Co., 26, 36, 82, 130
Pennsylvania, 9, 10, 36
Perkins, Jacob A., 94
PH&B RR, 121
Phelps Dodge & Co., 42
Phila. & Reading RR, 104
Phillips, Judge Samuel, 129
Phoenix Bridge Co., 53, 57, 86, 91
Photographs, 182
Pig Iron, 87
Pile Trestle, 26
Pilings, 36, 39, 73

Pine Plains, 10, 15, 17, 94, 110, 119, 122, 180, 188, 193
Pine Plains, Loco., 12
Pink Shirts, 46
Plate Glass, French, 69
Platform Cars, 96
Platforms, 39
Pleasant Valley, 20, 58, 94, 110, 134
Plum Point, 11, 12, 48, 153
Plumb Bob, 35
Plumb Point, 11, 35
Poaching, 79
Policy, Insurance, 44
Poor House, 149
Port Morris, 18
Portable Machinery, 46
Postcards, 59
Posters, 147
Poughkeepsie & Eastern RR, see P&E RR
Poughkeepsie & SE RR, 94
Poughkeepsie Baptist Church, 55
Poughkeepsie Bridge RR, 104
Poughkeepsie Electric Rwy, 134
Poughkeepsie Iron Furnace, 54, 57
Poughkeepsie Loco. Eng. Co., 10
Poughkeepsie RR Bridge, 38, 48, 79, 83, 94, 108, 110, 114, 133, 153
Poughkeepsie, 10, 11, 20, 56, 94
Poughkeepsie, Hartford & Boston RR, 20
PR&NE RR, 105, 114
Prentice Tool Supply Co., 41
President McKinley, 65
Pressing Wheels, 41
Price Fixing, 111, 123, 129, 133
Property Disposal, 55
Providence RI, 76
Proxy, 26
Pusher Engines, 153
Putnam County, 10
Quarry at Winchells, 89

Quarry Breakneck, 90
Quartered Oak, 69
R&C RR, 110
Raceway, Matteawan, 88
Rail Breakage, 78
Rail Trail, 109, 156
Railbus, 154
Railroad Club, 46
Railroad Br.,Poughkeepsie, 38, 48, 79, 83, 94, 108, 110, 114, 133, 153
Railroad Commissioners, 41
Railroad Timetables, 29
Railway Ed. Assoc., 47
Railway Express, 147
Ralph, J. E., 19, 31, 30, 60
Rate Agreements, 115
Rebuilding CB RR, 57, 59
Red Ink, 81
Refrigeration, 141
Refrigerator Cars, 119
Register Books, 76
Rent, Delinquent, 39
Rental Checks, 34, 76, 106, 115, 82
Repair Shop, 35
Reporter, 73
Reports, Management, 39
Restoration, 157
Retrenchment, 66, 93
Reynoldsville, 83
Rhinebeck & Connecticut RR, 15, 20
Rhinebeck, 11, 20, 133
Rhode Island Loco. Works, 63
Rico, Joseph, 57
River Access, 39
River Barges, 48
River Ice, 133
Road, C. B., 30
Rockville Bridge, PA RR, 91
Rocky Glen, 87
Rogers Loco. Works, 32, 61
Rolling Stock, 44
Rolling Stock, James Brown, 33
Rondout Landing, 15, 20, 130, 134

Ross, Ed, 150, 151, 152
Rosters, 159
Rotten Meat, 143
Roundhouse, 35, 43, 45, 48, 115, 154
Route 376, 100
Route 82, 49
Rowing Races, 46, 144
RR Bridge, Poughkeepsie, 38, 48, 79, 83, 94, 108, 110, 114, 133, 153
Rumsey Family, 83
Rutland VT, 17, 44, 50
Safety Hazard, 82
Salary, 120
Salt Point, 110
Salvage Crew, 57
Salvaging, 53
Santa Fe Engines, 153
Sawdust Insulation, 120
Scaffolding, 47
Scale, Track, 44, 53, 59
Schenectady Loco. Works, 33, 62
Schenectady, 30
School Taxes, 114
Schoonmaker, S. B., 47
Schultze, John, 9, 18, 25, 32, 40, 46, 49, 72
Scows, 26, 36
Scrap Metal, 48, 57, 60, 92, 109
Screens, 81
Seats, Bridge, 90
Second Engine #1, 66
Second Engine #9, 66, 68
Second Engine #8, 135
Selling Equipment, 60
Semaphore, 116, 129
Servicc Facilities, 153
Sewage, 146
Shared Trackage, 76
Sharon CT, 10
Sheffield Farms, 120
Shekomeko, 113, 119, 137, 181, 188, 194
Shelf Rock, 114

Shelter, Passenger, 48, 103, 104
Shenandoah Mining Co., 142
Shirts, Pink, 46
Shop Crews, 48
Shovels, 139
Shunpike, 133
Signal Tower, 103, 106, 128
Signals, Crossing, 100, 107, 108
Silvernails Bridge, 94, 110, 113, 123
Skidmore, Mrs., 145
Smoked Meat, 143
Smoker and Baggage Car, 68
Smokestack, 81, 113
Snow Goggles, 139
Snow, 124, 136
Snowdrifts, 124, 137
Snowshoes, 136
Soda Fountain, 79
Sousa, John Philip, 147
Southern New England, 9
Spanish-American War, 65
Specifications, 63, 69
Speed Limit, 77, 78, 86
Spencer, T. W., 53
Sprout Creek Bridge, 87, 88
Sprout Creek, 11
Stalled Train, 78
Stanfordville, 179
Stanton, J. C., 95, 101
Stanton, R. P., 93
State Fair, 146
State Hospital, 134
State Line, 9, 15, 20, 93, 94, 108, 110, 117, 123
Steam Gauges, 46
Steam Heat, 68
Steamboat William T. Hart, 75, 76, 131
Steamboats, 39, 119
Steamer Fanny Garner, 26
Steel Boiler, 42
Steel Bridge, 53
Steel Rails, 64, 78, 96, 137
Step Chairs, 101
Stewart, Inglis, 45

Stissing Junction, 58, 110, 179, 187, 192
Stissing, 20, 52, 121, 134
Stockholders Meeting, 26
Stone Abutments, 89, 97
Stone Smokestack, 113
Stop Signal, 80
Storehouse, 45
Storm, 136, 141
Stowell, 138
Straw Hats, 142
Stringers, Bridge, 67
Survey, 111
Surveyor, 35
Switch Keys, 77, 80
Switch Rods, 80
Switching Buffers, 80
Sylvan Lake, 11, 18, 22, 32, 49, 50, 52, 53, 54, 55, 59, 60, 95, 175
Taconic Parkway, 49
Tampering, 111
Teams of Horses, 57
Teamsters, 58
Telegraph, 38,, 76
Telephone, 38, 76
Tell Tales, 82, 88
Temperance Literature, 143
Temporary Tracks, 96
Tenement Houses, 35, 52, 39
Terminal Facilities, 27
Terra Cotta Curtains, 70
Terra Nova Drive, 96
Terry, George F., 57
Thieves, 102
Threaten to debar, 115
Thurston, George, 116
Ticket Office, 47
Tickets, 55
Time Signals, 141
Timetables, Railroad, 29
Tin Roof, 53
Tin Shop, 46
Tioronda Bridge, 27, 48, 85, 130, 153
Tioronda Loco., 12, 32, 60

*Index*

Tires, 40, 61
Tongs, Ice, 120
Tonopah & Goldfield RR, 108
Toolboxes, 70
Tools, 42, 46
Tournaments, Golf, 46
Towanda Coal, 132
Tower Bros. Iron Works, 59
Tower Brothers, 53, 54, 56, 58, 59
Tower Couplers, 70
Tower, A. E., 53, 54 , 58
Tower, Hopewell, 104
Tower, Signal, 103, 106
Town Meetings, 147
Town of East Fishkill, 71
Town of Northeast, 114
Track Crews, 48, 79
Track Scale, 44, 53, 59
Trackage Rental, 34, 76, 82, 106, 115
Trackage Rights, 34, 71, 110, 121, 131
Trading Equipment, 60
Training Facility, 156
Tramps, 145, 148
Transportation Council, 8
Trees, 56
Trestle Work, 43
Trestle, 26
Trestle, BH&E RR, 36
Trip Pass, 143
Troy NY, 54
Trucks, 48, 108, 129
Trustees NYB&M RR, 30, 31, 33, 40, 51
Turkeys, 76
Turner, N. R., 133
Turner, William, 151
Turntable, 35, 39, 44, 57, 78, 111, 115, 117
Typewriters, 23
Ukenas, John D., 57
Ultimatum, 96, 98

Undercutting,, 80, 110, 115
Underhill, Charles, 101, 99
Underhill, William, 58, 120, 144, 145, 157
Undersized Bolts, 87
Union Switch & Signal Co., 100
Upgrade Bridges, 78
Upgrade, Turntable, 39, 111, 117
Upholstery, 68
Urinal, 70
Used Coach, 41
USGS Maps, 13
Utility Corridor, 109
Vacuum Gauges, 46
Vail, E. Wright, 125
Van Benschoten, John, 145
Van Buskirk, W. G., 31, 33, 40, 61
Van Wyck Buildings, 137
Vandalism, 88
Vassar College, 134
Vending Machines, 148
Verbank, 11, 90, 93, 113, 120, 177, 186
Vicki Lane, 96
Violence Threats, 54, 56
Vulgar Language, 142
Wages, 120
Wagons, 57
Waiting Rooms, 47
Walton, Lake, 96
Wappingers, 94
Warwick NY, 90
Wash Bowl, 145
Washington, George, 45, 46
Washington, Loco., 13, 15, 30, 31, 52
Washington, Town Of, 12
Washroom Plans, 70
Waste Pipes, 42
Water Tank, 43, 45, 46
Waterbury CT, 13
Way, Larry, 24
Weak Points, 41, 64

Weather Reports, 141
Weather, 136
Weeks, Robert G., 142
Weigh Master, 59
Weldon, J. F., 108
Wells, G. S., 136
West Glenham, 86, 87, 92
West Point, 31
Western States, 9
Western Union, 76, 147
Westinghouse Brakes, 32, 42, 61
Westman, Victor, 158
Whaley Lake, 72
Wheel Press, 41, 42
Wheels, Flat, 80
Whortlekill Creek, 96
Wicopee Jct., 12, 27, 34, 37, 48, 71, 73, 118, 130
Wilkinson, Robert F., 94
Willard Lumber Co., 45
William Mann Co., 47
William T. Hart Steamship, 75, 76, 131
William T. Sellers & Co., 39, 117
Williams, G., 79
Williamsport PA, 89
Willow Blocks, 146
Wilmington DE, 69
Wilson, J. H., 78
Winchell Mountain, 13, 140, 181, 195
Winchells Quarry, 89
Window Shades, 68
Wing, Mrs John D., 145
Winter Ice, 40
Wire Tampering, 111
Wooden Legs, 146
Woodwork, 42
Wreck, 83, 84, 62, 148, 149
Wrecking Crane, 39
Wright, 45
Yard Tracks, 39
Yellow Pine Planks, 87

*207*

## About the Author

BERNIE RUDBERG grew up in a Swedish family on a farm in southern New Jersey. Railroads were a part of his family tradition for at least three generations. His great grandfather started with the Swedish railroads in 1874, and by 1894, was stationmaster in Polcirkeln, a small town where the tracks cross the Arctic Circle in northern Sweden. His grandfather was foreman of the station in the junction town of Boden near the Arctic Circle.

He served a tour in US Navy electronic systems during the Korean War. He spent four years in the Navy and never set foot on a ship, although he managed to fly to several naval air stations in California and the Pacific Islands. After leaving the Navy, he began a career with IBM engineering that lasted thirty-five years.

After retirement, at the end of 1991, he had time to get back to railroading. He is the current president of the Hopewell Junction Depot Restoration Inc. It owns the Hopewell depot and plans to restore it as a small museum and educational facility.

Bernie and his wife live in the Town of East Fishkill, within hearing distance of the Beacon line and the former Maybrook line. They have been married for forty-two years and have three grown children plus two grandchildren, who love to play with the model train layout in the basement.

## Another Hudson Valley Railroad Book

BRIDGING THE HUDSON: *The Poughkeepsie Railroad Bridge and Its Connecting Rail Lines* is the first comprehensive history of the first bridge over the Hudson below Albany ever published. It presents a narrative history, telling how construction plans gradually developed; how the bridge was built; how it served nobly over many years, carrying passengers and freight from near and far; and how its connecting rail lines made it a transportation hub for the nation. It also tells how a fire put the bridge out of use and how imaginative plans have been proposed for its future use.

Six years in the making, this is Pulitzer Prize-winning author Carleton Mabee's first bridge book, his second railroad book. His previous railroad book, *Listen to the Whistle*, a history of the gallant little Wallkill Valley Railroad which ran from Kingston, in Ulster County, New York, south through New Paltz and Walden to Campbell Hall, in Orange County, was also published by Purple Mountain Press.

*Bridging the Hudson* is a large-format book of 296 pages and contains more than 200 illustrations. It is available in paperback in stores or from the publisher for $25.00.

Purple Mountain Press, Ltd., is a publishing company committed to producing the best original books of regional interest as well as bringing back into print significant older works. For a free catalog, write Purple Mountain Press, Ltd., P.O. Box 309, Fleischmanns, NY 12430-0309, or call 845-254-4062, or fax 845-254-4476, or email purple@catskill.net.

http://www.catskill.net/purple